SIMONE WEIL

Simone Weil

And

The Intellect of Grace

By

Henry Leroy Finch

Edited by Martin Andic
Foreword by Annie Finch

Continuum New York

2001

The Continuum Publishing Company
370 Lexington Avenue, New York, NY 10017

Printed in the United States of America

Library of Congress Cataloging-in-Publication Data

Finch, Henry Le Roy.
    Simone Weil and the intellect of grace / by Henry Leroy Finch ;
  edited by Martin Andic ; preface by Annie Finch.
        p.   cm.
    Includes bibliographical references and index.
    ISBN 0-8264-1190-8   ISBN 0-8264-1360-9 (pbk)
    1. Weil, Simone, 1909–1943.   I. Andic, Martin.   II. Title.
  B2430.W474F54   1999
  194–dc21   99-32607
                                                    CIP

Contents

Foreword

by Annie Finch

O F ALL MY FATHER'S INTENSE and wide-ranging intellectual passions, outlined by Martin Andic in the introduction to this collection, Simone Weil was the object of his most enduring and devoted study. And yet, although he began work on a book about Weil almost twenty years before his death, this is the first book of his writings about Weil to be published.

I like to think that in the years during which my father was writing books on Wittgenstein and other subjects, and postponing the long-planned assembly of a collection on Weil, he was developing the life-wisdom he would need to address Weil adequately. Although it would have been wonderful if he could have finished editing this collection himself, at least, by the time he began to put this book together in his last months of life, he had attained a level of serenity and insight beyond that which had been available to him earlier.

When my father finally resumed work on Weil, six months before his death from cancer, he was too weak to carry a pile of books by himself. I cleared away the many stacks of books and papers around his chair (with his characteristic sense of duty and honor, he had been finishing another manuscript, on the mystic Da Love-Ananda, that he had promised and felt obligated to write). Under his direction, I carried books and manuscripts about Weil and arranged them in piles on the tables in his study. He told me that the Weil book would be easy, since he had been carrying it around in his head for many years. He asked me to bring him a legal pad, and he began to write.

In the last weeks of his life, he was too weak to write himself and dictated the remaining essays to my mother and to a dedicated nurse named Elie Joseph Hercule. He was still working on this book the day before he died—on

August 22, close to Simone Weil's own death-day. I told my father that I would get the Weil book published, and since I am a poet, not a philosopher, I was lucky that his devoted friend Martin Andic agreed to edit and introduce this collection, which impresses me anew with the vividness and intensity of my father's thinking. In conclusion, I offer the following elegy from my collection *Calender,* a poem which I wrote for my father's memorial service.

VIGILS

In memory of Henry Leroy Finch, August 8, 1919–August 22, 1997

> *"Bequeath us to no earthly shore until*
> *Is answered in the vortex of our grave*
> *The seal's wide spindrift gaze towards paradise."*
> —Hart Crane, "Voyages"

> "If a lion could talk, we couldn't understand him."
> —Ludwig Wittgenstein

Under the ocean that stretches out wordlessly
past the long edge of the last human shore,
there are deep windows the waves have not opened,
where night is reflected through decades of glass.
There is the nursery, there is the nanny,
there are my father's magnificent eyes
turned towards the window. Is the child uneasy?
His is the death that is circling the stars.

In the deep room where candles burn soundlessly
and peace pours at last through the cells of our bodies,
three of us are watching, one of us is staring
with the wide gaze of a wild sea-fed seal.
Incense and sage speak in smoke loud as waves,
and crickets sing sand towards the edge of the hourglass.
We wait outside time, while time collects courage
around us. The vigil is wordless. Once you

saw time pushing outward, that day in the nursery
when books first meant language, as your mother's voice
traced out the patterns of letters. You saw

words take their breath and the first circles open,
their space collapse inward. They sparkled. Your pen
would scratch ink deliberately, letters incised
like runemarks on stone as you heard, quoting patiently:
Wittgenstein, Gutkind, Gurdjieff, or Weil.

You watch the longest, move the furthest, deliberate in breath,
pulling into your body. You stare towards your death,
head arched on the pillow, your left fingers curled.
Your mouth sucking gently, unmoved by these hours
and their vigil of salt spray, you show us how far
you are going, and how long the long minutes are,
while spiralling night watches over the room
and takes you, until you watch us in turn.

He releases the pages. Here is the mail,
bringing books, gratitude, students, and poems.
Here are kites and the spinning of eternal tops,
icons, parades, monasteries and boardwalks,
gazebos, surprises, loons and unspeaking
silence. Pages again. The words come
like a scent from a flower. Geometry is clear.
Language is natural. The truth is not clever;

cats speak their own language. You are still breathing.
Here is release. Here is your pillow,
cool like a handkerchief pressed in a pocket.
Here is your white tousled long growing hair.
Here is a kiss on your temple to hold you
safe through your solitude's long steady war;
here, you can go. We will stay with you,
loud in the silence we all came here for.

Night, take his left hand, turning the pages.
Spin with the windows and doors that he mended.
Spin with his answers, patient, impatient.
Spin with his dry independence, his arms
warmed by the needs of his family, his hands
flying under the wide, carved gold ring, and the pages
flying so his thought could fly. His breath slows,
lending its edges out to the night.

Here is his open mouth. Silence is here
like a huge brand-new question that he wouldn't answer.
A leaf is his temple. He gazes alone.
He has given his body; his hand lies above
the sheets in a symbol of wholeness, a curve
of thumb and forefinger, ringed with wide gold,
and his face, which is sudden and beautiful, young
for an instant, is new in the light of the flame.

Abbreviations

EL *Écrits de Londres et dernières lettres* (Gallimard, 1957).

F *First and Last Notebooks* (tr. Richard Rees; Oxford, 1970).

FW *Formative Writings: 1929-1941* (ed. and tr. Dorothy Tuck McFarland and Wilhelmina Van Ness; University of Massachusetts Press, 1987).

GG *Gravity and Grace* (introduction by Gustave Thibon; tr. Emma Craufurd; Routledge, 1952).

GW *Gateway to God* (ed. David Raper; Fontana, 1974).

IC *Intimations of Christianity among the Ancient Greeks* (tr. Elisabeth Chase Geissbuhler; Routledge, 1957).

LP *Lectures on Philosophy* (tr. Hugh Price; Cambridge, 1978).

LPG "The Legitimacy of the Provisional Government" (tr. Peter Winch; *Philosophical Investigations* 53 [1987]: 87-98).

N *Notebooks* (2 vols.; tr. Arthur Wills; Routledge, 1956).

NR *The Need for Roots* (tr. Arthur Wills; Putnam, 1952; reprinted, Harper 1971).

OC *Oeuvres Complètes* (ed. André Devaux and Florence de Lussy; Gallimard, 1988-).

OL *Oppression and Liberty* (tr. Arthur Wills and John Petrie; University of Massachusetts Press, 1958).

PDL   "Prerequisite to Dignity of Labour," in *Simone Weil: An Anthology* (Virago, 1986), 264–276.

PSO   *Pensées sans ordre concernant l'amour de Dieu* (Gallimard, 1962).

PSV   *Poèmes, suivis de "Venise Sauvée"* (Gallimard, 1968).

S   *Sur la Science* (Gallimard, 1966).

SE   *Selected Essays: 1934–1943* (tr. Richard Rees; Oxford, 1962).

SJ   "Are We Struggling for Justice?" (tr. Marina Barabas; *Philosophical Investigations* 53 [1987]: 1–10).

SL   *Seventy Letters* (tr. Richard Rees; Oxford, 1970).

SN   *Science, Necessity and the Love of God* (tr. Richard Rees; Oxford, 1970).

WG   *Waiting for God* (tr. Emma Craufurd; Putnam, 1951; reprinted, Harper, 1973).

Introduction
by Martin Andic

THIS BOOK IS A COLLECTION of Roy Finch's writings about Simone Weil which he intended to pull together into a continuous study of her thought and significance; he was working on it through his final illness. Finch was one of the founders of the American Weil Society in 1970, and he was an active participant in its meetings. In his writings and discussion and conversation, he constantly compared Simone Weil (1909–1943) in importance to Martin Heidegger (1889–1976) and to Ludwig Wittgenstein (1899–1951), about whom he wrote three well-regarded books. Finch was educated at Yale and Columbia, and was a professor of philosophy for twenty years at Sarah Lawrence College and sixteen years at Hunter College, City University of New York. Like Simone Weil, he had the highest regard for Plato, though he also admired Pascal and Kierkegaard, Isaac Luria and Jacob Boehme, William Blake and D. H. Lawrence, Dostoevsky and Gandhi. Again like her, he took a deep interest in Taoism, Hinduism, and Buddhism, especially the work of Nagarjuna and Dogen. He studied Zen Buddhism with Daisetz Suzuki at Columbia and said that one day we would examine and discuss Dogen here the way we now do Aquinas and Kant. He also explored Jewish philosophy, particularly the thought of Martin Buber, Franz Rosenzweig, and Eric Gutkind, whose papers he edited; as well as ancient Gnosticism, medieval Catharism, and Islamic Sufism; and alchemy, Kabbalah, and the occult philosophy of the Renaissance, including that of Boehme and Newton. For eighteen years Finch chaired a Columbia Faculty Seminar on Religion, bringing together scholars from all over New York, and he constantly and tirelessly sought to define the differences between the major religious and philosophical traditions while he looked out for a deeper unity. He was convinced that Simone Weil is the genius we need to show us how to rethink religion, politics, history, and culture. This collection of his best work gives some idea of how he began to do this with her help.

Roy Finch was drawn to Simone Weil by her freedom and openness of mind, her power of analysis and criticism, her clarity and precision, her love of truth and her hunger and thirst for justice, her concern with nonviolence, and her attempt to be a pacifist, as he himself was through the Second World War. He also shared her mistrust of technology and abstraction and the reduction of all values to those of commerce, her concern that philosophy should be practical as well as contemplative, her interest in the religious dimension in mathematics and politics, her regard for everything and everyone marginalized or excluded by orthodoxies and establishments, whether it was world religions and heresies or the colonized peoples of the Third World. He saw these intellectual and moral qualities, based on a profound love of truth, in Plato and to a great extent in Wittgenstein. He felt that Weil's *Notebooks* would one day stand beside the *Pensées* of Pascal, presenting the same baffling obscurity to those who do not read earnestly and luminous clarity to those who do.

The following chapters fall into three broad categories: religious and moral epistemology; the criticism of politics, society, and culture; and renewal through a spirit of truth, justice, love, and freedom.

For Finch the center, the point of departure, and the goal of Simone Weil's thought is what might be called *an epistemology of grace*.[1] Truth is to her a matter both of attention and contemplation and of action and life.[2] It requires an impersonal, loving intellect, where our love seeks out what is truly good and moves us to realize it in life, and as a condition of this—or perhaps it is partly the same thing—truth frees us from self and its fantasies of prestige and power and wealth, acquisition and superiority and compensation; our intellect for its part must find true good, carefully discerning these false worldly images from it in order to see it as it is. Intellect must be illuminated by love (this is the traditional view);[3] but even so we can do no more of ourselves than to turn away from such shadows and to surrender to God's love who alone can show us that pure Good that is in him and that he is.[4]

> Those who love truth more than life itself turn away from the fleeting things of time with all their souls, to use the expression of Plato.
>
> They do not turn toward God. How could they do so when they are in total darkness. God himself sets their faces in the right direction.[5]

But if grace alone fulfills our intellect in this way, we need grace even to begin exercising it. Even the love of truth by which we turn from falsehood, or at least desire to turn, is an implicit love of God, his own love obscurely and confusedly self-conscious in us (though the obscurity and confusion are ours, not his).[6] Three of the most important ways in which Weil says God breaks the hold of our egoism and awakens our impersonal intellect are the encounters with necessity he provides in mathematics, beauty, and affliction (if it is not so great as to destroy us); these three acquaint us with the necessity that defines the world he has created as an act of love that leaves us free to give or refuse our consent to his order. Stirring our attention and desire, they give us a precious opportunity to see him in these, as Goethe thought that God is visible to Reason in elemental phenomena. For they define the world that represents the distance between God as Creator and ourselves as his creatures, a distance created in love and for love and crossed only by it. But without his initiative, we could do nothing. It is a *grace*, given freely, for we have not earned it, nor is it conditional on any response, nor could any response be fully adequate to it, or equal it and repay it.

Finch examines Weil's account of the Greeks' use of mathematics as a way for the intellect to and from God, first, to understand the idea of precise truth about realities beyond our imagination, and beyond the certainty of daily and nonreligious experience, and, second, to explain the idea of a mediator between incommensurables, a proportional mean, above all between God and humanity.[7] He follows her discussion of ancient Greek mathematics and goes on to show how she looked for and found among the Gnostics the idea of a religious knowledge or *gnosis*.[8] She shares their sense of the world as fallen from God but goes beyond them in seeing this distance between him and the world and his absence within it (except secretly) as the best and clearest proof of his reality and his love, that he should have made the worst of all possible worlds in which his love is still possible.[9]

Gnosis is a participation in divine knowledge, beyond "perspective"; Weil means beyond partial, egoistic perspectives, which are to her only appearances and illusions; she means the abandonment of *finite*, worldly perspectives altogether.[10] She follows Pascal and Kierkegaard in regarding infinity as a criterion of God;[11] and this makes it easy for her to draw on the transfinite mathematics of Cantor to describe religious truth. In his valuable discussion of this, Finch perhaps emphasizes Weil's attention to God's infinite greatness in himself to the neglect of what she says of his infinite smallness, God's *infinitesimalness* compared to and by the criteria of the finite, if one may put it this way.[12] For she recurs constantly to the thought that here below God is powerless and acts non-actively; that in humility God comes to us as a beggar with no force but that of love; that he neither compels us to love nor is compelled to love us by any other force; that he is heard only in silence. Finch elsewhere shows his awareness of this, however; for example, when he says (in chapter 10) that, for Weil, God is not in a worldly sense *powerless* so much as he is *powerfree*, or beyond all power but that of love.[13]

Finch goes on to show how Weil and Cantor fit into the Platonic tradition of an *actual* infinity in what might be called a qualitative sense of a *superlative* free of the limits that define what proceeds from it: on this showing, God is a

Good that is nothing but good and in no way evil, and the source of the good in all other goods that variously qualify it. And Finch discusses more particularly Weil's idea of the way mathematics can be mysteriously and providentially "appropriate"—precisely where it is "ponderous" (or necessary in a way that is otherwise brute or nontransparent to our intelligence)—to the Good and to God in his relations to himself and to the world and to us. This is one of many generally neglected topics in Weil's writings that Finch opens up for further investigation.

His study of Weil's critique of culture, society, and politics begins with her admiration of T. E. Lawrence, who shared her struggle to understand how to act in truth, how to be faithful to moral ideals and clear of wrong in dealing with force. He too found in ascetic discipline and purification a model for this greater ordeal of moral integrity and freedom, and in suffering for these ideals a fuller self-knowledge. He likewise, and this is very significant, needed to live with others in relations of equality.[14] Both emphasize will—the resolution that is earnestness, wholeheartedness, integrity of purpose and desire—and yet speak of genuine action, the best and truest, as that in which "we have no choice," in which, as Descartes would say, we are not "indifferent" but "spontaneous" in being drawn irresistibly to what presents itself to our purest and fullest and most "equal" attention—that is to say, most detached from self and complete and just—as the best we can do in our circumstances. The evil we then must do is *purified* only by the conviction that we have to do it in order to avoid doing even greater evil (and by the prayer that its consequences fall only on ourselves). Weil means to follow Krishna's teaching in the *Bhagavad Gita*, as well as Socrates in the *Gorgias*, and to contrast the cases in which evil is purified of wrong with those in which it is not, citing, for example, the massacres in Canaan that the Hebrews of the Old Testament said that they did at the command of their God. Evil is not purified of wrong, she would say, when it is not necessary in order to accomplish what is best for everyone affected by what we do.

Finch next examines Weil's assessment of the work of Karl Marx. She commends his idea of a mechanics of social forces, the relations of power between producing and ruling classes, while rejecting his notion that the triumph of justice and the working class is historically inevitable. The first is a stroke of genius, she says; the second is merely wishful thinking, for what is mechanically necessary will never of itself produce what is good. Marx has sacrificed truth to his love of justice. Weil tries to complete Marx's great idea by developing a general theory of oppression. It is turning human beings into *things*, that is to say, depriving them of freedom to *think* and *act* as they themselves will; it is degrading them by using the power of secrets, money, arms, and prestige against them to evoke admiration and fear of those who have it for now, though no one has it for long nor is truly made great because of it. The prestige of power is thus egoistic and exciting to the imagination; but it is imaginary or false. The end of oppression requires a critique of the greatness defined by power, and an alternative definition by regard for freedom and for the limits within which human beings exercise it and through which they encounter the world and one another. It requires a transformation of our idea of labor. Weil draws on her own experience in the factory and the fields, in picturing a free society as one in which people think and act for themselves, and while they have to work for their living, their work is free labor not slave labor—not, as for Marx, because they own the means of production, but because they are craftsmen who understand and value the whole process and the contribution they make to it and to society, individually and together; their hands and heads and hearts are at one in truly human labor. Their work has meaning as part of human work in the world.[15]

Finch notes with approval Weil's point that Marx in his mechanical determinism failed to allow for the individual thinker like himself who acknowledges necessity but also judges it, as if we cannot transcend our society and class but must think and judge as it does, as if it is our society and class that do this in and through us; but, so Weil objects, nothing *social* thinks, only the *individual* does. It should be said, however, that we are social beings, we act and live and think *with* others, and thus we often mean to think through *together* what to judge or do about something *as* a group, such as a family or a business enterprise or a nation; we can take a purely private role or a more public one, and then we speak as individuals on behalf of all of us—as individual members of our group—inviting consensus by offering reasons that should be reasons for any of us. In this way we can think for our society, though it is in and through us that it does it, or because you and I do. This is or can be thinking responsibly, and not a piece of make-believe.[16]

Weil concedes this in effect in her discussion of nationalism, the true nationalism that roots the soul in the world, as opposed to that which merely exalts the collective ego in the use of force that really uproots both oppressor and victim. For there are universal needs that only nations can rightly fulfill, nourishing the soul with traditions, language, places, and personal relationships. She prefers not to say that we have *rights* to the fulfillment of these needs, but rather that we have *obligations* to see to it that they are met. To her, rights are in themselves egoistic and amoral and are asserted in a spirit of bargaining and contention that is backed by force or the threat of it and blocks movements of human generosity on both sides. To say that what is wrong when a girl is forced into prostitution is that her rights are violated is to say too little: it is she herself who is violated. What is wrong is that she is being denied her due as a human being, the protection that any deserves and is owed by and expects from any; for to be a human being is to be morally connected to human beings in a way that is both impersonal (because it is due to

anyone from anyone simply because both are human) and personal (because
it calls for earnestness, wholeheartedness, integrity of response). As we shall
see, Finch constantly returns to this point in order to bring out more and
more from it.

Weil seems to say that it is wrong to uproot others, and yet it is right to
uproot ourselves when it is from the false nationalism of collective violence
and worldly domination, for this blinds us to the true rooting and nourishment that nations alone can give, as mediators of love and truth from the eternal. We should see our country as something unique and infinitely precious,
but fragile and perishable and an object of our compassion and love. For most
of her life as a Marxist radical, Weil had been an internationalist and a pacifist, but when the war came she was eager to come to the aid of her country
and sought to join saboteurs behind enemy lines or even to lead a team of
nurses to tend soldiers of both sides at the front lines. George Steiner says that
at the fall of Paris in 1940 she declared it "a great day for Indo-China"; but
André Devaux points out in correspondence that the closest she comes to this
in writing is in an article she had published in 1937:

> When I think of an eventual war, I admit that the fear and horror such a thought
> causes one is mixed with another comforting thought. It is that a European war
> could show the great revenge of colonial people to punish our thoughtlessness,
> our indifference, and our cruelty.[17]

Criticism of the patriotism of national glory is compatible nevertheless with
a patriotism based on justice and freedom for *all* peoples.

Finch is rightly concerned about Weil's proposal to limit freedom of
speech by punishing politicians and journalists for willful lying and deceit,
at the same time that she means to defend this freedom for everyone seeking
to discover and declare the truth. As he explains it, however, the first is meant
to be justified by the second, and she intends precisely to protect the freedom
of the mind from interference by indoctrination, propaganda, and the techniques of mass suggestion, especially from totalitarian motives. And as he
points out, we can add today the management of public opinion by leaks and
half-truths, spin-doctoring and disinformation. These corrupt the spirit of
truth and are intolerable. When members of an organized body like a church
that is charged with the preservation and transmission of truth question or
deny that institution's principles, it may remove them from teaching functions, but it cannot rightly silence them, or require them to *adhere* intellectually to its principles. Nothing can rightly restrict the freedom of the intellect
(indeed, it is an obligation) to *attend* to everything and let each show itself for
what it is. We must want to see things as they are and not as we want to see
them. In this, Weil is following Plato and Kant.[18]

To see things as we want to see them, always only as we want them to be and want to make them, is the spirit of modern science and technology as they are criticized both by Simone Weil and by Martin Heidegger as reductive and grasping. To her they are alien to the Good, while to him they are closed to Being, which accordingly conceals itself from them. Finch shows how both thinkers find the fault in a false individualism: Weil in a personalism that considers nothing in us but the worldly *I* and *we* and makes us vulnerable to commercial and political oppression by the collective; Heidegger in a subjectivism that isolates us from the real and seeks a metaphysics of it that defines it as what we know. She relies on the religious dimension of Plato, which he ignores, while he emphasizes the phenomenological element in Aristotle disregarded by her. Both call for renewed receptivity to a reality that is beyond and more than we can make of it. She would say that we have no human essence but our love and desire of pure Good; he would find it in our openness to and freedom in Being. They both see our only rescue in the breathing of this true spirit of humanity into science and technology, and into our entire culture and politics and society. But both are pessimistic about the prospects that this will happen.

If the Promethean Will to master nature and bend it to our will seen in modern technology and science shows a typically masculine attitude, the receptivity to nature that freely cooperates with it can be thought of as feminine, as in modern environmental and ecological writings (as well as ancient Chinese Taoism). In what may be his boldest discussion, Finch explores this idea by comparing Simone Weil to the twelfth-century Hildegard of Bingen, who speaks of the greening freshness of the living cosmos. But where Hildegard views the world as created in love that shows God's presence throughout, Weil calls it *abandoned* in love that is shown precisely in God's *absence* throughout. In explaining this Finch mentions the sixteenth-century Kabbalist Isaac Luria, who spoke of God's *Zimzum,* or creation by withdrawal to make room for a world other than himself, even allowing it to fall away into a would-be complete independence in a *breaking of the vessels* unable to contain the beauty that is in him and in selfless obedience to him. To Weil this abandonment of the world itself shows the love of God, who has made a world for us in which the greatest love can be shown in response to his, a world in affliction in which our love has the greatest distance to cross to him.

In developing this, Finch considers the love of a parent for a child, whether in raising it or in abandoning it to make a life that is better for the child. (He refers here to John Boswell's careful history of this practice in medieval Europe, *The Kindness of Strangers*.) A parent's and especially a mother's love is freely given rather than earned, and it is impersonal or directed to the child because it is one's child rather than because of its personality likable or otherwise, and equally to this child and to its brothers and sisters, who are loved just as much. And this leads Finch on to the contrast between the New Testament God of love and the Old Testament God of wrath. The God of Hildegard and Weil is forbearing and forgiving; the God of Moses is rewarding and punishing, with infinite severity and jealousy. If (as is often said, though it needs many qualifications) the Jewish God is generally a strict and unsatisfiable and often angry Father, the Christian one is more like a loving Mother; the one a God of power and intolerance of pagans and heretics, the other a God of nonviolence and inclusion.[19]

The true God for Simone Weil is a God of love and peace who welcomes everyone and everything and accepts every religion and every heresy formulated in good faith, and who even allows hatred and violence and intolerance in his world as part of the evil that defines the distance his love has to cross in order to be as great as it can be. Finch shows how Weil's view was partly anticipated by the Christian heretic Marcion, who was attacked by Tertullian for his criticisms of the Old Testament God and his attempt to contrast the false God of power with this true God of love. (William Blake tried something similar fifteen centuries later.) For Simone Weil God's justice is not vengeance, it is love. Human justice has no other origin. For the only thing that stops us from wronging one another when we can get away with it and get something out of it for ourselves is our shared *expectation of good* from one another simply because we are equally human beings; it is the recognition of our common humanity, and thus the human kindness that we owe each other without having earned it or done anything to deserve it. We are born with this expectation, and we are *given* what we need, for no reason other than that it does us good, and for no reward other than to give it and so to do what makes both good. This expectation of good and the love that acknowledges and fulfills it, which is really and implicitly the love and desire of pure infinite Good, is the only sacred thing in us; it is the basis of genuine human community, the foundation of real religion, the ground of true humanism and culture.[20] This divine element in us is at once impersonal and personal, as we saw earlier. It is much to Finch's credit that he has worked so tenaciously to clarify this idea.

He resists attempts to explain the life and thought of Simone Weil in psychological terms, in effect to explain her away without examining what she means and whether it is true. He gives a close reading of her letter to Father Perrin presenting a spiritual autobiography that is intended to clarify her decision not to enter the church, though as she says she loves God, Christ, the Catholic faith and its liturgy, hymns, architecture, rites, and ceremonies (WG 49–50; LP opening). In this letter she describes the Christian attitudes in which she was born and grew up and remained all her life; she tells of three decisive contacts with Catholicism and her mystical experiences; and she formulates her understanding of the incarnation of Christianity in everyday life and society, and of her call from God to be a Christian *outside* the church. She is concerned about the totalitarian tendency of the church to limit the free thought of its members and to exclude those with whom it disagrees, at the risk of rejecting the truth it does not understand.[21] Finch notes that words of God are liable not to mean the same to the public even within the church as they do to the religiously earnest individual who speaks or hears them, a point often made by Kierkegaard. Considering the death of Simone Weil, Finch mentions the so-called terrible prayer for total annihilation in God and obedience to his will that she wrote in New York as an example to show what prayer is; he explains that this amounts to the same as the Lord's Prayer that God's will be done in us in time as it is in him in eternity. This is also the meaning of her prose poem about Christ's taking her to the attic to talk with her for a few days and then sending her away for good; perhaps it was a mistake, it could not have been *she* he came for, and yet she cannot prevent herself from thinking with fear and trembling that despite everything she has his love.

In the final chapter we see Finch applying the thought of Simone Weil in comparing the four great religious traditions of Judaism, Christianity, Hinduism, and Buddhism, in their treatment of time and the timeless. Whereas the Jews carry their past with them in a historic present they share as a people, Christians see the present as the only time they have in which to act, a time in which they are *free* from their past and from self and free simply to do right, as individuals that can interact in deeper community. If Christians mean to recover the time of childhood when we rely on the care of those who love us, Hindus recover a time before birth, perhaps best understood as a birth of self with its dualisms of subject and object, subject and subject. This impersonal consciousness, they say, remains with us without our knowing it, beneath or above our ordinary one, and it is the purification of this from our obscurity and confusion, its clarification and sharpening in focus, that fulfills us as our greatest reality and our truest knowledge and our fullest joy. Buddhists are intent on this movement beyond self, but they prefer not to speak of emergence from it into a deeper or higher Self because all words and imagination objectify and reduce that Self, whereas it is pure subjectivity. Zen Buddhists free this by attention to *koans*, or questions to which this freedom is itself the only answer, when we suddenly see that we get nowhere by our own efforts, but everywhere when we surrender to the living truth. It comes suddenly and from *beyond time*, in renunciation of self-regarding regrets and resentments of what *was* and of desires and hopes for what *will be*, when we long for Good and do what there is rightly to do and then receive and enjoy what rightly has to be *now*.[22] This everyday loving attention to what is given to us and fulfills us, an attention that is itself given—for both come from beyond our egoistic materialistic self—is the intellect of grace.

Finch's conclusion that we should accept all four traditions, and learn from all human traditions, is not a casual remark. It sums up his idea, taken over from Simone Weil, of receiving everything and making room for all, and permitting them to reveal themselves for what they are and to find their own level. This requires detachment from our own private egoisms and our regard for an impersonal Good that is not measured by them and not limited by them. It is clear that Roy Finch himself sought this detachment and regard, and found Zen and Christianity set very high. It is clear also that he understood openness to all religions to be a criterion of authentic religion, and openness to all human traditions a criterion of full humanity. This openness is a willingness to enter into dialogue with one another as equals deserving our attention (at least initially), a willingness to be contradicted and corrected where we see that we are wrong, to owe others our opposition and reasons when we think that they are wrong, to make and listen to appeals to experience, to learn from each other. It is part of sharing a world that is common to all who are awake to it and to one another and to themselves, so truly that without this receptivity there is no real world for human beings, and no real human beings either, no real dialogue, and no real action; and that is no life for a man or woman to live.[23] Everyone who knew Roy Finch would say that *he* knew how to talk and listen and learn, knew how to receive, was very much awake and alive and human.

A word in closing about the title of this book. The editor considered "The Grace of Intellect," which catches Simone Weil's and Roy Finch's idea that our best knowledge is *given* to us, and shares in the beauty, and so in the life, of the giver. But "The Intellect of Grace," modeled on Dante's phrase *intelleto d'amore* (in *La Vita Nuova* 19.10 and *Purgatory* 24.51), connoting as it does a transforming knowledge concerning grace as well as inspired and lit by it, seemed preferable in the end, as it seems to combine both meanings.

All notes in the text that follows are the editor's, except those marked with an asterisk.

CHAPTER 1

Affliction, Love, and Geometry

S IMONE WEIL HAS BEEN CALLED a saint of the intellect, and the description is apt. For intellectual clarity with her had a spiritual significance; and she herself had the gift to be simple, and at the same time she had a remarkable intellectual sophistication: a rare combination. We are reminded of one of her favorite poets, George Herbert, and also of a philosopher whom she did not know but with whom she had much in common, Wittgenstein.

To say that Simone Weil is a simple writer is only to say that she is simple in the way that Einstein's equations are simple. *Her* equations of course apply to the realm of the spirit, where we are not used to lucidity—or at least to her degree of lucidity. On matters of religion we have long since given way to sloppiness, to emotion and sentimentality. Nobody takes the time to be clear. Simone Weil delivers formulae as impersonal and enigmatic as the formulae of mathematical physics. Some readers are annoyed; they feel that she is writing in a code for which they do not have the key. They can see how they would not understand the equations in mathematical physics; in religion, however, shouldn't everybody understand immediately?

The similarity between religion and mathematics is indeed one of Simone Weil's central points. In her view the supernatural is allied to the realm of the intellect, and propositions about it should be more clear, more precise, and more lucid than propositions about the natural. And this is even true, even it is most true, when we are dealing with the paradoxical. For Simone Weil, who had an extraordinary, analytic mind, mathematics starts from and terminates in paradoxes; and this is what makes it, as we shall see, an ideal analogue for religion. To her, Greek geometry was one of the supreme prophecies of Christ.

Simone Weil saw the spiritual significance of the impersonal intellect, most of all the mathematical intellect, which frees us from the biases and prejudices of egocentricity, both individual and collective. The awesome, impersonal order and beauty of the natural world teach us a lesson that we could never learn from the psychological and social worlds, infected as these are with the delusions of the human ego (and it was also her view that the psychological and social worlds in this respect are as mechanical and necessary as anything in nature). One of the great teachers of the human soul is the impersonal truth of mathematics and science when seen in its proper spiritual perspective.

What concerned Simone Weil was what had the power to pierce the soul from without. She had no illusions about human nature. She knew that what we tell ourselves about ourselves is, in one way or another, almost always pleasant, while what we find out about ourselves from outside is almost always a shock. It is one of the main lessons of Greek tragedy. Only what pierces the soul from without has a chance of revealing to us what we really are. Mathematics and science come from without in this way; so do art and beauty; and a third thing, perhaps most important of all, pain and humiliation. Mathematics, beauty, affliction—they have the power to break through the shell of the ego. Thus she writes:

> It is the same truth which penetrates into the senses through pain, into the intelligence through mathematical proof, and into the faculty of love through beauty. (SN 186–187)

The scientist has no claim to spiritual insight as long as he restricts his impersonality and objectivity to specialized areas of science and refuses to turn it on himself and his own life. Pure thought, like pure affliction, can either drive us into ourselves and desolate us, or it can shatter our pretensions and liberate us. In the latter case, it orients us toward the Good, in Plato's sense of the term. This is the meaning that science and mathematics had for the Greeks, especially the Pythagoreans and Plato, and which modern science and mathematics have forgotten.

We must consider the religious significance of doubt and skepticism in this process of stripping away. We become attached to ideas as if they were personal possessions, and we are not willing to see them harmed. But there are pitfalls in skepticism too. The great French poet Paul Valéry questioned the religious skepticism of Pascal because he detected in it Pascal's hidden motive to frighten himself and others into religion. This cannot be said of Simone Weil. She makes no cosmic wagers.[1] The infinite spaces do not frighten her. And she does not try to justify prejudices which she already holds on religious grounds.

Criticizing in another way another skeptic, Descartes, the American philosopher Charles Peirce once said, "Let us not pretend to doubt in our heads what we do not doubt in our hearts." Descartes' doubt was in the head and for this reason did not reach the feelings where our ultimate rationalizations and subterfuges are hidden.[2] Simone Weil is very critical of the personal in religion—not because she is against feelings or thinks that only ideas matter, but because she knows how easily feelings express deep individual and collective prejudices.

Furthermore, she saw that this process by which we conceal from ourselves our deep-seated attachments or conditionings is as necessary as water flowing downhill. We do not control the automatic workings of the imagination. We always see things, as it were, in our own favor or in favor of our own group. It is, therefore, virtually a miracle if anything penetrates through this, and there are only a few things that can penetrate through it: the scientific and mathematical intellect, impersonal beauty and love, and the power of suffering when it does not close us in and degrade us. In these three places the Greek mind, anticipating Christianity, saw the supernatural acting in the world.

It follows that the personal, the psychological, and the social and historical are not of intrinsic value for Simone Weil because they are all infected by the ego. Nothing in these spheres can lay claim to universality or spirituality. They all fall under the illusions of perspective brought about by the conditioning that controls human life. Only the impersonal intellect, selfless feeling, and pride-shattering affliction can break through.

The "outside" is not, as we might be tempted to imagine, the material as such. It is the divine beyond it when it is transparent to the intellect, that is to say, material necessity reflecting divine necessity when what is furthest removed from the Good is seen to be an image of perfect obedience to the Good. It is the mind that is the mediator between blind necessity and divine necessity.

The Good, the supernatural,[3] is beyond all power and force and is therefore of a completely different order from human and material powers. It has no place in the world at all. And yet, Weil says, there is a "secret complicity" between the Good and the world. Here is one of the pairs of contradictory truths that have to be held in the mind at the same time. On the one hand, the Good does not belong to the world, as we can see, for example, in the case of Christ (or as she sometimes puts it, it touches the world only as something infinitely small). On the other hand, it decisively "steers" the world. As Plato knew, it is these two truths together that make up wisdom. Anyone who knows only one of them is not wise.

The material world is completely under the sway of power and force, as are also the psychological world and the social world. Here all is necessity, though this necessity has a different character when seen from the standpoint of the Good. It is Simone Weil's most profound contention that we owe no allegiance to this power and force, none whatever. We owe allegiance only to the Good.

Those who have criticized Simone Weil have done so mainly for three reasons: first, for her apparent Manicheanism in setting matter as far away from God as possible; second, for her opposition to personalism and all forms of inner-worldism; and third, for her rejection of the social. All three rejections come from the same source: the refusal to make any concessions to the powers of the world. She will not bow down to the great gods of today—the material world, power, the nation, or the person—only to the Good.

Simone Weil, it may be said, puts a negative sign over all the powers of the world, as does the Platonic philosophy, the New Testament and certain later books of the Old Testament, and in other ways the *Bhagavad Gita*, the *Upanishads*, the *Tao Te Ching*, and the Buddhist sutras. Her *epochē*, or "bracketing," is more radical than Husserl's, extending to the transcendental ego, history and the dialectic, the people, and the whole cult of the psychological.

It is here that we meet Simone Weil's most surprising and most characteristic idea: that God is completely absent from the material world, and yet this very absence is the most perfect expression of God's love. In other words, God is most God when he permits the existence of what is at the furthest remove from him. This is how Weil's Christianity embraces Manicheanism. We do not have to do with an evil material world, but with a greater paradox. To be at the furthest remove from the good is not to be in opposition to the Good but to be a still more profound expression of the Good. Those who have been most abandoned have the greatest opportunity to love. They may, though it is never likely, be given something that reaches across this abyss. This, which is beyond human capacity, can only be a supernatural gift: the Divine Love itself. Human capacity in itself does not extend so far as to love that which afflicts and abandons us. At the human level the only result is Nietzsche's resentment.

The meaningless, blind necessity of brute force which is the extreme absence of God in the material world is paralleled by affliction, which is something worse than suffering because it is permanent, a permanent maiming, combined with the social humiliation that is the extreme absence of God in the human world. It is only if these two together, necessity and affliction, can be given meaning that there is any meaning in speaking about God. That this ever happens has to be experienced to be believed. To the afflicted's agonized cry of Why? Why is this happening? Why am I abandoned?—a cry that was wrenched even from Christ—there is no answer. But Weil says that if the afflicted nevertheless persists in the orientation toward the Good, something more miraculous than the creation of the world will be revealed.

In Simone Weil's eyes Christ became completely human and completely divine only in his cry of abandonment: "Why hast Thou forsaken me?" Then "in the very silence there was something infinitely more full of significance than any response." Thy will be done.

We see how Simone Weil came to regard Christianity as something like a science of affliction. It is the only religion that finds a use for (or meaning in) suffering instead of trying to escape from it. However oddly the words ring, they capture the possibility of exact thought about these extremities as understood by Christianity. God is evident to us only then, when we are remote from him. He shows himself only when all human help is completely cut off. Hence Weil says:

> Christians ought to suspect that affliction is the very essence of creation. To be a created thing is not necessarily to be afflicted, but it is necessarily to be exposed to affliction. . . . Affliction is the surest sign that God wishes to be loved by us; it is the most precious evidence of His tenderness. (SN 193)

It may take a saint fully to understand this (and it certainly takes one to practice it), but the logic is clear enough. Affirming divine order in the midst of blind materiality and force, and divine love in the midst of permanent agony and loss, is not what we would expect from human beings, at least not without help.

Material necessity and intellectual necessity are ultimately opposite. ("There is no relation at all between the necessity that 1 plus 1 equals 2 and feeling the weight of two kilos falling on your head.") By *material* necessity she means force and gravity, war and fate, the human stretched out on space and time, the crucifixion, and the powers of the world; by *intellectual* necessity, light and grace, translucence and vision, order and beauty, the harmonies and proportions of the world.

Human beings, utterly fragile, at the mercy of every material accident and at any moment exposed to the possibility of affliction, have only two tiny points where they are linked to something else. One is the capacity for impersonal, impartial attention, the waiting that is an intense receptivity to that which comes from outside; the other is the ineradicable expectation in every human being that Good will be done to us. These are the only things in us that are worthy of total respect and that cannot be taken away. By comparison, "rights" are superficial and finally at the mercy of power. Simone Weil does not believe in "rights." It is the expectation that good will be done to us which she regards as the basis of justice, and not what John Rawls calls "fairness." The expectation of Good is impersonal. The demand for fairness arises from the personality and is connected with calculation, possessiveness, and envy.

The infinite distance between the divine and the human was bridged by Greek mathematics, Greek tragedy, and the death and rebirth shown in the mystery religions. Greek civilization saw as its task to mediate between the power of the world and the beauty of the Good.

> Here is the very center of all Greek thought, its perfectly pure and luminous core. The recognition of might as an absolutely sovereign thing in all of nature,

including the natural part of the human soul, with all the thoughts and all the
feelings the soul contains, and at the same time as an absolutely detestable thing;
this is the innate grandeur of Greece. . . . This double movement is perhaps the
purest source of the love of God. (IC 116)

What is it about geometry that makes it the model for the relation between
the human and the divine? In what way does mathematics itself express the
divine? These questions require us to look into Simone Weil's philosophy of
mathematics.

Her view is that mathematics is not only *a* science; it is the *only* science. For
nothing is a science except to the extent that it is mathematical. (This echoes
the Platonic against the Aristotelian conception, that at bottom there is only
one science, or one scientific method, instead of many sciences or methods.)
But equally important, she says, mathematics is not an isolated subject concerned only with itself, as many now believe; in its very essence it is *the science of nature*. When this is ignored or forgotten, we get the empty formalism
that we see in modern logic and mathematics. Cut off from relation to nature,
it becomes a trivial game.

As the science of nature, mathematics is no longer a product merely of the
human will. It is what it is because the world is what *it* is. Almost from the
start Greek mathematics is concerned with one main question: the question
of infinity, that of numbers and that of the continuum (infinite divisibility).
The Greeks were not bewildered by this: they thought with the utmost precision, rigor, and exactness about this question. Nothing reveals the significance of the human mind and its relation to the natural and supernatural
better than this, that our most exact thinking has to do with just this, and that
from just this arise our most practical results in arithmetic, geometry, calculus, and modern logic. While we may say that the infinite remains incomprehensible to the imagination by generating contradictions, what is really
important is that it is the subject of our most exact and fruitful thinking. In
all the various crises in the history of mathematics, beginning with Zeno's
paradoxes and the Pythagorean "scandal of incommensurability," through
the irrational numbers of Cardano, the "infinitely small quantities" of the calculus and the imaginary numbers of Hamilton, down to the paradoxes of
modern logic and set theory—the question of infinity has remained central
and has continued to produce the best of human thinking.

The Pythagorean discovery of the incommensurability of the third side of
a right triangle with the sum of the other two sides may be taken as proto-

typical. Since the triangle is finite, the third side certainly has an exact length; this length may be measured, but it cannot be expressed in the same units as the combined lengths of the other two sides, that is, in any whole numbers or fractions. This gave Greek mathematics the shock that led to its greatest achievement. We would say that infinity does not defy thinking but becomes its truest expression. In modern terminology the length of the third side has to be expressed as a non-recurring, non-repeating infinite decimal.

When today we think of mathematics as a mediation between the finite and the infinite, or a way of expressing the latter in terms of the former, we sometimes forget that these terms "finite" and "infinite" had for the ancient Greeks very different meanings from what they had for the Middle Ages and for the modern world. For the Greeks the finite was the divine and the infinite the material, the reverse of the later understanding. But the problem was the same.

The most natural image of divine mediation was the possibility of relating all numbers to the number 1. This involved the search for the *mean proportional*—that is, the number which mediates between 1 and any other number in such a way that 1 has the same relation to this as this has to the other number. Thus, between 1 and 4, the mean proportional is the number 2, since 1 is related to 2 as 2 is to 4. But, the Greeks asked, what is the mean proportional between 1 and 2? Here it looks as if our thought falls apart and we can find no such number. It is the same question as the one about the measurement of the length of the third side of the right triangle that is a half square. It looks as if mediation fails.

But mediation does not fail. It finds an exact expression for even these wretched numbers, as Simone Weil calls them, alluding to the human condition which resembles theirs.[4] We learn to see that the meeting takes place in "another dimension," what we now call the dimension of the real numbers, which includes the misnamed irrational numbers.

The Greeks understood the significance of the fact that it is in the very stronghold of reason, in mathematics and logic, that we encounter impasses and contradictions and our imagination fails us. Our reason, however, does not fail us. For the Greeks these contradictions and this failure of imagination were not an excuse for mystification or pseudo-religious patter. What saved the Greeks from that was reason that could see the beauty and intellectual clarity of mathematics. Commenting on the situation in mathematics in our day, Weil says:

> The demand for perfect rigor which obtained in Greek geometers disappeared with them, and now, only within the last fifty years, are mathematicians returning to it. . . . The requirement of rigor is not something material. When that requirement is absolute, its use in mathematics is too obviously disproportion-

ate to its object. . . . In mathematics this exigence destroys itself. It must one day appear there as an exigence in a void. On that day it will be close to being ful-filled. The need of certainty will then encounter its true object. (IC 165)

This is one of many passages in Simone Weil that have a prophetic tone. She tells us that mathematics is reaching the point where it is becoming an "exigence in a void" and that this is the moment when it will again find its true understanding of itself.[5]

For the Greeks mediation between the human and the divine is the very idea of the *cultural* (in contrast to the *social,* which is the home of the collec-tive ego). In Greek philosophy and science it is the mind that is the mediator, while in Greek tragedy and mystery religions life itself assumes this role when nemesis and death lead to redemption and rebirth. All are anticipations of Christianity, in which there is a full revelation of the living divine mediation. Weil points out the actual stylistic form of the proportional mean in the New Testament, adding that a single relationship unites God to Christ and Christ to his disciples.

From this I conclude that just as Christ recognized himself in the Messiah of the Psalms, the Just One who suffers in Isaiah, the bronze serpent of Genesis,[6] so in the same way he recognized himself in the proportional mean of Greek geome-try, which thus becomes the most resplendent of the prophecies. (LP no. 7)

If among the Greeks, mathematics and science had a religious meaning, how did the modern split between religion and science come about, and the turn of science toward technologism and the service of the pseudo-religion of nationalism and the nation state?

The principal reason, as Simone Weil saw it, was the misunderstanding of Greek culture that appeared in the Renaissance and has persisted to the pres-ent day. This misunderstanding sees the Greeks as "humanistic" or "human-oriented" in contrast to the supernaturalist or revelation-oriented Bible. Thus arose the division between humanistic culture and revealed religion. It was a division that for a time seemed to strengthen both, but now is revealing the fatal weakness on both sides.

What has to be done is to reexamine our understanding of the Greeks in order to recognize the religious inspiration of Greek culture and the funda-mental Christian themes anticipated in it, an inspiration as genuinely reli-gious as the biblical inspiration. This is Weil speaking:

All our spiritual ills come from the Renaissance which betrayed Christianity for the sake of Greece, but having sought in Greece for something of a different nature from Christianity, failed to understand what was truly Greek. The fault lies with Christianity which believes itself to be different from Greece.

We shall only remedy this evil by recognizing in Greek thought the whole of the Christian faith. (N 465)

Even Renaissance Platonism tended to interpret Plato in humanist terms, failing to understand, for example, that the aspiration for the Good has to come as a gift of grace from the Good itself and cannot come merely from human desire.

It should be noted that Simone Weil does not believe that our civilization came from Greece alone but from pre-Christian antiquity (Germans, Druids, Rome, Greece, Aegeo-Cretans, Phoenicians, Egyptians, Babylonians), pre-Christian but Christian in essence, and all of them containing prophecies of the essential teachings of Christianity. In fact, Weil believes that there was never a time when there was not redemption upon earth and that Christ is always present unless people drive him away, wherever there is crime and affliction.

God's wisdom must be regarded as the unique source of all light upon earth, even such feeble lights as those which illumine the things of the world. (LP no. 7)

The Greeks regarded geometry as a divine gift and not merely a human achievement, because like poetry and art it was the product of genius, and genius like wisdom was a divine grace.[7] When the Renaissance secularized science and mathematics by cutting them off from religion, in the long run the effect was to impoverish both science and religion, science because it lost its relation to the Good and became unbeautiful, and religion because it lost its relation to culture and become individualistic or nationalistic. Simone Weil says:

Nothing is more foreign to the Good than classical modern science, which makes the elementary form of work, slave labor, the very principle of its representation of the world. . . .

In such a picture the Good is altogether absent. Therefore classical science is without beauty; it neither touches the heart nor contains any wisdom. (SN 12, 16)

While the essence of our science is technology, which means power, the essence of Greek science was measure and proportion, and nature was therefore already a kind of religion. In our science, she says, jewels of thought are treated like hammer and nails, subject to our wills. The Greeks desired to contemplate in sensible phenomena an image of the Good; we desire to exploit and use. Ancient science expressed a sufficiency, modern science a lack that deepens with the passage of time. As she observes in *Oppression and Liberty*, the power that grows is collective, and, by some unknown law, as collective power grows individual power shrinks. Therefore ours is simultaneously the most powerful and the most powerless generation in history. The more powerful we get, the more powerless we are.

In looking to see how this comes about, Simone Weil says there are three features of the modern world that have grown up together and which she calls the "three monstrosities of contemporary civilization" [F 30]. They are *algebra, money,* and *machinery.* In each of these cases something that started out as a means to serve other ends, began to grow monstrously on its own as a cancer does.

In *algebra* it is the process of symbolization itself, proliferating like an independent power, developing for its own sake and getting further and further away from any human meaning, or indeed from any meaning at all. What we call "information" is a good example. Information is quantitative order, entirely apart from meaning, and, like computers, something to which it becomes harder and harder to give meaning.[8]

Since the human mind cannot comprehend a science built on signs it does not understand or misunderstands, it is no wonder that modern science itself is not understood even by scientists and leads to so many results that are not prepared for. The feeling that we have that technology is out of control has its roots in a mistake about the nature of algebraic symbols. We believe mistakenly that the value of an algebraic variable may represent a full concrete particular, whereas actually it is only an abstract representation.[9] The whole of modern science and philosophy is infected with this mistake.

Something similar applies to the second "monstrosity," *money.* It was originally an intermediary, but now like an algebraic symbol it has taken on a life of its own. We have the phenomenon of money generating money and, even more oddly, money itself becoming irrelevant and being replaced by credit, and by credit to the second or third degree. The effects are to produce unreality by separating human effort from its results. We see this particularly as finance capital replaces industrial capital. Weil writes:

> Among the characteristics of decadence in the modern world do not forget the impossibility of envisaging concretely the relation between effort and the result of effort. Too many intermediaries. As in all the other cases this relation, which no thought can encompass, is found in a thing, in money. (F 30)

Finally, there is the third "monstrosity," the *machine,* in which methodicalness escapes understanding and also assumes a life of its own. The best example is the modern factory, which Simone Weil studied first-hand. The "fragmentation" of the work, isolating each worker in a tiny, seemingly unrelated part, creates the situation in which these broken-off pieces can be taken over by machines, or the workers themselves become more machine-like in doing them. It is not that the machines are not methodical—nothing could be more so; but their method is something we do not understand and do not need to understand. The result is to starve the worker intellectually and spiritually and above all to destroy the proper relation of mind and body, which is an essential part of satisfying work. Weil's analysis of what constitutes satisfying human work is one of her major accomplishments and far in advance of anything in Marxist literature.

The strength of Simone Weil's position is that it *addresses* what is already in our civilization, though in a truncated and now badly distorted form. Western civilization, she indicates, has misunderstood the nature of both science and religion by accepting the rift between them. One result is the unholy alliance now obtaining between science and nationalism—that is, between a secularized inhuman science and fanatical pseudo-religious nationalism.

In Simone Weil's view science and religion have a great deal more in common than either does with nationalism or any ideology. What they have in common is that at their best they each challenge the illusions of the human ego, individual and collective. The religious virtue of humility is paralleled by the intellectual virtue of skepticism, and the enemy of each is the ego-serving imagination which manufactures illusions.

Christianity has now to discover its true universality in two directions. First, to establish again its affinity with the spirit of mathematics and science and to recover the sphere of culture for religion. And second, to accept and affirm the forms of the spirit in all the world's religions, not as something hostile to Christianity but as having deep affinities with it. The road to humanity goes through the transformations of science in its proper relation to religion and through the acceptance of the spiritual content in all the religions of the world.

Christianity has failed in universality on two counts according to Weil: in allowing itself to be separated from mathematics, science, and culture; and in understanding its relation to other religions in an exclusivistic and even hostile way. The true instruction of Christ to his disciples, Weil says, was that his glad tidings were to be *added* on to other religions, not to *replace* them (LP no. 9).

In her *Letter to A Priest* sent to Father Couturier in New York, Simone Weil gave as her principal reason for not being baptized in the Catholic Church that the church did not recognize sufficiently the spiritual significance and validity of other faiths. Such terms as *polytheism*, *pagan*, and *primitive*, not to mention *superstition* and *heathen*, are still used to disparage other religions.

We know full well that there is genuine spiritual content in all religions, but our theology has not kept up with this. Some Christians even pride themselves on their ignorance of other faiths. Many theological schools, for example, do not acquaint students with them or do so only peripherally.

When Simone Weil died in a sanitorium at Ashford Kent in 1943 at the age of thirty-four, the coroner wrote on her death certificate under the heading of religion, "None." This is perhaps the supreme image of our religious situation today.

CHAPTER 2

Gnosis

L IKE WITTGENSTEIN, SIMONE WEIL BELIEVED that the most important thing is "to teach the meaning of the word *know* (in the scientific sense)" (F 364). But, also like him, she did not believe that the way modern science has understood this *is* the correct "scientific sense." The "knowledge" of modern science is removed from the Good; it is obsessed with power and utility and subverted to the illusions of progress and technological expansion. The center of gravity of Simone Weil's understanding of science (and, to the extent that it relates to the New Testament, of religion too) is the Pythagorean and Platonic *gnosis*, which sees the mathematical and philosophical intellect as a means[1] of grace.

In discussing Plato we distinguish between his two main terms for knowledge, *epistēmē* and *gnōsis*, the former suggesting measure and the latter inner appropriation. The notion that it is only *epistēmē* that gives exactness and precision (a notion that is part of the modern heresy) is precisely that notion that Simone Weil and the Pythagoreans and Platonists rejected. It is the *gnosis* of intellect that has to do with the infinite and the paradoxical in the most exact way, and thus has most to do with the divine.

We may take as our text for these propositions a passage from Simone Weil's notebooks:

The most important truth:
The mysteries of the faith can be and have been used in the same way that Lenin used the Marxian dialectic (in both cases contradiction as a logical criterion of error is eliminated); they are used by shrewd manipulation of the anathema for the total enslavement of minds. By the elect who disdain both rebellion and servility of mind, they are turned into koans by contemplation. But their secret lies elsewhere. It is that there are two different kinds of reason.

23

There is a supernatural reason. It is the knowledge, *gnosis* of which Christ was the key, the knowledge of the truth whose spirit was sent by the Father.

What is contradictory for natural reason is not so for supernatural reason, but the latter can only use the language of the former.

Nevertheless the logic of supernatural reason is more rigorous than that of natural reason.

Mathematics offers us an image of this hierarchy.

That is the fundamental doctrine of Pythagoreanism, of Platonism, and of early Christianity; it is the source of the dogma of the Trinity, of the two-fold nature of Christ in one person, of the duality and unity of good and evil, and of transubstantiation, which have been preserved by almost miraculous protection, one might think, of the Holy Spirit.

Natural reason applied to the mysteries of the faith produces heresy.

The mysteries of the faith when severed from all reason are no longer mysteries but absurdities.

But supernatural reason only exists in souls which burn with the supernatural love of God. (F 109–110)

Weil's text continues in a most astounding way to relate supernatural reason, not only to Christ, Paul, and John of the Cross, but to Odin, Osiris, Dionysus, and Prometheus.

That mathematical knowledge may be *redeeming* knowledge is a secret lost to the Western world since the mistaken humanism of the Renaissance split apart science and religion and paved the way for the madness of modern nationalism.

Simone Weil's *gnosis* is not the attempt of the human will to assert itself beyond all limits, to seize and possess and control everything, but rather an awareness that what belongs to the supernatural comes as a gift. The signs of this are the paradoxes and self-contradictions encountered by exact thought. Students of modern logic know what difficulties have been created by the paradoxes discovered by, and bearing the names of, Bertrand Russell, Burali-Forti, Grelling, Tarski, and others. Logic has felt itself brought to a dead stop, unable to cope with problems of self-reference, consistency, completeness, and non-denumerable infinity.

The Pythagoreans, as Simone Weil pointed out, faced with similar paradoxes, dealt with them as metaphors or analogies of the relations between the human and the divine. This was the significance of incommensurability, the impossibility of finding a whole number or fraction which, multiplied by itself, gives the number 2. That there is no such number may be regarded as a defeat for the intellect and for exactness of knowing; or it may be understood as indicating a further *gnosis*, a further opening of possibilities.

What is a scandal to natural reason becomes a valuable clue to super-

natural reason. The insoluble problem becomes in another sense a wholly sat-
isfactory answer. This is the grace bestowed on mathematics.

Every great religion in a sense "squares the circle": by thus "solving the
paradox." And what was found in Greek mathematics has another expression
in the New Testament, in the Sufi teaching story, and in the Zen koan. The
answer is no sacrifice of rigor or of intellect, but much more like a greater clarification. What is the sound of one hand clapping? It is like asking: How can
one become two and still remain one? How is one contained in two?[2] When
the student sees the answer—that the "how to" is not the last word or even the
first word—he or she may be inclined to say "Nothing easier!" The "solution"
requires an act of acceptance that occurs, it seems, by grace, for it is nothing
that we could have anticipated in advance or thought up alone. And is not this
the character of grace and revelation—that what we could not have done for
ourselves is nevertheless available and fully adequate?

Simone Weil, in keeping with all the major religions, declares that we have
no way from the natural to the supernatural, no technique, no method, nothing that we can accomplish by our own efforts—except to keep looking.[3]
Greek geometry, like the figure of Jesus Christ, or the Zen koan, or Osiris in
the Egyptian religion, or Krishna speaking to Arjuna—they can all be misin-
terpreted or fail to speak to us at all. There is nothing that we can take hold
of or grasp or make to serve our egoistic purposes or designs.

Since the publication and fame of Anders Nygren's *Eros and Agapē*, it has
been a frequent practice to contrast the possessive striving of Platonic *desire*,
seeking to make part of itself the immortal, the beautiful, and the good, with
biblical *agapē*, which comes as an undeserved gift, a grace freely bestowed
upon us. It is this "one-way" understanding of Platonic desire and knowing
(particularly in the *Symposium*), as "taking possession" even with regard to
the Good, which Simone Weil rejects. We who are not the Good can only
desire the Good by the grace of the Good—this is the deeper message of the
Symposium. At this point the supposed contrast between the Platonic and the
biblical breaks down, for it is only the Good's movement toward the world
that could inspire the world's movement toward the Good. And there is no
doubt in Plato about which comes first, for in the *Republic* he even tells us that
the Good is "beyond Being in dignity and power."[4]

It is *genius, wisdom, the paradoxes of the infinite, impersonal love* and *grace*
which belong to supernatural reason—all of them finally arising from the gift
of the Love of God—while talent, ordinary knowledge, finite measures, personal love, and will belong to natural reason and are tied to the human ego
and persona. The vision of the Good, which is the acme of Plato's philosophy,
like the Love of God in the prophets and in the New Testament, is not possible for the ego. The order and beauty of the world, best revealed by mathe-

matics, are a form of the Love of God. Mathematics is for Weil the supreme science of nature and is only valid insofar as it *is* the science of nature; but this means that it is supremely beyond our power to create, though not beyond our power to misuse and misunderstand.

It is the *impersonality* of science and mathematics, their freedom from egocentricity, ethnocentricity, and anthropocentricity, which ultimately validates them. This itself is a genuinely religious element in them. There can be no true *gnosis* that serves personal ends, or natural or racial ends. Nothing personal or ethnic or social can be sacred. It is what breaks down the ego, individual or collective, which alone can free us for truly scientific knowledge, and for one form of the Love of God.

It is clear that Simone Weil's *gnosis* is not of the kind of the non-Christian Gnostics of Alexandria, who developed the vast semi-mythological systems we associate particularly with the names of Valentinus and Basilides. It is more like the Neoplatonic Christian Gnosticism of Clement and Irenaeus. Speaking of Clement, Thomas Merton described his thought in words, which could apply to Simone Weil, as "a living apprehension of the central underlying significance of all reality and all history in the one light of the mystery of Christ."

There is indeed, however, another element in Simone Weil's *gnosis* which is indeed closer in spirit to the non-Christian Alexandrian Gnostics and hence to what is called Gnosticism in the more limited sense in which the term is used in the history of philosophy. This is the special flavor of her philosophy which is seen as related to the ancient Manicheans, to the twelfth-century Cathars or Albigensians, and to all those descended from the Alexandrian Gnostics. The best way to describe this is the attitude of *cosmic alienation*, the all-pervading sense of the far-awayness or absence of God, something not known to the Greeks, Hebrews, or Christians, but peculiar to the Alexandrian (and Syriac) Gnostics.[5] Connected with this is the feeling of our vast separation from God represented by matter and space and time, which, if not evil, are nevertheless the source of the intractable necessity that separates us from God.

Simone Weil's philosophy may be described as a remarkable blending of this ancient sense of alienation from God with the Christian doctrine of the Love of God. Her almost unique religious experience and teaching are that it is in God's *absence* that his love is most strongly and wonderfully shown. She presents a christianization (and Platonization) of the ancient non-Christian (and non-Platonic) Egyptian and Syriac Gnostic alienation.

We understand this better if we distinguish cosmic alienation from other kinds, such as Marx's social and Heidegger's ontological alienation. What matters for her is not separation from the products of our work or from "authentic existence," but separation from our source, our home and destination, by the vast gulf of the physical world. The supreme symbol of this is the vastness of cosmic space and time. The Gnostic experiences an overwhelming homesickness like a continuous sense of loss. The order and beauty of the world may be enough of a consolation for the Greeks, and for Simone Weil they are an expression of the Divine Love. But the light which "lighteth every human being who comes into the world" is for the Gnostic (and for this side of Weil) often more like a far-off gleam that is almost drowned in the darkness.

The Gnostic philosophers spare no pains to emphasize the lostness and abandonment of the human situation. This is expressed by Simone Weil in the enormous emphasis she puts on *affliction*, as the second main form of the Love of God. While we cannot understand an earthly parent manifesting love for a child by abandoning it, this is just what in Simone Weil's view is the highest form of the Divine Love. Love that loves despite being abandoned (as Weil understands Christ to have done) must itself be of divine origin. In the human situation we are confronted by the possibility of being able to love despite the worst afflictions, and since this is clearly beyond our own power, it can only be Divine Love itself that makes it possible. It is therefore not the resurrection but Christ's expression of abandonment on the cross that is the supreme expression and evidence of the Love of Love. The furthest possible point removed from God turns out to be the point at which Divine Love shows itself to *be* divine (i.e., beyond human power but real nevertheless).

The cosmic world is itself in Weil's vision a manifestation of this same situation. The Spirit is, as it were, crucified on the vast distances and necessities of space and time (a very Manichean picture). And only if the Spirit had truly a divine character could it survive this abandonment and keep its eye on the Light.

All this is bound to be disturbing to those who still link God with power, and for whom he is the thundering, tyrannical, power-wielding God of the Old Testament. But there is nothing admirable about power, nothing we should worship there. God is entirely removed from power, altogether free of it. Worldly power is illusion and borrows its reality from necessity. Necessity, showing itself in death, disease, hunger and separation, is not God's punishment but God's absence, which ensures the reality of his Love. Imagining God in terms of nations or peoples or powers is projecting collective egotisms. The images of Pure Light and Pure Love do not tolerate this.

Simone Weil does not see God directing human history and interfering in the wars and movements of people and events in the manner of Hegel's Universal Spirit. All that belongs either to the sphere of human illusions or to the necessities of the social world (which Simone Weil thought Marxism at its best had begun to deal with). This does not mean that the Spirit has no influence on human history, but that its influence is very unnoticed and very mysterious, like another dimension touching this world only at singular spots, as grace touches human lives only in unpredictable and unexpected ways.

In the Alexandrian Gnostic system, the Ultimate God is separated from the world by 365 aeons or cosmic space-time dimensions. This is a mythological expression of how far away the realm of grace is from the human world. As we contemplate the wars and horrors of history we can understand this. In the Manichean system, formulated by the Persian teacher Mani in the third century of our era, messengers come from the far-away Light to remind us of our ultimate home, messengers including Jesus, Buddha, Zoroaster, and Mani himself.

For Simone Weil the darkness is not an independent reality struggling with the Light; but the role of the World Redeemers is the same for her, and she sees them all as many versions of Christ. And the gap between the divine world and the human world, with its individual and collective egos and its endless struggles for illusory power and glory, is just as vast.

Among the medieval Cathars in the south of France (apparently originating from the Bogomils in southeastern Europe), there was a strong tendency to regard the physical body itself as an impediment to the spirit. Hence those who aspired to sanctity or perfection abstained as much as possible from the physical—particularly from food and sex. Some Cathars practiced the *endura* or dying by refusing to eat. There is no doubt that Cathar ideas exercised an influence over Simone Weil (as they did over Samuel Beckett), but they were also balanced by an awareness of the sacramental and incarnational aspects of Christianity. The more Gnostic and the more Christian were clearly in a strong tension at certain points.

Among modern Gnostics there is evidence in Weil's notebooks that she was acquainted with the teachings of P. D. Ouspensky and G. I. Gurdjieff, apparently through Mme. de Salzmann (the "Mme. de S." of the notebooks) and René Daumal. What seems to have interested her most is the idea of transformations of energy, or the ways in which energy may either be degraded (turning into what Ouspensky and Gurdjieff called "negative emotions") or made available for spiritual possibilities. As in the plant world sunlight acts as an energy transformer of the food which the plant receives from the soil, so Ouspensky and Gurdjieff said, the energy of negative emotions, like anger, hate, and fear, may be transformed by acts of conscious attention into spiritual developments. Much as the life of the plant is lived between *gravity* and *sunlight*, so the human story takes place between the poles of *gravity* and *grace*.

∞

A third feature of Simone Weil's *gnosis* is her universalization of Christianity and her rejection of the intolerance and exclusiveness of the original biblical God, still found in some versions of Judaism, Christianity, and Islam. She rejects the God of wrath and fear in Deuteronomy and Leviticus, who threatens the unrighteous Hebrews with every kind of punishment. But she also rejects the God who denounces pagans and heathens, whose example has justified not only the Christian persecution of the Jews but also the exploitation of those belonging to other nonbiblical religions and ways of life.

As many of the ancient Gnostics rejected the Old Testament God, so Simone Weil says that any God who orders the extermination of human beings (as the Old Testament God does in a number of places) cannot be the true God. It is the Hebrew prophets who first in the Bible opposed this narrow and anti-human divinity. The denial of the validity of the spiritual traditions of the ancient pre-Christian nations of Europe, Asia, and Africa is an aspect of the biblical point of view which she entirely repudiates.

The principal reason Simone Weil gave for not being baptized into the Christian church (despite her acceptance of Christ and of the essential Christian teachings), she says in her *Letter to a Priest*, was the Christian church's intolerance toward other faiths, intolerance it inherited from the Hebrew Bible. This "contempt toward the Gentiles" was continued against pagans and heathens as well as against the Jews themselves. It has blinded Christians to the spiritual values to be found in other traditions.

One of the most important sentences in Simone Weil's writings appears in the *Letter to a Priest* (no. 9). It is her statement that Jesus' disciples misunderstood him when they thought that his teaching was meant to *replace* other religions, when in fact what he meant was that his teaching was to be *added* to them. This single change would have made Christianity a religion that recognized itself in all others, rather than one that sought to supplant them. Christianity would not then have thought of itself as superior to other faiths (and destined to "final victory") over them, but rather as helping to bring out what was best in them.

In Simone Weil's view there can be no conflict between the valid spiritual teachings of any of the great religions of the world. Whether we are talking about the Celts or the Druids, the Norse or the American Indians, African folk religions or the great spiritual traditions of Asia, in every case there is something that belongs to universal religion and that, properly understood, is found to be in harmony with the inner truth of Christianity and the biblical prophets, Greek religion, and Buddhism. We can learn from all of them.

In place of the dominationism built into the biblical traditions, which see themselves as destined for ultimate *triumph*, since they remain infected by the veneration of power, Simone Weil points to a universal Christianity in which all the other traditions *retain* their identity and place in the light of a supernatural Love that accepts and makes room for them all.

What has been added here to both traditional Christianity and traditional Gnosticism is an all-embracing humanism, a point of view that affirms all religions and all peoples in the fullness of the human pleroma. In the age of nuclear weapons the deadly exclusivism and spiritual elitism and claims to metaphysical superiority promise only endless wars and eventually suicide. The traditional God takes sides with one religion or people against others. Only the Spirit that puts all traditions and peoples in relation to Divine Love and grace makes possible the fullness of humanity. This is the full ecumenical content of Simone Weil's *gnosis*.

CHAPTER 3

Intellect as Grace

The Kingdom of Truth

SIMONE WEIL GREW UP IN A FAMILY where the word *genius* was often used to describe her brother André, who showed remarkable mathematical gifts before he was nine. She was three years younger than he, but very close to him, and she must have wondered often about the meaning of this highly charged word which was spoken of him so reverentially by the members of her family. It is not surprising that in time the "crisis of adolescence" should have come upon her as a question about her own intelligence. As she later described it, the episode was portentous for her whole future:

> At fourteen I fell into one of those fits of bottomless despair that come with adolescence. . . . The exceptional gifts of my brother, who had a childhood and youth comparable to those of Pascal, brought my own inferiority home to me. I did not mind having no visible successes, but what did grieve me was the idea of being excluded from that transcendent kingdom to which only the truly great have access and wherein truth abides. I preferred to die rather than live without that truth. (WG 64)

Here the word *truth* has the special weight that it retained until the end, and here too appeared the pattern, which was to be repeated again and again, of darkest despair giving way to new plateaus of insight.

> After months of inward darkness, I suddenly had the everlasting conviction that any human being, even though practically devoid of natural faculties, can penetrate to the kingdom of truth reserved for genius, if only he longs for truth and perpetually concentrates all his attention upon its attainment. He thus becomes a genius too, even though for lack of talent his genius cannot be visible from outside. (WG 64)

31

Coming from a Frenchwoman raised in a typically irreligious, not even nominally Jewish, agnostic home, the expression "everlasting conviction" is striking; but even more is the anticipation, so early on, of the parameters ("genius without talent") within which the struggles and agonies of her short life were to take place.

Everything that happened from that time on (with a degree of coherence that takes the breath away) is like a gloss on this text. Twenty years later, nearing her harrowing end brought on by spiritually imposed starvation (which it seems to me only those who have studied the Cathars can even begin to understand), she had come to see, nakedly and without evasion—in that very double light of which she speaks, intellectual detachment and identification with the sufferings of others—what her own role had been.

> Today it is not nearly enough merely to be a saint, but we must have the saintliness demanded by the present moment, a new saintliness, itself also without precedent. . . . The world needs saints who have genius, just as a plague-stricken town needs doctors. (WG 99, italics added)

Simone Weil's life followed three distinct but inwardly united tracks, any one of which would have been impossible for her without the others: (1) the scholar and teacher and writer on philosophy and religion, science and history; (2) the social activist, revolutionary, and critic of Marxism; (3) the manual laborer on assembly lines and in the fields. All of these for her equally essential activities expressed her rejection in her own body and mind of the distinctions between *pure* and *applied*, *theoretical* and *practical*, and *abstract* and *concrete*, which no modern philosopher (neither Kierkegaard, nor Marx, nor Nietzsche) had been able fully to escape. Like Wittgenstein and Tolstoi (with both of whom she had so much in common in her love of common people and simplicity and gospel Christianity), she saw in *the spirituality of work* (which she attempted to define precisely) the missing factor in our civilization, and without which there is no true civilization. As others have said, her epistemology begins with work, not knowing. This crucial factor, which it is no surprise to find eluding intellectuals, is the meeting place of the economic, cultural, psychological, and religious.[1]

If we look for the secret of Simone Weil's intellectual vitality and remarkable output and intellectual authority—there are ten large volumes of her writings in the *Oeuvres Complètes* now being published by Gallimard, and none of her writings are "inferior" or can safely be ignored—I think that we will find it in her first beginnings in philosophy under the tutelage of the great French thinker Alain (Émile Chartier, 1868–1951), with whom she studied at the Lycée Henri IV in Paris in the years 1925–1928. In her writings for him we first encounter the marvelous quality of freshness and precision that characterizes her genius. And we also see her characteristic ways of thinking about imagination and perception and will, thinking and action, the individual and society, psychology and science which she inherited from Alain, as well as her veneration for Plato and for Greek mathematics, and her high regard for Kant, Spinoza, and Descartes (on whom she wrote her dissertation for the École Normale Supérieure). A number of these early essays written for Alain are reprinted in the first volume of the *Oeuvres Complètes*. In them her genius is already fully evident.[2]

It is in one of these writings, the *Fragments on Freedom* written in 1926, that she comes closest, I believe, to giving us the decisive clues. It shows how she understood *thinking*, the thinking that was continually born in her, and came to her as a gift and not as an effort of will, and to which she already knew herself to be dedicated. It was so closely connected with absence of self or self-effort as to make the terms "thinking" and "freedom" virtually interchangeable in her grammar. We must bear this in mind when we read "This freedom is God." The thinker here is not the Cartesian ego ("the self which knows the self") but the inspiring source itself, manifesting through us only when no ego or agent is in the way. (If we qualify it in intellectual and Christian terms, it is not far off to describe Simone Weil as shamanic and charismatic.)[3] Speaking in intellectual tongues, she says that

> God is above all determinations, since he does not limit himself to a single idea; he is thus free; better expressed, he is freedom itself. . . . I can agree to call God my own freedom. This convention has the advantage of freeing me from every God object. . . . If God is my freedom, he is and exists every time that my freedom manifests itself in my ideas and movements, which is to say every time that I think. (OC 1.89–90)

No higher value could be placed on *thinking* and *freedom* than this. They lie beyond logic and law, ego and will, eros and mythos, in the place to which genius and sanctity alone have access and of which she says "only by convention" can it be called "my own," since nothing there belongs to anybody. Freedom and thinking are not objectifiable, controllable, or possessable.

This text does not speak of truth as the source of freedom, but implies more provocatively that freedom is the source of truth. Detachment to a superlative degree (for example, from every past and every future) permits the opening of what William Blake called "the Intellectual Fountain of Humanity" and "the Universal Poetic Genius" that both Blake and Weil regarded as "the Only True God" and identified as the New Testament Christ.

Like Blake, she understood that these gifts are given only on condition that we do not intend them for worldly sense and do not seek to "use" them. Like Blake, she recognized that in the Greek phrase for "daily bread" in the Lord's Prayer (*arton epiousian*), the Greek word *epi-ousian* is better translated "super-substantial" or "super-essential." For, as Blake said, "I should suspect that I worshipped the devil if I asked God for worldly things."[4] Freedom in Simone Weil's lexicon is freedom from the world—that is, from attachment to the world, where "world" includes all social groups and identification as well as all forms of individual ego-enhancement and prestige. It is the game of ego, collective as well as individual, which blocks our relation to Truth.

Simone Weil was attentive and a listener, like the poet; but she also had intellect. Her words do not grasp or seize or attempt to persuade or influence; they do not express an opinion or perspective or point of view. They manifest the detachment of freedom and real openness, impersonal and honest and incorruptible.

Some will say (we have heard it all our lives from the existentialists) that it is still her truth, implying that every truth has to be somebody's truth. But this is not the case, for her truth has no owner (nor does it come from the senses or the mind or the unconscious). Arising in the void of freedom, where there are no hidden commitments and nothing to defend or gain or lose, no social or economic or psychological attachments, it is nobody's (that is to say, it is God's).[5] Words from there require no defense. They are untainted by any ancestry or ideology, any hope or fear or desire. They are a pure gift, not belonging to any community or race or nation, any church or book or creed or system; they do not belong to any individual.

This is a long way from what is called *thinking* or *truth* today—problem solving or rearranging existing opinions to support preconceived conclusions. When it is not technical calculation or trying to sell something, it is to some degree or other apologetics or propaganda. Simone Weil's truth breathes a different air because from the outset she does not care how it comes out.[6] We might well speak of a divine recklessness. (We see her walking on the high wire and watch fascinated. But it is always we who blink. Far up, almost out of sight, she is sustained by the opposite of gravity. It prevents her missing a step.)

As Simone Weil understood it, the word *truth* sums up everything we would rather not look at (and that turns out to be just about everything). Truth is what opposes all our weakness and hypocrisy and cowardice, our self-serving and self-deceit. It is the harshest ingredient in human life, the most costly and the most dangerous. The Fool and the Child are only preliminary images.

> A village idiot is as close to truth as a child prodigy. The one and the other are separated from it only by a wall. But the only way into truth is through one's own annihilation; through dwelling a long time in a state of extreme and total humiliation. (SE 27)

In the last year of her life, writing to an old friend, Maurice Schumann, we find her expressing the same marvelously impersonal love of Truth:

> Truth only comes to us from outside, and it always comes from God. . . . Life for
> me means nothing, and never has meant anything really, except as a threshold
> for the revelation of truth. (SL 170, 178)

But now something else joins this, a feeling that anticipates her impending
death, and even the grim and enigmatic conditions surrounding it:

> I feel an increasing sense of devastation, both in my intellect and in the center
> of my heart, at my inability to think with truth at the same time about the afflic-
> tion of men, the perfection of God and the link between the two.
>
>   I have the inner certainty that this truth, if it is ever granted to me, will only
> be revealed when I am physically in affliction and in one of the extreme forms
> in which it exists at present. . . .
>
>   I am outside the truth; no human agency can bring me to it; and I am inwardly
> certain that God will not bring me to it except in that way. (SL 178–179)

Although what this means remains obscure to those of us who have no comparable experience by which to understand it, how can we not think that her
inability to eat at the end of her life in the sanitorium at Ashford Kent, was the
extreme final ordeal she had spoken of?[7]

   Despite this extraordinary and nearly incomprehensible death-circumstance,
Simone Weil's best epitaph, it seems to me, nevertheless might be the dying
words of the young priest in the book *Diary of a Country Priest*, by Georges
Bernanos, an author whose writings she deeply loved and with whom Weil
briefly corresponded: *Grace is everywhere.*

The World of Necessity

It is all too evident that we do not live in the kingdom of truth. We live in what
Simone Weil calls the world of necessity.[8] This is her designation for the natural world and the human world, which, in its darkness and ignorance, so
often resembles it, but without the "obedience" that ennobles the natural
world. The world of necessity is the world of uncaring nature, the vast cold
reaches of space and time, the indifferent cosmos, loss and death, illness and
suffering, and all that goes with them. She speaks of it as

> the necessity which is the substance of the world but which is only felt by us in
> the form of blows.[9]

In this world we experience for the most part not truth and love and justice
but only the appearances of them.

> Our world is the kingdom of necessity. The appearance of justice is of this world.
> Real justice is not of this world. (IC 142)

Human life is cast in a third world, the world of illusions. This is the world of power and prestige and privilege, the system of social lies which fills our day with the pretensions of vain pride. The rulers of the social world employ the weapons of necessity—force and death and different kinds of enslavement—to maintain their illusory systems of self-importance. Only here and there do we catch glimpses of truth amidst the fantasy systems of human imagination.

To see all this clearly, to realize all the lies and corruption and power seeking, without ever going down on our knees to it; this is the mark of authentic spiritual leaders—Homer, Sophocles, Plato, Jesus, those who refused to succumb to the idolatry of brutality and force.

In this imaginary world of idolatry, there is no Platonic realm of ideas.[10] There is only natural necessity, materiality with all its gravity and force bearing down on us. But the illusions of the human ego, collective and individual, have no reality but only the appearance of it. As if across an infinite abyss, traces of the Truth and the Good, known only by grace, reach us in our darkness and blindness.

We may thus distinguish three realms [or levels, or dimensions]: human illusion, the natural world, and supernatural truth— in other words existence, necessity, and impossibility:

Existence, or shadow reality: illusion, the imaginary, prestige, social power, gold, pride, lies, war, ideology, the appearance of justice, fame, opinion.

Necessity, or solid reality: matter, space and time, gravity, causality, force, affliction, birth, eating, disease, death, loss, destruction.

Impossibility, or manifest reality [sc. manifest only to love, by grace]: transcendence, divine love, anonymous love of neighbor, order, beauty, truth, humility, friendship, paradox, attention, affliction as a means of grace, school studies as development of attention.

The realm of Existence has the character of a dream, as in Plato's Cave. Imagination rules, as it does in social life and in war. It is significant that it was a military man, Napoleon, who said, "Imagination rules the world."[11] Simone Weil's illustration for the unreality of this social power or prestige is a box of old medals, for which men fought and died, now a child's plaything for a rainy afternoon. A reality test is, How would it look from the Great Nebula in Andromeda? But even Necessity cannot wake us from our dreams of glory. Only what is humanly speaking Impossibility, the supernatural, can do it:

We must touch impossibility in order to emerge from the dream state. (N 410)

In the realm of natural necessity we come up against what is not ourselves, obstacles and hardships that we cannot do anything about. In the social world this is force, and evil. As the Greeks understood (and, Simone Weil adds, the Old Testament and Romans did not), the important thing for any civilization is not to unite God with force and power.

It is the inability to tell this difference that characterizes the sophists opposed by Socrates and Plato, and rulers and politicians throughout history. They are the attendants upon Plato's Great Beast of public opinion that has to be humored and pandered, for at any moment it may turn upon the powerful and tear them to pieces. Believing only in power, they are ignorant of the subtle guiding wisdom of the Good.

> The herd imposes its values, in one way or another, in all societies without exception. There are two moralities, social morality and supernatural morality, and only those who are enlightened by grace have access to the second. . . . The wisdom of Plato is nothing other than an orientation of the soul toward grace. (SN 99)

Mathematics and science "sublime" necessity[12] in order to reveal the supernatural order and beauty of the world. But while the Greeks saw the clues to the beyond in just this way, our science has seen the necessity only in terms of utility, human collective power, and the analogy to human work.

> Classical [modern] science in the end was able to subsume the study of every natural phenomenon under the simple notion of energy, which was directly derived from that of work. . . .
>
> Nothing is more foreign to the good than classical science, which makes the most elementary form of work, slave labor, the very principle of its representation of the world; it finds no place for the good, even by way of contrast, as an opposing term. (SN 7, 12)

(The fact that the "slave labor" metaphor has been so "successful" in physics tells us no more than that it was "successful" in the same way that it was in human affairs—at what cost in humanity?—and that our science and our society very well reflect each other.)

Despite the differences between them, Greek and modern science both recognized what the common man experiences as Necessity. Twentieth-century quantum theory, on the other hand, has abandoned this and set up what Simone Weil regards as an unintelligible notion of probability, detached from all [concrete] meaning. (Apart from necessity, she says, probability becomes a meaningless notion.) A science without necessity in short order will lose both meaning and truth and cease even to attract students (SN 49-65). It is one thing to give up "representing" the world, as modern science has done, and another to give up "making sense" of it. (For the latter we need relevant metaphors and human relations.)

If truth cannot be defended by power (and truth is indeed the first casualty of power), then does it need metaphysics to defend it? The question itself rests upon a confusion between the *metaphysical* and the *supernatural*, somewhat like that between the psychological and the spiritual, or between the social and the moral. Within the metaphysical lies the idea of taking possession of the world, of knowledge that grasps and consumes. The supernatural, on the other hand, is what reveals itself, it comes as a gift, it is an inspiration or illusion. As the word "Being" epitomizes metaphysics, so the word "Spirit" does the supernatural. Spirit no longer belongs to the human will. What the Franciscan Joachim of Fiore called the Third Age begins with the end of metaphysics.

It is a characteristic of Simone Weil's philosophy, as it is of the later Wittgenstein's and the later Heidegger's, that it begins with meanings as given, not having to be constructed or explained or justified. Whether they are given by language (Wittgenstein), history and poetic thinking (Heidegger), or by Truth, Love, and the Good manifesting in the world (Weil), it is meanings that we have to examine. Metaphors and analogies become more important to the establishment of paradigms, frames of reference, and ways of thinking and looking.

The Decline of Perspective

Along with the model of mechanical work, the modern world has been dominated by the idea of *perspective*, a metaphor going back to the Greeks, but only fully realized in the Renaissance with the invention of new geometries and the science of optics. It was a truly integrating idea, of the kind that creates "reality." Both scientists and artists, dealing for the first time with three dimensions representationally, could imagine that they had taken control and for the first time saw it as it really was.[13]

Descartes' *Geometry* (1637) opened the possibility of algebraic equations, representing all possible paths of all bodies in two-dimensional space, which could be extended to any number of dimensions. As he stated at the very beginning of his book,

> Any problem in geometry can easily be reduced to such terms that a knowledge
> of the lengths of certain straight lines is sufficient for its construction.

He is referring to what we now call the use of coordinate systems. Combined with the Newton-Leibniz calculus for dealing with the infinitely small in space and time (i.e., the lack of nextness [sc., of points, thus for dealing with continuity and its infinite divisibility], this provided the basis for the new science. It was a new "objective world" we looked out upon.

> Measurable material quantities assumed the metaphysical status of "what is really there," replacing the medieval intellectual forms as true Being seen by the eye of the mind.

The first sign that this so-called reality itself was cracking up (even before it happened in physics, for Cartesian coordinate systems themselves were given up by Einstein) was the abandonment of perspective in the arts. There has been no more daring step than the return of flatness, the realization that two dimensions are "more real" than three are, and that it is the latter that are the construction or the abstraction. When Cézanne's apples, although painted in two dimensions, nevertheless appeared as solid as, if not more solid than, Giotto's (a fact noticed by D. H. Lawrence and Rainer Maria Rilke), a new epoch began in art and culture.

In philosophy even such a great innovator as Nietzsche was unable to break the hold of perspective and believed that the end of metaphysics (the one ultimate perspective) would certainly produce a chaos of relativism and moral nihilism, as human perspectives multiplied indefinitely, with no way of determining that any was truer than any other. (The analogy in music was the chaos of atonality, regarded as evil by some conservative musicians in the 1920s and 1930s.)

Simone Weil saw the significance of the return to Greek plane geometry and its analogies everywhere.

> The fixed point of view is the root of injustice.
>
> Plane geometry is an exercise in thought without a point of view. Everything is on one plane.
>
> In every sphere, it is an indispensable purification of thought to set out the subject on one plane, thus eliminating any point of view about it, by the use of deductive intelligence.
>
> But several cross-sections have to be taken, as in a mechanical drawing. A single cross-section leads to error. (F 270)

(The conflicts generated by different conceptions of justice from different points of view clashing with each other is a political expression of a failure of perspectivalism.) Multiperspectives and the composition of perspectives in the same picture are only the beginning of dealing with this. The abandonment of perspective altogether is the more drastic step.

Simone Weil speaks of the "loss of the sense of reality when the mind submits itself to a perspective" (N 234). The following clarifies this: "The position of indifference is the one which is outside any point of view" (N 224).

More radically and cryptically she says, in a statement that makes sense only if we see "grace" as the "supernatural justice" that overcomes perspective:

> Supernatural justice, an operation analogous to the overcoming of perspective. No center anywhere in the world, only outside this world. (F 87)

And finally this:

> It is impossible that the whole of truth should not be present at every time and every place, available for anyone who desires it. (F 302)

The intellectual cul de sac anticipated by Nietzsche with the end of metaphysics—relativism and chaos—has been avoided most successfully by the later Wittgenstein, the later Heidegger, and Simone Weil. With certain precursors, but no immediate ancestors, all three of them succeeded in getting through to a postmodern aperspectivalism, in no way anticipated by Nietzsche or any other nineteenth-century philosopher.

Learning to Think in a New Way

It was Albert Einstein who said that "we must learn to think in a new way or perish." He did not say what the new way was. Nevertheless, it would be surprising if after the catastrophes of the century just passing there were not profound changes in human thought. There is indeed a new way of thinking emerging to be seen most clearly among philosophers and artists, of whom Wittgenstein and Simone Weil are among the most well known.[14] Despite the vast differences in what they wrote about, there are remarkable similarities between these two.

We see a widening consensus that the following must be given up:

1. *Ideological thinking*: systems of mythical causality in the manner of Freud and Jung, Marx and Lenin. These lack the detachment to be true science and the honesty to be religions; they are disguised belief systems. Suitably qualified, their descriptive insights would be valuable, but they serve well-established prejudices.

2. *Metaphysical thinking* and its latest variant, the anti-metaphysics of Nietzsche and Derrida. The anti-metaphysical cannot free us from metaphysics since it makes the same absolute claim, but in a negative way. We cannot deny what we claim is nonsensical.[15]

3. *Foundationalism* and *representationalism*, twin pillars of tradition—"the absolute ground" and "the absolute picture"—indicating doctrinal ortho-

doxy. Appropriately, it is modern logic and modern mathematics which have shown both to be illusory.

4. *Perspectivalism*, claiming that "to think is to take up a perspective," generated the insoluble epistemological problem of how to unite the private subject with the detached object that it confronts.

The key word for the new way of thinking is "description" when this word has lost all of its overtones of complete logical mapping. We are looking not for exactness but for description so detached, so penetrating, so obvious that it has the character of revelation.[16] This is a kind of seeing in which the ordinary becomes translucent, a kind practiced by Simone Weil and Wittgenstein. Their thinking itself becomes a kind of looking.

Such "seeing" entails and invokes metaphors and analogies that change our structures of meaning. The day is past when philosophy was concerned with knowledge.[17] It is concerned now with meaning and understanding. We see now that knowledge itself does not bring understanding, that "every day we know more and more but understand less and less."

The facts that are bringing about the disintegration of our civilization have gained the upper hand in this century, and it may be too late to reverse this. It was Simone Weil's belief that [in all human probability] our civilization will not survive, but one day will simply stop working and break down completely. To understand how this came about, to take inventory of our failures and mistakes—that would be worth doing so that we would not go down wholly in the dark and those who come after us might still learn from us (OL 108–124).

With the Renaissance the sense of what lies beyond the human will was lost, and instead the extension of scientific knowledge and power appeared to be without limits. This has led to the loss of human proportions, the fragmentation of culture, and technology out of control. As this spreads to the mass media and the power of political manipulation grows, our culture sickens with unreality and the inability to discern reality from it. Renaissance *hubris* has been overtaken by its *nemesis*.

Our civilization will only be revived by and rebuilt on a renewed humility (in Simone Weil's words, "the only supernatural virtue"). Only by finding this again in the original sources of our civilization will we be able to survive and pass into the new world of the post-technological age.[18]

CHAPTER 4

Cantor, Infinity, and the Silence

ONE OF THE FOREMOST MATHEMATICIANS of our time, David Hilbert, once described mathematics as "the science of the infinite." The statement is justified by the fact that each of the great moments in the history of Western mathematics has been characterized by a discovery and a scandal bearing on the question of the infinite: the sixth century before Christ, when the Pythagoreans discovered the "incommensurability" of certain lengths or what later came to be called irrational numbers; the seventeenth century of our era, which introduced the infinitesimals that became the basis of calculus and modern science; and the nineteenth century, the period of Georg Cantor's transfinites.

To describe each of these three dealings with the infinite as a shock, both mathematical and cultural, would be an understatement. Plato saw the philosophical implications of incommensurability as important enough to shake up a whole civilization and labeled anyone who did not know about it a "pig."[1] George Berkeley in the eighteenth century poked fun at the idea of any quantity being infinitely small, while partisans of Newton and Leibniz fought over which one deserved the priority in having made these discoveries first. The reaction of some mathematicians to Cantor was that he belonged in a mental hospital (where in fact he did spend some time).

What has made this subject of the infinite, when connected with our most exact science of mathematics, so touchy? Is it not because we have here the most paradoxical and mysterious of results attached to ultimate things in a precise way? Consider the Pythagorean discovery. In its simplest and most shocking form we have a right angle triangle with two sides equal in being one unit long each. Now it turns out that there is no exact number which can represent the third side, the hypotenuse, no combination of integers and fractions. Certainly the third side has an exact length. We can see it in front of us. But there does not exist any ordinary number to express this.[2] Instead we have "a number that is not a number," the square root of two, which is a non-terminating, non-repeating decimal. The infinite is present in the most simple, the most ordinary measurement we can imagine. This was a shock for Plato, who was forced to conclude that the infinite and the finite are mixed together to make a world.[3]

To take a contemporary example, Hilbert imagined a Grand Hotel. It has an infinite number of rooms and is all filled up. There comes one more guest asking for a room. The proprietor says: "All I have to do is to ask each guest to move up one more room and I can give you room number 1." And so it is. Next door is another hotel also with an infinite number of rooms all filled. But this hotel only has even-numbered rooms, whereas the first hotel has both even- and odd-numbered rooms. It might seem that the first hotel contains twice as many rooms as the second does. But this is just what is peculiar about the infinite: *a part is equal to the whole.*[4] This is the initial definition, the first distinction between the infinite and the finite. The Hermeticists used to say, "the whole is everywhere." How could this be unless by a peculiar arithmetic?[5]

Before we discuss the marvelous innovations of Cantor and how Simone Weil reacted to them, let me say a word about her names for God and how they relate to what the scholastic philosophers called the Transcendentals, or the six main Names or Divine Attributes for God as they came down through the Christian tradition. First of all, of course, is Plato's name *The Good*, probably the name Weil most frequently used. Second is Plotinus's designation, *The One*. Plotinus was not a Christian and, in fact, was hostile to Christianity, but his writings, and the writings of others influenced by him, played a large part in early Christian philosophy. Weil, of course, could think of the Divine Unity without also thinking of the Trinity, Three-in-One. Third, we have Augustine's favorite name for God and also one of hers, *Truth*. Anyone who has studied Augustine will recall the importance to him of the Truth within. The fourth transcendental is *Beauty*, which is not so easy to connect with a single theologian, but my choice would be the Franciscan Bonaventura.[6] Simone Weil deplores the relative absence of Beauty in the Christian theological emphasis in recent times; she regards Beauty as a manifestation of the divine and one of the ways by which God seduces the soul. The fifth transcendental that carried the day through the triumph of Thomas Aquinas was *Being* understood in terms of Act, and leaning heavily on Aristotle. It is a striking fact how seldom Weil uses this term by comparison with some of the others.[7] Sixth is Duns Scotus's favorite term for God—*Infinity*. The issue between Thomists and Scotists has been a running battle, the former charging the latter with pantheism and the latter the former with agnosticism. Most disturbing to Protestants has been Thomas's conception of "the analogy of Being," which Karl Barth called an invention of the devil since it asserts that Being is a universal common denominator between God and creatures. Scotus believed in "the univocity of Being," which means that Being may have a [single] meaning, not only analogically.

Let us note parenthetically that three of the most innovative thinkers of our time have been Scotists: Gerard Manley Hopkins the poet, Charles Sanders Peirce the American philosopher, and Martin Heidegger the German philosopher. Heidegger began his book *Being and Time* with the question, "What is the meaning of Being?"—not "What is the meaning of the word 'Being'?" but "What is the meaning of *Being?*" This question could only be properly asked and answered by a Scotist. And Heidegger wrote his doctoral dissertation on Scotus. Heidegger's philosophy finds the meaning of Being to be *presenting*, a decision for which there is New Testament authority.

And now to Cantor. If we simply imagined an arithmetic in which adding infinity to infinity gives infinity, subtracting infinity gives infinity, multiplying infinity and so on, the result is always just infinity again. Cantor's initial great discovery was that there are different *powers* of infinity—different *kinds* of infinity—and he was able to establish this mathematically.

Imagine a ruler graded in such a way that between any two numbers smaller and smaller fractions are packed, so that it would seem that all spaces are entirely filled up with fractions, and between any two fractions we can imagine an infinity of others. It is one way of imagining an infinity of points in space.

Now comes Cantor to tell us that nevertheless the line is still empty. When we look at the line in terms that include the irrational numbers, there are more empty spaces than filled ones. If we fill in all the irrational numbers as well as the rational ones, we will have a line with infinitely again more points on it than before. With a very simple argument known as the Diagonal Proof, Cantor was able to establish this amazing result. He did it by showing how to construct sequences of infinite decimals, each decimal differing in at least one place from the decimal preceding it. Each one of these infinite decimals represented a new number that could not be matched to any previous number. While the even numbers could be matched one for one with the whole numbers, these irrational numbers could not be. The first kind of numbers were denumerable or countable in this way. The second kind could not so be matched and counted and therefore constituted a still greater infinity.

The paradoxes connected with the real number continuum are, if anything, even more startling than those connected with the ordinary or so-called natural numbers. In infinite terms,[8] even the smallest distance between two points is equal to the distance from here to the farthest galaxy. Here is a genuine mystery, comparable to the mysteries of religion and theology.

Adopting the name of the first letter in the Hebrew alphabet, Cantor called the ordinary infinity *Aleph null*. The infinity of the real numbers was designated *c* for *continuum*. Cantor called this second infinite number *Aleph 1*. The first two cardinal infinite numbers were set up in this way. But what was the connection between them? Cantor found this connection when he found that *Aleph null* raised to the *Aleph null* equals *Aleph 1*. The same procedure gives us *Aleph 1* raised to the *Aleph 1* producing *Aleph 2*, a third degree of infinity. And this process can go on into more and more dizzying heights.

Cantor was a religious person. He was born and baptized a Lutheran and remained a devout Christian all his life. He said that his transfinite mathematics had come from a divine inspiration. And this is what made him so certain of it. In the 1880s he corresponded with Roman Catholic theologians who, under the guidance of Pope Leo XIII, took an interest in his mathematics. What particularly concerned the theologians was whether the actual infinity that Cantor spoke about applied to the natural world in its concreteness or only to God. Cantor said that the application to the natural world could only be a reflection of the far greater Divine Infinity which was beyond human conception and comprehension.

At an International Congress in Rome in 1908, Cantor repudiated the idea of a *Genus Supremum* embracing all transfinite numbers. He said:

> I have never proceeded from any "Genus Supremum" of the actual infinite. Quite the contrary. I have rigorously proved that there is no "Genus Supremum" of the actual infinite. What surpasses all that is finite and [all that is] transfinite is no "Genus"; it is the single completely individual unity in which everything is included, which includes the "Absolute" incomprehensible to the human understanding. This is the "actus Purissimus" which by many is called "God."[9]

It may help to clarify what is meant by the actual infinite in its concreteness if we consider three separate cases: consider all the grains of sand on all the beaches of the earth. This is a huge number and it is very unlikely that we will ever know what it is. But it is certain that it is finite. Now consider all the possible moves in all possible chess games. This too is a large number. And it too is finite and we know exactly what it is. But what about all the stars in the sky? Is this finite or infinite? This we do not know. But it could be one or the other. It is perfectly conceivable that it might be infinite.[10] Would this be the supernatural infinity of God? No, that would still be a far greater Infinity.

Simone Weil's explicit references to Cantor in her notebooks are so condensed that it is often difficult to tell what she is getting at. It seems clear,
however, that [to her] the relation between Cantor's transfinitism and theology is one of analogy. For example, the following:

> In "Cantor's Paradise," the mind has got to be very much clearer, more exact and
> intuitive than anywhere else. (As in the case of the mysteries of theology.) (N
> 362)[11]

Note the phrase in parentheses. And this:

> Transfinitude. Cantor. Something lies behind the very highest. (N 420)

The expression "the very highest" must be referring not to the finite but to
Cantor's infinites.[12] And again:

> Analogy tending toward the non-apprehensible. Eudoxus. Cantor. Use of mathe-
> matics. (N 252)

The "use of mathematics" must refer here to analogy, and her examples are
Eudoxus and Cantor. Eudoxus, an associate of Plato in the fourth century B.C.,
developed the "method of exhaustion" (called by Diogenes Laertius the "theory of crooked lines") for squaring the circle by making smaller and smaller
segments of the circle into tangents, until we could see that when these
become infinitely small, a square becomes a circle, or reversing this, vice
versa. Coupling this with Cantor, we have two analogies for the relation
between the infinite and the finite, and thus between the divine and the
human. We must not confuse even infinite numbers with the divine. Weil
says, "There is no superlative in Number" (N 622). As in Plato, the divine
attributes, such as Goodness, Truth, and Beauty are beyond any numbers,
even the infinite numbers. The transcendentals lie beyond even them, and of
course beyond Aristotle's ten categories, to which the scholastics counter-
posed them.

It seems to me that Weil distinguishes between Cantor's mathematics and
the supernatural when she speaks of Grace as something infinitely big of the
second order. This is to be understood analogically.

> [Order of infinities (*read Cantor*).]
> [My misery is infinite with respect to my will, but it is finite with respect to
> grace. . .] Grace is something infinitely big of the second order.
> But my misery is with respect to Grace, finite, not infinitely small. (N 249)[13]

Cantor's series of infinities are certainly being referred to in the following
entry:

A mathematical series (recurrence through analogy), with or without passage to the extreme limit, and spiritual problems.
Must study Cantor. (N 325)

Why is she telling herself that she must study Cantor? Perhaps just because of this relation between the mathematical and the theological, the natural and the spiritual, which, as we have already seen, Cantor was careful to keep apart, although, as we have already noted, he believed that his transfinite mathematics had come to him as a divine revelation.

There are several places where, without mentioning Cantor by name, Weil uses the expressions "infinity beyond infinity" and "infinity of higher degrees." This brings us to one of the climactic points in her spiritual life, an ultimate moment portrayed in her Spiritual Autobiography.[14] Here the appeal is not to Goodness or Beauty or Truth, though these meant much to her, but, quite in the manner of Duns Scotus, to *Infinity*. She is speaking about her morning practice of reciting the Lord's Prayer before going into Thibon's vineyard to pick grapes, reciting it with her purest attention:

At times the very first words tear my thoughts from my body and transport it to a place outside space where there is neither perspective nor point of view. The infinity of the ordinary expanses of perception is replaced by an infinity to the second or sometimes the third degree. At the same time, filling every part of this infinity of infinity, there is silence, a silence which is not an absence of sound but which is the object of a positive sensation, more positive than that of sound. Noises, if there are any, only reach me after crossing this silence. (WG 72)

Let us mark Weil's use of the word "sometimes" in the second sentence in distinguishing between infinities of the second and third degrees. I take it this is characteristic precision which parallels Cantor's precision. (It reminds me also of the different levels of *samadhi* in the Hindu system.) Not only does perspective vanish but so also does dimensionality.

Finally we have to notice that she links infinity to *silence*—silence as a positive sensation, more positive than sound. What could this mean? When Beethoven was stone deaf he wrote his last Quartets, though he couldn't hear a single sound. Many critics and listeners have commented on these pieces that they express a "music beyond music" or a "music beyond sound," a movement of spirit. When Simone Weil speaks of a silence "which is not an absence of sound," is this what she experienced? We recall also the Pythagorean "music of the spheres," which is so omnipresent that it cannot be heard.[15]

We approach here the mystics' "Abyss of Unknowing" where form and formlessness, affliction and love, past, present, and future disappear altogether in incomprehensible harmony.

How are we to think of mathematics in relation to the supernatural? Weil calls mathematics an "image of reality" and as such it is a principal revelation of the beauty of the world. We will recall that for Plato, as much of a Pythagorean as he was, numbers ranked below the Forms or Ideas because they are not as universal and separable, unique and unitary, as the Forms.[16] One of Plato's primary uses of the word *metaxu* is to refer to numbers which for him stand "between" the Forms or Ideas and the sense world. Weil vastly extends the use of the word *metaxu* to cover all mediators between divine and human.

Let us take a moment to look once more at the question of necessity. For Simone Weil necessity is experienced by us as the blows of the world; but it is known to intelligence and best revealed through mathematics. It is thus connected on one side to the horrors and miseries of human life and on the other to the beauty of the world. Such necessity is a first incarnation of the divine —God's first showing—by withdrawal and abandonment. Christ, who revealed the meaning of this as Love, is the second incarnation. We may describe Greek geometry as a prophecy of Christ through its anticipating necessity as Divine Love.

All necessity is intellectual necessity, even that which is felt and seen within the various kinds of brute force in the world. But the beauty of the world, which she says is the only real beauty there is,[17] goes far beyond this— the sea, the mountains, the trees, the night sky—and we commit a crime by not seeing all this and contemplating it. For we can find hidden in this force and necessity and beauty the mathematical concordances which, even though ultimately incomprehensible to us [fully], make them images of perfect order and the Good.

This is summed up in the following passage:

> One does double harm to mathematics when one regards it only as a rational and abstract speculation. It is that, but it is also the very science of nature, a science totally concrete, and it is also a mysticism, those three together and inseparably. (IC 191)

What does this word "mysticism" mean here? Surely that which leads us to participation in the supernatural—a *metaxu* and an incitement to knowledge of the third kind, as this idea appears in philosophers and saints, in Plato and Spinoza and John of the Cross. When Weil speaks of modern mathematics as concerned only with rational and abstract speculation, she is referring mainly to algebra, which she believes since the time of the Babylonians has been on the wrong track, though now it has practically taken over the whole world.

Finally, we come to one of the most profound and mysterious passages in

Simone Weil, one that connects mathematics and the Good (N 513-515). There is a tradition that Plato intended to give a lecture on mathematics and the Good but did not. In Weil we do not have the lecture, but hints and insights.[18]

She draws a distinction between *demonstration*, which is always conditional as all proofs are, and *appropriateness* (the French word she uses, "convenance," connotes fittingness and concordance).

Contemporary mathematicians are obsessed with demonstrations and proofs. To show this, someone recently went through the fifty or so current mathematical journals and found that in one year more than two thousand proofs were printed. The point is that no one could put them all together or judge which were the most important and which were the unimportant ones. So fragmented and specialized has mathematics become, like many other subjects, and indeed like our whole culture, its domination by algebra being not least to blame.

Weil begins the mysterious passage I mentioned in this way:

> Demonstration belongs to the order of necessity. It is conditional. Appropriateness eludes it absolutely and always. Appropriateness has reference to good. Mathematics displays to us the mystery of the persuasion exercised by good over necessity. Demonstrative necessity and appropriateness form the opposites which are the terms of mathematical harmony. (N 513)

She goes on to say that beauty lies in the concordance of harmony and necessity without either intervening in the domain of the other, and "[t]his concordance alone contains for us the fulness of reality" (N 514). "The essence of reality lies in beauty or transcendent appropriateness" (N 515).

We need an example of this appropriateness of mathematics to the Good. She gives us one, which is repeated in the essay on Pythgoreanism.[19] It has to do with the mysterious way in which right angle triangles lying on the diameters of circles as their hypotenuses determine and are determined by the points of the circle. There is nothing in the concepts of a circle and a right angle in themselves that would lead us to expect this. We could never have created it; we simply came upon it, like a sign or a gift. If the right angle apex falls outside or inside the circle, it will no longer be a circle or the right angle a right angle. Looking at the two, circle and right angle, separately, there is no reason to suppose that any such relation would have to exist between them.

Weil points out that there are two sides to this mysterious appropriateness in this example, as in many other such examples found in mathematics, one relating to the natural world and our technology, and the other to the supernatural. Thus, the way in which circular motion translates into alternating motion, which is basic to our technology, is a direct consequence of this appropriateness. It is illustrated every time someone sharpens a knife on a grindstone or weaves cloth in a factory. This side of it she calls the ponderous element. The other side is in the transcendent concordance, known by grace. The appropriateness, as we see, is in the sensible world, but also in the transcendental one. Both are subjects fitting to deepest contemplation.[20]

Both Simone Weil and Georg Cantor, our survey shows, are firmly anchored in the Platonic tradition of *actual infinity*, both natural and supernatural, the tradition of Augustine, Scotus, Cusa, Bruno, and Pascal, and both rejected the potential infinite of Aristotle, Averroes, and Thomas.[21] The Divine Infinite and the natural infinite are for them two forms of the actual infinity.

When Simone Weil, in describing her ultimate and most complete religious experience, spoke of entering an infinity beyond infinity, and even an infinity beyond that, and a silence beyond silence, and even a third degree of silence beyond that, she was clearly echoing the translucent mathematics of Cantor. Through the means of this most recent intellectual understanding of the infinite she was conveying her total spiritual participation in the supernatural.

CHAPTER 5

T. E. Lawrence and the Purification of Evil

O F ALL THE FAMOUS MEN AND WOMEN whom Simone Weil might have singled out to "wholeheartedly love and admire," it tells a great deal about her that the only one of whom she speaks in this way was the British military genius (as Churchill called him) and epic anti-hero T. E. Lawrence. It may seem surprising that a soldier-scholar who went to such lengths to create and then to repudiate a mythic persona near the summits of military power in World War I should have been a leading inspiration for a left-wing Parisian intellectual immersed in pacifism, trade unionism, Marxism, and finally Christian spirituality. Yet there were deep affinities between them and, like André Malraux, who also was fascinated by Lawrence, Simone Weil could not avoid the problem that Lawrence epitomized and struggled with all his life—how to preserve purity of action in the midst of whirlwinds of force.[1]

It was in 1938, just after the publication of Lawrence's *Letters* (he died in 1935 after many years of seeking anonymity as a private soldier and air force mechanic), that Simone Weil wrote to the editor of that volume, David Garnett, a long letter (in English) beginning:

> Shall I own that my real reason for writing to you with inexpressible gratefulness [is] for editing the letters of Lawrence? I hardly knew more than his name before reading the *Seven Pillars,* and at once recognized that here was the one man famous in history, I won't say in our time, but in all times known to me, whom I can wholeheartedly love and admire; and I am scarcely able to bear the knowledge that he is dead. . . . I am always tortured, about past and remote as well as about present and actual things, between admiration and horror; for cruelty and cowardice are alike horrible to me, yet as all human relations are more or less based upon some form of slavery, it is impossible not to be either cruel or cowardly or both. . . .[2]

51

In this letter Weil mentions two things that made her love and admire Lawrence: first, his effort while engaged in the most savage desert warfare to keep killing and cruelty to a minimum, and, second, his strong sense of human equality and his inability to live in company with others except in relations of equality. He was, she said, "one of those most rare men . . . for whom equality in all human relations is as necessary as the very air they breathe." It was this necessity that came in conflict with Lawrence's most striking and enigmatic feature, his remarkable charisma, which, when he wished to use it—for it was apparently in his control—could hold people (even people like Churchill) in a spell. Remarkable as the charisma was, more remarkable was the refusal to use it. Weil's letter tells why.

> Lawrence was clear-sighted enough to know that among men in general not equality, but power and crushing subordination has been, is and will be the rule; so life was impossible for him. . . . Having used men, either enemies or servants or allies, as material to be grinded [*sic*] for his own ends, though the ends were not personal, he could not forgive himself that he had gained glory in this way; and that he found unvoluntary [*sic*] pleasure in the glory was poison for him.

For Weil it was Lawrence's double awareness of the extent to which power rules the world (both in nature and the human soul) and the fact that this was nevertheless "an absolutely detestable thing" which made her admire him, as she admired the same combination in the ancient Greeks.[3] The extra turn of the knife for Lawrence was precisely his being a natural leader with a magnetism like a force of nature, which made many think of Alexander and Napoleon. (As Churchill discerned, there is no telling where it might have taken him.) But this power spelled domination over others, the very breach of human equality that was most repugnant to him. Weil was on the mark when she asked, "Who knows the whole extent of the empire of might and at the same time despises it?" and answered, "T. E. Lawrence, the liberator of Arabia, was one" (IC 116).

Lawrence's life and world-view turn on the same duality as Simone Weil's: on the one side the hardship and misery of the world and the illusions and falsity of the human world brought home to us in our bodies, and on the other hand the unrelenting requirement to discover and maintain non-egoistic freedom and integrity. For both of them life was an ordeal: a series of trials in hostile circumstances where they were held (by what?) to impossible demands.[4]

The supreme symbol of this was the desert, with its implacable indifference and awesome austerity, where Lawrence's ordeal reached its first apogee. This was the setting for grueling hardships described in *The Seven Pillars of Wisdom*: endless miles of forced marches in killing heat alternating with freezing nights; long periods of thirst and hunger, disease and delirium; ambushes and betrayals; and the daily and nightly immediacy of death and dying. When he returned to England, Lawrence had over sixty wounds on his body, including thirty bone injuries, and had been wracked by seven or eight serious diseases. Only an unbelievable will and the cause into which it seemed destiny had thrust him kept him going. Living beyond human limits (and particularly an episode of torture and sexual violation at the hands of the Turks) had all but destroyed him, even as it satisfied some deep longing for purification and emancipation and self-knowledge through suffering.[5]

In a letter to a friend, Lionel Curtis, Lawrence said that like a "lay monk" he had discovered asceticism. What happened in the desert was that "the body was too coarse to feel the utmost of our sorrows and our joys. Therefore, we abandoned it as rubbish."[6] But, far beyond this, both Weil and Lawrence, it seems from opposite poles had come upon the deep connection, known to the Greek tragic dramatist but in our own time all but forgotten, between suffering—called by Weil, in order to include the social dimension of humiliation, affliction—and self-knowledge.

Simone Weil's desert, as real in its own way as Lawrence's, was *within*. As she described it, it was a void from which the illusion of self and collectivity had eventually disappeared like mirages, an inner vacuity in which the imaginings of ego and society were silenced and the promptings of the spirits could at last be heard. Only under conditions of such extreme detachment, going far beyond what is usually meant by skepticism, could human beings speak the bare truth: a happening so rare and so upsetting to normal illusions that every effort is made to prevent its being spoken or not to hear what is said. All lesser attachments had to disappear in this nothingness, from which alone truth about matters of any importance could emerge. In her mind, genius and saintliness alone could sustain living with the void, which becomes in them a "divine plenitude."

Such a practice was not without its price. For most of her adult life she suffered from excruciating headaches that for years and years never let up even at night. She located this pain in the pineal area behind the bridge of the nose and seemed to believe that there was some relation between the "hatred and repulsion . . . recoiling on myself" generated by the pain and what she called the "pure gold" of some of the insights that came to her. Some of her most remarkable writings were composed in a context of continuous pain.[7]

Weil too was driven by the "necessity for equality," in her case the need to experience life as workers do by getting jobs on factory assembly lines, although she was temperamentally and physically unsuited for this. She found it to be far more enslaving and humiliating than revolutionaries could have imagined who had never had such experiences (she mentions Marx, Lenin, and Trotsky). The importance of the working environment seemed never to penetrate revolutionary circles, obsessed as they were, like capitalist bosses, with who gets the profits. The need to share a common lot propelled her into the Spanish Civil War, where she caught a glimpse of the random brutality of war before being mustered out by a random camp accident.[8] Her final ordeal as a manual worker, of picking grapes in the vineyards of Gustave Thibon in the south of France, she confessed she was able to complete only "by the help of grace."[9]

Lawrence's adult life was spent in the military (writing in his spare time) but in impossible situations, first leading a strange and difficult foreign people, and then as a private soldier under an assumed name among his own.[10] *Seven Pillars* is about the Arab Revolt, but it is also a study of the Arabs, their mentality and spirit, undertaken with the detachment of a poet and historian who never forgets the distance that separates him from the people he leads.[11] It is fair to say that this second side of Lawrence was of no interest to Simone Weil, while it was of very great interest to friends like E. M. Forster and C. M. Doughty, who with other prominent literary figures of the day, Henry James and D. H. Lawrence,[12] to name only two, were always centrally concerned with "national character."

In her notebooks we find Simone Weil many times referring to T. E. Lawrence in remarks on the nature of action and the purification of evil. What constitutes genuine action, she says, is not what we imagine that we would do in a given situation, but what in moments of decision, in the light of an "equal attention,"[13] we find that we cannot help doing. Genuine action is what there is no alternative to doing. Weil offers as an example Lawrence going back to look for the Arab who had lost his way (N 29–30).

Such actions are imposed by the situation itself clearly perceived. They spring from it and express it, she says. In terms of her multilevel perspectivalism, and one of her favorite metaphors, such actions bring the otherwise chaotic elements of a situation into a unique balance and then the scales themselves tip one way or the other. The body, which can only do one thing at a time, is the pointer on the balance, while motives, desires, and inclinations are the weights.

The essential condition is the equal attention in which the "I" is absent and, as she puts it, the person behind it does not appear. The choice is now not just an arbitrary personal one, but necessary. It is not a leap of desperation but the result of thinking that is much more than what is usually called by that name. (For what most people call thinking is simply consulting their prejudices and attachments and individual or group interests.) Lawrence's thinking could be called *pondering* (thus *Seven Pillars of Wisdom*, chapter 33) and is certainly what Robert Graves had in mind when he said, "In all my acquaintance I know no more than three people who really *think*, and these three include Lawrence." Weil observes that "Hamlet does not know how to contemplate in this way."[14]

As an example of genuine "detached action," nonetheless decisive for being detached and all the more whole for being impersonal, she cites the *Bhagavad Gita* and paraphrases it:

> If one situates oneself at a given moment of time, one no longer has the choice. . . . At a given moment one is not free to do anything whatever. And one must accept this internal necessity, accept what one is, at a given moment, as a fact, even one's shame. (N 56)

What makes both thinking and action pure is the absence of self, which is at the same time the absence of force. But it is not in the way in which self may sometimes seem absent from criminality or fanaticism. "Not to be present in an action" means not to be attached to it in any respect, whether as a cause, an idea, or a belief. Lawrence's attachment to the cause of the Arabs, surely wholehearted enough, was nevertheless detached enough to be the subject of continuous awareness and study. To "remember who you are" in Hindu, Gnostic, Sufi, or Christian parlance always carries this "remove" with it.

Would Lawrence have been able to act in this way if he had been on the losing side or anticipated losing? We forget that he *was* on the losing side and that he *did* anticipate this. He knew that whoever had the most power at the war's end would determine the terms of victory, regardless of who got to Damascus first or what promises had been made. Power, not justice, would settle the outcome.

Not being present in action does not mean being immunized to the suffering involved, but rather the contrary—the suffering is vastly increased because the human bond is not set aside.

> One must be very pure to do evil. And if one is pure, doing evil is torture. Lawrence. What remedy exists? A good deal of constraint is necessary, and few beings are sufficiently pure to be able to handle force. (N 87)[15]

The remove from self and hostile group identification establishes and reveals equality with the enemy; more particularly, it adds to one's suffering, for one feels then that the enemy's suffering is as significant as a friend's. Criminals and fanatics, on the other hand, assume the omnipotence that isolates and privileges the victimizer before his victim.

Simone Weil found this impartiality belonging to the right action that purifies evil—symbolized by the equal mind and the golden scales of Zeus—in the texts both of *The Iliad* (about which she wrote one of her most brilliant essays) and of the *Seven Pillars*. Such impartiality is very difficult to achieve and maintain and carry out fully in practice. Even when Lawrence was unable to stop acts of revenge and cruelty and unnecessary force by others under his command, he knew that it was *his* failure.

In a broader historical context Simone Weil reminds us that the principal attempts to purify evil have been by methods of force sanctified by religions, such as holy wars and crusades, inquisitions and religiously backed colonial and imperialist missions that were often genocidal.

> God making evil pure—that is the idea behind the Gita. It is also the idea animating Moses and Joshua, the Crusades and the conception of H(itlerism).

She means to draw a line between the *Gita* and the rest, and she continues:

> Jehovah, the Church of the Middle Ages, H(itlerism)—all these are earthly Gods. The purification they effect is an imaginary one. (N 502)

Why is the *Gita* genuine purification and the others not? It is because God in the *Gita* is wholly Good [despite requiring us to do evil], while the biblical God is complicit with evil, permitting gratuitous atrocities and even ordering them.[16] We sometimes forget that when the biblical God ordered the complete extermination of whole nations (e.g., Deuteronomy 7.16; 20.16–17; Psalm 106.34), he set an example for the medieval church and for modern totalitarian regimes which only now fully revolts us, making us realize how deeply rooted in religion our inhumanity has been.[17] Probably nothing has contributed more to discrediting the biblical God, not only for Lawrence and Weil but also for large numbers of young people in recent generations: Have so many crimes have been committed in his name or under his orders that we cannot recognize him any longer as true God?[18]

Does it have to be said again that justice is not possible for a God or a religious institution or a secular state whose ultimate resource is force?

> There is something in us which lies completely outside the range of relationships of force, . . . and that is the supernatural principle of justice; for force is injustice. Force is the evil principle. It reigns everywhere, but is never able to defile Love by its contact. (N 457)

> The false God changes suffering into violence: the true God changes violence into suffering (N 507).[19]

Up until the fall of 1938 when she had her culminating religious experience (for which all her past life had been a preparation), Simone Weil said that

> the word God had had no place at all in my thoughts. . . . Until then my only faith had been the Stoic amor fati as Marcus Aurelius understood it, and I had always faithfully practiced it—to love the universe as one's city, one's native

country, the beloved fatherland of every soul. . . . (Letter to Bousquet, SL 140-141)

Lawrence might have described his own outlook in the same way, not only during his years in the Arab Revolt but afterwards, with one important addition, the influence of Nietzsche. What he called his "Titanic books" were books of *will* and *doubt*: Dostoevsky's *Brothers Karamazov*, Nietzsche's *Zarathustra*, and Melville's *Moby Dick*.[20] We will look in vain through *Seven Pillars*, the *Letters*, or *The Mint* for anything beyond will and doubt.

The will can endure any hardship of the body. This thought is best expressed in a passage at the end of chapter 83 of *Seven Pillars*, where the Nietzschean word also appears:

Into the sources of my energy of will I dared not probe. The conception of antithetical mind and matter, which was basic in the Arab self-surrender, helped me not at all. I achieved surrender (so far as I did achieve it) by the very opposite road, through my notion that mental and physical were inseparably one; that our bodies, the universe, our thoughts and tactilities were conceived in and of the molecular sludge of matter, the universal element through which form drifted as clots and patterns of varying density. It seemed to me unthinkable that assemblages of atoms should cogitate except in atomic terms. . . .

The practice of our revolt fortified the nihilist attitude in me. During it, we often saw men push themselves or be driven to a cruel extreme of endurance: yet never was there an intimation of physical break. Collapse rose always from a moral weakness eating into the body, which of itself, without traitors from within, had no power over the will. While we rode we were disbodied, unconscious of flesh or feeling; and when at an interval this excitement faded and we did see our bodies, it was with some hostility, with a contemptuous sense that they reached their highest purpose, not as vehicles of the spirit, but when, dissolved, their elements served to manure a field.

These words could have been echoed by many of Lawrence's generation— Malraux, Hardy, Flecker, Jeffers, Mencken, to name a few—but would have found no resonance in the later Weil, for whom *attention* had replaced will, and *love* and *grace* molecular sludge, all of this without her ever having read the mystics.

The closest Lawrence came to meeting the spirit that imbued Simone Weil was an encounter, described in chapter 63 of *Seven Pillars*, with "a greybearded ragged man, with a hewn face of great power and weariness" who wandered into the desert camp one day and sat down groaning the only words he seemed able to articulate clearly: "The love is from God, and of God, and towards God."

Lawrence was shaken, not by the message (though he treated the wanderer with tenderness), but by the challenge to one of his long-cherished ideas.

> The old man of Rumm loomed portentous in his brief, single sentence, and
> seemed to overturn my theories the Arab nature. . . . I had believed Semites
> unable to use love as a link between themselves and God, indeed, unable to con-
> ceive such a relation except with the intellectuality of Spinoza, who loved so
> rationally and sexlessly and transcendently that he did not seek, or rather had not
> permitted, a return. Christianity had seemed to me the first creed to proclaim
> love in this upper world, from which the desert and the Semite (from Moses to
> Zeno) had shut it out: and Christianity was a hybrid, except in its first root not
> essentially Semitic.

(The expression to "use love" gives Lawrence away here; this is an expression
which would never have been allowed to cross the lips of a Sufi or a Christian.)[21] Years before he had intended to write a book on the background of
Christ, and now its main thesis was questioned by the strange old man. The
thesis was that Jesus was far more Greek than Jewish, coming as he did from
Galilee, "Syria's non-Semitic province, contact with which was almost
uncleanness for the perfect Jew." Brought up on Galilee's intellectual freedom
among the "products of an intense if very exotic provincial and corrupt Greek
civilization," Jesus picked up "the tang of humanity and real love that made
the distinction of his music."

Unfortunately the old man wandered back into the desert late that night,
"meaning strange things, not knowing day or night, not troubling himself for
food or work or shelter." Lawrence was not able to get out of him anything
more than the single sentence. And thus went by the best chance he probably
ever had to know the spirit which in a brilliantly intellectual and articulate
form was also the spirit of Simone Weil.[22]

CHAPTER 6

Marx, Oppression, and Liberty

S IMONE WEIL MADE HER FINAL RECKONING with Karl Marx in London
in the winter of 1943 in the last essay she wrote before her death in
August of that year. She had been studying and writing about him since
the 1930s, when as a young teacher she was involved in trade union struggles
in collaboration with the PCF, the French Communist Party. Most of her criticisms had taken shape even at that early stage (though without the further
religious additions they would have later) in a series of essays written in 1934
and brought together under the title *Oppression and Liberty*. These essays, by a
twenty-five-year-old, remain what Albert Camus said they were—"more penetrating and more prophetic than anything since Marx."

The late essay "Is There a Marxist Doctrine?" puts the earlier critique even
more succinctly. She means to separate the wheat from the chaff in Marx and
to claim him for the Western philosophical tradition. She makes it clear that
she herself rejects Marxism as a doctrine (or as we might say, a system, world-
view, or paradigm).

> Marx was checked when still a young man by an accident very common in the
> nineteenth century; he began to take himself seriously. He was seized by a sort
> of messianic illusion which made him believe that he had been chosen to play a
> decisive role for the salvation of mankind. Thenceforward it was impossible for
> him to preserve the ability to think in the full sense of the word. (OL 169–170)

Today when with the collapse of Communism it is evident that Marxism—
which has always made philosophers, and not merely reactionary ones,
uneasy—finds itself more seriously questioned, there could be no better
restarting point than the writings of Simone Weil. Many students will have to
put to themselves now the question she asked herself: What is "solid and inde-

structible" in Marx (if anything) and what is "meager, superficial and mediocre"? What is permanent and what is obsolete?

The line between the two, the permanent and the obsolete, we will find she drew decisively and unequivocally. She is unstinting in her praise of what she regards as Marx's "great discovery," his "idea of genius," his thought "of infinite value." But she feels only scorn for the "nonsense" and "foolishness" and "superstition" into which she believes he also fell. Probably no one has ever praised Marx so much in one respect while criticizing him so mercilessly in others.

The great achievement of which she cannot speak too highly was his discovery of *social matter*—that is, of a *mechanics of social forces* to which we are all subject, analogous to the mechanics of physical forces known to the physicist. Social behavior in this sense is subject to laws as determined and prediction-supporting as any in nature (laws having to do with, e.g., different kinds of social power and the way they push us around). This realization is a method or instrument of incalculable value. No one, least of all any Marxist, she says, has as yet made any significant use of it (Foucault might now be an exception). Marx himself had no inkling of its full possibilities as it might be applied to phenomena of war, gender, education, race, and mass culture.

While in possession of this priceless method, it was Marx's misfortune that he allowed himself to fall victim to

> the most ill-founded superstitions of his day, the cult of production, the cult of
> big industry, the blind belief in progress (OL 148).

And when this was combined with the messianic illusion, his great discovery was soon wrapped in "the wretched cult of science" and surrounded by "metaphysical clouds" and "formulas devoid of meaning," in a misguided attempt to create a fictitious connection between socialism and science. Mythology and mystification had carried the day.

Simone Weil tells us that Marx deceived himself by trying to invoke the prestige of science and mythic history to guarantee a happy outcome for justice in a world of purely material forces. He could not bear to admit that justice should not have (what it so manifestly does not have) big battalions on its side.

At the core of this wishful and ultimately sentimental thinking were two nineteenth-century shibboleths—"progress" and "production." Marx slipped into a religion of production, believing that more and more production is inevitable and that this is the driving force of history, so that productive forces will go on expanding indefinitely, although there is no good reason to believe that they will. (It was simple nineteenth-century middle-class optimism.) Finally, he thought that these productive forces would inevitably fall into the hands of the largest group in society, the workers, who would know how to use them justly, having no further enemies.

This last idea of the "chosenness" of the proletariat, who might otherwise seem a trampled group not particularly well prepared for moral leadership, she says, was largely the result of another illusion to which Marx succumbed, the idea that *number* as such is a force. (She might also have referred to the prestige of large numbers.)[1] But the truth is that millions of oppressed people do not become a force simply by being a large number:

> Marx's revolutionary materialism consists in positing, on the one hand, that everything is exclusively regulated by force, and on the other that a day will come when force will be on the side of the weak. . . .
>
> If the absurdity of this does not immediately strike us, it is because we think that number is a force. But number is a force in the hands of him who disposes of it, not in the hands of those who go to make it up. (OL 193–194)

Marx sets up this absurdity by imagining history as a process in which larger and larger, but also weaker and weaker, groups progressively take over until finally at the limit only the largest group is left, now unopposed. Of this she says scornfully:

> The limiting process, when applied to a relation one of whose terms it eliminates, is altogether too absurd. But this wretched form of reasoning sufficed for Marx, because anything suffices to persuade the man who feels that, if he were not persuaded, he could not live. (OL 194)

This whole mythology constitutes for Simone Weil an "inferior religion" designed to soften (what in her view should not be softened) the bitter disparity in human life between *force* and *justice,* or in Plato's language between *necessity* and the *good.* Hence the imaginary role assigned to the proletariat. And hence also Marx's failure to look more closely at the concept of revolution itself, which, she says (and as Marx himself understood on occasion, but did not wish to see steadily) never takes place until the social power transformations it legitimates have already occurred (OL 148). Nor did he even seem to notice such other forms of oppression as war, conscription, bureaucracy, and factory work, not to mention social discrimination such as that against women.

In trying to make room for and account for his own role and that of other leaders of the proletariat who were not themselves of that class, Simone Weil says, Marx gave way to one of the things he hated most, professional morality. Setting up a new priesthood of professional revolutionaries, he opened a snake pit of evils.

> He was struck by the fact that social groups manufacture moralities for their own use, thanks to which the specific activity of each one is placed outside the reach

of evil. There is thus the morality of the soldier, that of the businessman, and so on, according to the rules. . . . one accepts as an absolute value the specific morality of the social group of which one happens to be a member. One's mind is then at rest; but morally speaking one is dead. (OL 156)

Other professionals who have emerged in our time with their own rules by now include concentration camp guards, secret agents and spies, high financiers, arms dealers, advertisers and public relations consultants: all notorious liars and deceivers.

Marx fell into this trap because he failed to balance properly the social and the individual and to make room for the free independent mind and judgment, which ultimately does not have to give way before any necessity, whatever its lot in the world. It is the individual mind (and there *is* no other mind) that acknowledges necessity and in this act frees itself from it.

The frozenness of Marxism as a doctrine, its cultural and philosophical sterility, has been due not merely to the heavy hands of Lenin and Stalin, but to Marx's own omission of a place for individual responsibility. Without it we have a closed system. And although, in Simone Weil's words, the social condition is "the fundamental fact" and "determines almost everything," it cannot completely define the human situation. The social does not think, and it has no conscience. As a thinker, Marx failed to defend the thinker: the only kind of thinker there is, the *individual* thinker.[2]

If physical forces and social forces were the last word, no one would be in a position to judge the truth of this, nor to distinguish between what *is* right and what only *seems* right. If a small elite undertakes to decide "truth" ("party truth" or "revealed truth"), then we are on the road that leads to the crimes of the gauleiters and commissars.

> But Marx was a generous soul. The sight of injustice made him suffer really, one might say in his flesh. This suffering was intense enough to have made it impossible for him to live had he not harbored the hope of an imminent and earthly reign of complete justice. For him, as for many, need was the best of proofs.
>
> The majority of human beings do not question the truth of an idea without which they would literally be unable to live. (OL 172)

Has Simone Weil found Marx's weak spot, his passionate need for *justice*, for which he would be prepared, even unknowingly, to sacrifice the *truth* itself? Such wishful thinking would not be her own way. To her Western civilization rests upon something else: never to refuse to see and acknowledge necessity, though never to call it good.[3] That is the same thing as to endeavor not to deceive ourselves.

As Marx understood things, social morality is infested with lies and propaganda, though for him the proletariat (and its leadership) could not lie because history was on its side. But evidence and reason forbid us to make an exception for them. Every social group will behave shamefully in order to enforce its own interests if it can, and to the extent that it can. It was clear to Simone Weil that no revolution will ever change *that*.

Marx opened the door to the analysis of social oppression, but, as everyone knows, he mostly confined himself to the subject of capitalist oppression in its economic aspects in the last century. He did not go into the question of oppression in its multifarious forms, which lay in wait for communists, socialists, fascists, and everybody else in the next century. He and his followers never tried to develop a general theory of oppression or even to ask what oppression really is. In the light of what happened, it was an amazing oversight, for we have lived to see regimes, calling themselves Marxist, as oppressive as any societies in human history.

The changes brought about by the Russian Revolution simply did not get down to anything basic. As Simone Weil wrote, the institutions of this insurrection

> did not perhaps effectively function for as long as a single morning, and . . . the real forces, namely big industry, the police, the army, the bureaucracy, far from being smashed by the Revolution, attained, thanks to it, a power unknown in other countries. (OL 78)

To this we have to add that the development of weapons of propaganda, indoctrination, secret police, torture and murder, used to establish mind control of an entire nation, all that we have come to call totalitarianism, were also completely unanticipated by Marx.

Simone Weil's writings attempt to fill this vast lacuna with a general theory of oppression. Before we have gone very far we discover that the question does not concern merely capitalism and economics but our entire civilization: for this is what has produced Hitler and Stalin, world wars, genocides, arms races, drug cultures, and ecological suicide. The truth is that we have a "civilization" the entire foundation of which has begun to quake. The relevant text here is the most prophetic of Weil's writings, "Sketch of Contemporary Social Life" (OL 108–122), a text that should be required reading now.

What is *oppression*? Simone Weil suggests that we start with Marx's idea, of Kantian origin, that oppression is what turns a human being into a *thing*. And this means one is no longer able to think or act as one will.[4] The limiting case is the corpse on the battlefield; for war is the supreme example of oppression or the reduction of humans to things, and the preeminent Western epic, the *Iliad*, deals with just this, how human beings on both sides are put at the mercy of chance, force, and necessity. So too the slave, the conscript, the detainee, the factory worker, the brain-washed person are turned into things, though living things. A society in which people are no longer able to think or act for themselves is a society of slaves, of oppressed people, no matter what it is called.

How do these conditions come about? Historically, she says, we find privileged groups in every society which command, with others obeying. They become privileged through (1) secret knowledge (magical or technical secrets), (2) wealth, (3) weapons, and (4) status. None of these constitutes oppression as such, since any may be restrained and accepted. For oppression we need something else, turning privilege into "a harsher form of necessity than that of natural needs themselves." This is the struggle for *power*, the exercise of domination for its own sake. Here is a truly demonic factor, for, as Nietzsche too observed, unlike all other human desires, the desire for power has no limits and cannot be satisfied.

Simone Weil says that power initially is a means of action to supplement limited individual force. It can be lost in an instant by the merest accident, and it is continually threatened by inferiors and rivals and betters. It cannot be an *end* because there is no security in it and there is never enough of it. Yet this is just what in the social world is treated as the *supreme* end.

> It is this reversal of the relation between means and end, it is this fundamental folly that accounts for all that is senseless and bloody right through history. Human history is simply the history of the servitude which makes men—oppressors and oppressed alike—the plaything of the instruments of domination they themselves have manufactured, and thus reduces living humanity to being the chattel of inanimate chattel. (OL 69)

In her later writings Simone Weil broadens this, basing her understanding of oppression not on the struggle for power but on something even more fundamental, the struggle for *prestige*. The significance of this change she explains in this way:

> The necessity for power is obvious, because life cannot be lived without order; but the location of power is arbitrary because all men are alike, or very nearly. Yet power must not seem to be arbitrarily allocated, because it will not then be recognized as power. Therefore prestige, which is illusion, is of the very essence of power. (SE 168)

In the human realm, she says, force derives two thirds of its strength from prestige.

The emergence of this concept is important because it links Simone Weil's social philosophy with her psychology and religious philosophy. It adds to the social situation the dimension of the psychological. We have now to do not only with "social matter" but also with "psychological matter." Three aspects of prestige are paramount.

First, prestige is intimately connected with the defense and promotion of the human *ego*, which is what keeps the individual and social worlds going. When individuals strive for honor, position, rank, recognition, and fame, they are striving for what, in her view, is entirely a social illusion. Prestige has no more intrinsic significance than a box of old medals. There is a circle of illusion by which those who are important are sustained by the adulation of the others who are not, while these others derive their ego satisfaction from knowing the important ones. This is what keeps the social wheels turning. The celebrity game is only the public version of what has been the game all along in business, politics, academia, literature, and the rest.

Second, prestige, like everything illusory, is based on *imagination*. It is the imagination that gives people the fascinating power to seem more than human, enabling them to treat with contempt the nobodies below them who accept this treatment with pleasure. In the political realm almost the whole task is to capture the public imagination, as not only Napoleon and Hitler but democratic leaders everywhere have found. Napoleon said that "imagination rules the world," knowing full well that millions would be ready to die for him if the proper chords of national glory could be struck. (The precedent of Napoleon was irresistible to Hitler, as was that of Alexander to Napoleon.) Imagination, fragile as a cobweb, binds like steel chains when it holds sway. Skill in public relations is a skill in manipulating archetypal images. Simone Weil's philosophy attempts to break such spells and free us from this manipulation and willing self-deception, the basis of all oppression.

Third, lies and propaganda are the substance of politics. Plato's image of "the Great Beast" (*Republic* 6.492f) is a metaphor for the public opinion that has constantly to be assuaged and flattered lest it turn on the politician and tear him or her to pieces. Weil imagines different groups and leaders stroking or tickling different parts of the Beast, some his paws, others his muzzle, others again the back of his head, all depending on what has most to be appeased. For the Beast is supreme on earth and has one principle, *force*, which is fickle, unstable, inconstant. The all-powerful dictator may one day be found swinging by his heels or poisoned by his valet. Democratic politicians continually test the winds of public favor lest the Beast (now the media, the rival politicians, and the voters) turn against them in the night.

We cannot leave the subjects of oppression and prestige without looking at what Weil describes as the most effective means of oppression and the most reliable sources of prestige—*fear*, *cruelty*, and *terror*. And this we see best by looking at its chief practitioners in world history, the ones from whom these ways of ruling have principally been learned, the Romans.

> The Romans have never been rivalled in the shrewd employment of cruelty. When anyone is cruel from caprice, or a disordered sensibility, or rage, or hatred, the consequences are often fatal to himself. But cold, calculated, systematic cruelty, never mitigated by change of humor, prudence, shame, or pity—cruelty that can neither be stayed by courage, dignity, or force, nor mollified by submission, supplication, and tears—cruelty of this kind is an incomparable weapon of domination. (SE 106)

It is a major comment on what millennia of false "greatness" have done to us that we admire this, in the same way that in the presence of our children we call Hitler and Stalin great.[5] Education, still permeated with the adulation of Roman "greatness," is hardly designed to prepare generations which will be immune to oppressive leaders. What could be said of the Romans can still be said of us:

> All these cruelties were ways of heightening prestige. . . . With unswerving resolution, they always sacrificed everything to considerations of prestige; they were always inflexible in danger and impervious to pity or any human feeling. They knew how to undermine by terror the very souls of their adversaries, or how to lull them with hopes before enslaving them by force of arms; and, finally, they were so skilled in the policy of the big lie that they have imposed it even on posterity, and we still believe it today. (SE 112, 102)

We are being reminded that the big lie has not died with the Romans. Nor with Hitler.

Extending the concept of oppression to include all forms of systematic degradation of human beings provides a pluralistic framework for post-Marxist social philosophy. In the spirit of the science of his day, which looked for single causes rather than new sets of conditions, Marx focused on the ownership of the means of production. This led generations of leftists into abstract regions, fertile fields for sectarian fighting, far from the workplace as it is actually experienced. (Splinter groups could spend whole events in "principled" arguments about who will turn off the lights at night.) Weil took as her focus the endless, unsatisfying, monotonous drudgery and degradation of wage labor, which is what most workers experience it to be. She asked, How does the worker become a thing in the workplace? And what are the conditions of work fit for human beings? What is free human labor?

> It is not in relation to what it produces that manual labor must become the highest value, but in relation to the man who performs it; it must not be made the

object of honors and rewards, but must constitute for each human being what he most essentially is in need of if his life is to take into itself a meaning and value in his own eyes. (OL 104)[6]

The measure of civilization looked at in this way is not gross national product but workmanship and craftsmanship, which involve the total human being in all aspects of producing. To link the hands and head and heart in the work is to make the work truly human.

These are themes that also concerned the young Marx, though he dropped them later: integrating the intellectual and the manual in each individual's labor; worker participation in the entire range of company planning and policies; interest and variety in daily work routines. (These Fourierist and anarcho-syndicalist ideas, labeled "utopian" by orthodox Marxists, become more relevant as their "orthodox" themes become less so.)

Simone Weil's ideas at this point are drawn from her own firsthand experiences of factory and field work. She came to feel that as with affliction and love, childbearing and bereavement, so factory work has to be experienced to be understood as it is: a narrow, rigid enslavement that kills mind and soul. She pointed out that neither Marx, Lenin, nor Trotsky ever did actually experience it. If they had, their philosophies might have been different, although we do not know in what way. (Would it have decreased their abstract sectarianism?)

One thing that makes factory work exhausting and humiliating is that it requires just enough attention to hold the mind fixed motionless, but not enough to keep it interested and alive. (Those who imagine that work on an assembly line permits the mind to be free to think of other things are entirely mistaken.) It is the fact that both mind and body are stunned into unwilling acquiescence that makes such labor enslaving and inhuman. As Weil says in her "Factory Journal," the natural reaction is rebellion, but even this is suppressed. Such work destroys what is human in us; it destroys the soul.

> Revolt is impossible, except for momentary flashes (I mean even as a feeling). First of all, against what? You are alone with your work, you could not revolt except against it—but to work in an irritated state of mind would be to work badly, and therefore to starve. (FW 171)

The overall lesson that she took away from the factory is that it is not resistance and dignity that are learned there but humiliation and submission. Nor is there room for concern for fellow-workers. (There is not enough mental and spiritual space for this.) The occasional spark of solicitude or fellow feeling is so rare that it is like a precious jewel in memory.

Marx said that products come out of the factory ennobled, while workers come out debased. But then he looked at the ennoblement (the surplus value) of the products and forgot the debasement of the workers. Today, especially after what has happened in Eastern Europe, we must find our way to the labor that is humanly satisfying.

> There thus emerges a new method of social analysis which is not that of Marx, although it starts, as Marx wanted, from the relationships of production; but whereas Marx, whose conception is in any case not very precise on this point, seems to have wanted to classify the modes of production in terms of output, these would be analysed in terms of the relationship between thought and action. (OL 100)

This phrase, "The relationship between thought and action," provides the key to the difference between *slave labor* and *free labor*. Only if thought freely eventuates in action in accordance with an individual's own mind and choice, and is not imposed from outside, do we have what deserves to be called *free labor*.[7]

In her essay "Theoretical Picture of a Free Society" (OL 83–108), Simone Weil presents three implicit pictures or models of tendencies in our society, the first two in her view leading away from liberty. Although Marx regrettably did not allow himself or his followers to speculate about the future, the first is a picture that he occasionally presented with favor; the second is an extrapolation of a tendency now increasing; the third is her own vision.

In the first picture, liberty means "the possibility of obtaining without effort what is pleasurable," that is to say, what will satisfy our desires, whatever they are. Here the ancient curse of labor has been lifted, and people work as little as possible, having leisure to do whatever they may wish. In one of his few utopian flights Marx envisaged a life of culture and learning for even the average man who learns ancient languages and cultivates the classics, or takes extension courses.

Simone Weil rejects this picture of liberty as the satisfaction of desires in both its cultural version ("reading Shakespeare") and its hedonistic one ("gratifying physical appetites").

> We have only to bear in mind the weakness of human nature to understand that an existence from which the very notion of work had pretty well disappeared would be delivered over to the play of the passions and perhaps to madness; there is no self-mastery without discipline, and there is no other source of discipline for man than the effort demanded in overcoming external obstacles. (OL 84)

Even science, art, and sport, which require discipline, she says, must imitate what is required in the correct performance of work, or become unreal.

The second model imagines a society in which everyone has become technically expert and cultivates only technical virtues.

One might conceive, as an abstract limit, of a civilization in which all human activity, in the sphere of labor as in that of speculative theory, was subjected right down to matters of detail to an altogether mathematical strictness, and that without a single human being understanding anything at all about what he was doing; the idea of necessity would then be absent from everybody's mind, and in far more radical fashion than it is among primitive tribes which, our sociologists affirm, are ignorant of logic. (OL 94–95)

The third vision, which is Simone Weil's, envisions a free society that is built around neither consumption (either of pleasure or culture) nor mindless technology, but productive labor, considered as the highest human activity, bringing all human faculties into play. Manual labor would be given a new meaning in terms of what might be called an *epistemology of work* (and not, as in classical philosophy, perception), in which this wholehearted work constitutes the fundamental human relation to the world.

The most fully human civilization would be that which had manual labor as its pivot, that in which manual labor constituted the supreme value. . . . Thought is certainly man's supreme dignity, but it is exercised in a vacuum, and consequently only in appearance, when it does not seize hold of its object, which can be none other than the universe. (OL 105)

The idea of conquering nature or establishing human dominion over the world was a nineteenth-century dream that turned into a twentieth-century nightmare. We are under more constraints than we know. We cannot wish away necessity, whether it is in the form of affliction, love, death, the weight of the past, the vastness of the cosmos, the overwhelming vistas of time, the horrors and injustices of life. (To the extent that we suffer less from natural disasters, it appears that we suffer more from social ones, Weil says.) There is no question of dominating nature or submitting to it, but rather of trying to live in balance with it, as we also have to live in balance with each other.

CHAPTER 7

Nationalism

A NOTHER WAY IN WHICH SIMONE WEIL distinguishes herself sharply from Marx is in rejecting his internationalism in favor of a nationalism that is benign, not militaristic or exclusive but providing roots in this world for the soul. Instead of thinking of nations as resting on natural necessities of collective behavior such as Marxist historical and economic forces or fascist blood and soil, or on supernatural covenants or social contracts as in classical and modern theories, she thinks of them in relation to universal needs of the *individual* human being, and especially the need to be, in a religiously qualified sense, *at home* in the world. This is the framework that we have to bear in mind as we read her late text *The Need for Roots*, which poses the question What is a nation? and How shall we evaluate the success and failure of nations? seeing as we do more failure today than success.

The tenacity and power of nationalism in this century have surely been a surprise. For while empires and supranational movements have declined or barely held their own, nationalism has spread and deepened. At the beginning of the century the Austro-Hungarian Empire, the last shadow of the Holy Roman Empire, still comprised thirteen peoples and twenty-four countries, including besides Hungarians and Austrians, four North Slavic peoples, three South Slavics, three Romanics, and vast numbers of western and eastern Jews. This empire was a casualty of the First World War, which also saw the beginnings of the breakups of the overseas colonial European empires. There were some 150 nations, at last count, and the end of the Soviet Empire has added another dozen.

Four questions arise: (1) Why has nationalism revived? (2) What should nationalism and the nation be today? (3) Why has nationalism been so violent and destructive? (4) What is the relation between nationalism and religion, and Christianity in particular?

As we examine Simone Weil's answers to these questions, we will see that there is little ground for the kind of optimism with which some have greeted the downfall of Communism and the apparent triumph of democratic capitalism, since the very factors that produced totalitarianism and destructive nationalism are still present and as strong as ever. In Weil's view these factors are spiritual and cultural failures going back to the Renaissance and embedded in our modern ways of life. They are like land mines still live and dangerous, and unless nations meet the legitimate needs of the human soul, which nations alone can meet, there will be more of the collective violence of which we have already seen too much, and on a more terrifying scale than ever.

It was World War II and the initial victory of Hitler over France that forced Simone Weil to recognize the depth and strength of the human need for roots, a need which had not been sufficiently recognized by intellectuals, which only nations could fulfill. That this need was unfulfilled was the principal cause of the appearance of the modern disease of totalitarianism.

Up to this time, as a trade unionist and pacifist in the 1930s, Weil had been a brilliant radical Marxist internationalist. It was this orientation that led her to join an anarcho-syndicalist column in the Spanish Civil War. But along with this went a lifelong abhorrence of violence (at the end of her life she still called it "the only evil"), following her teacher Émile Chartier (1869–1951), who wrote under the name of Alain. And although she renounced Alain's pacifism,[1] she did not change this hatred of force, but only deepened it. In a similar way she never gave up her internationalism, but only incorporated it into her nationalism.[2]

The supreme specific evil of the modern world, she came to see, was the monstrous power of the nation state, which first showed itself in World War I:

> a State, the object of hatred, repugnance, derision, disdain, and fear, which under the name of *patrie*, demanded absolute loyalty, total self-abnegation, the supreme sacrifice, and obtained them, from 1914 to 1918, to an extent which surpassed all expectations. It set itself up as an absolute value in this world, that is, as an object of idolatry; and it was accepted and served as such, honored with the sacrifice of an appalling number of human lives. A loveless idolatry—what could be more monstrous, more heart-rending? (NR 128)

The dominance of this Moloch seemed intolerable in the 1920s, and most thought it impossible that it should rage again. And yet the conditions that produced it were actually worsening all the time, and the steps taken to counter it were wholly superficial and ineffective. Within a bare generation the demons broke loose again, but at the same time, to Simone Weil, something else was revealed, that losing one's country was like having one's skin torn away.

> Today every Frenchman knows that . . . one part of his soul sticks so closely to France, that when France is taken away it remains stuck to her as the skin does to some burning object, and is thus pulled off. . . . All Frenchman have come to feel the reality of France through being deprived of her.[3]

The nation state has become an idol, not only militarily but in another way too, which is finally catching up with us, as a limitless cornucopia from which everyone expects benefits while resenting that others are getting more while one is not getting enough. This development, which is now reaching a critical point in the United States and Western Europe, Simone Weil described in 1943 in this way:

> The State had ceased to be, under the title of nation or country, something infinitely valuable in the sense of something valuable enough to be served with devotion. . . . it had become in everybody's eyes of unlimited value as something to be exploited. The quality of absoluteness which is bound up with idolatry remained . . . and assumed this new aspect. The State appeared like an inexhaustible horn of plenty, pouring out its treasures in direct proportion to the pressure put upon it. So people always had a grudge against it for not providing more. (NR 155)

Writing before the final defeat of Germany, but when it was evident that this was inevitable, Simone Weil attempted to describe another kind of nationalism—lawful, critical, humane, and world-oriented, based on love of nation and willingness to die for it when its existence is threatened, but unafraid to challenge the nation's "injustices, cruelties, mistakes, falsehoods, crimes, and scandals" (NR 173).

The principal quality of this nationalism is that it should correspond to deep human needs, the most important of which is the need to feel at home in the world, surrounded by traditions, language, places and persons that we love and that are food to our souls.[4] A nation is an instrumental good, not an end in itself. It is like food in serving the purposes of life, no more and no less valuable than this.

> Even when a total sacrifice is required, no more is owed to any collectivity whatever than a respect analogous to the one owed to food. (NR 8–9)

The phrase "any collectivity" also includes families, peoples, churches, political parties, and the like. When a nation or any collectivity ceases to be food and begins instead to devour souls, or when it supplies poison instead of nutrition, Simone Weil tells us that there need be no more obligation.[5] Such a nation should be reformed or destroyed. Nations that do not meet the needs of individual souls should disappear.

> We owe our respect to a collectivity of whatever kind—country, family, or any other—not for itself, but because it is food for a certain number of human souls. (NR 7)

She recognizes two needs that take precedence over all others, which she describes as supernatural. They represent the limits of nations. The first is the need to be respected as a *human* being just because one is human. The second is the need for the spirit of *truth*. These needs apply equally to all nations, races, and religions, whatever their diversities. With the first goes the corresponding obligation to respect every human being

> for the sole reason that he or she is a human being, without any other condition requiring to be fulfilled. . . .
> This obligation is the one and only obligation in connection with human affairs that is not subject to any condition whatever. (NR 4-5)

There is no human being so peculiar, so evil or depraved, that his or her conjunction with the human continuum can be canceled. Not even Haman or Genghis Khan or Hitler. And there is no act, however wrong, that can remove us from the claim on this respect. No souls can be read out of humanity, for any reason whatsoever.[6] This is not merely a collective responsibility or an individual right. It is a supernaturally infused need and obligation.

Simone Weil does not believe that a true nation or civilization in the West—that is, one that is true to its roots—can be built on the idea that has for several centuries dominated Western political and social thought, the idea of *rights*. This concept, she believes, is too superficial and too legalistic to satisfy our yearnings and correspond to our deep needs. The moral and political concept proper to needs is not rights but *obligations*.

What is wrong with the concept of rights, which, after all, was invoked in both the American and French Revolutions and before that in the very reasonable spirit of the Enlightenment? Why does Weil say that it belongs to an inferior part of the soul and puts human relations on the wrong basis?

We can disentangle three reasons for the superiority of obligations to rights. First, rights have a *contentious* character. To be effective they have to be imposed by force. This often leads to what she calls the shrill nagging of claims and counterclaims when different people's rights come into conflict.

Rights that are recognized by no one count for nothing, however shrilly they are asserted.

Second, no *moral* weight attaches to people struggling for their own rights, no more than attaches to them when struggling for their own interests as individuals or groups. A moral aspect appears only when they struggle for the rights of others, and this already presupposes obligation. Simone Weil agrees with the philosopher Kant that obligation, and its corollary conscience, is the basis for morality. Rights are tainted with egoistic self-interest, as obligations are not.

Third, and perhaps most important, rights often act to "inhibit any possible impulses of charity on both sides." Instead of making room for sympathy and understanding, they frame relations and problems legalistically, often failing to come anywhere near the true dimensions of human needs. For example, Simone Weil points out how inadequate it would be for a girl being dragged away into prostitution to complain that her rights were being violated.[7] If the situation were not so horrible, this would seem ludicrous. For something much worse than that is being done to her: her soul is being violated. She is being violated. The proper response is a human one that speaks to her on a sacred human level. When a human violation occurs, it is *human interconnectedness* that is being violated, as happens in various types of war crimes such as genocides and attacks on civilians.[8]

All this helps to explain why Simone Weil says that rights are alien to the Good. Human communities that know of no stronger bonds than rights are poorly prepared for emergencies. How can they defend human beings as such when their humanity has not even been fully recognized, either by those who need defense or by their attackers? If people helped each other only because of rights, there would be no help.

The Greeks, she points out, did not have the concept of rights. Justice, which means the recognition of the full equality of all human beings, including strangers, was enough for them. In the best of the Bible, strangers too are recognized with full equality,[9] but too often in other biblical passages they are not.

> Just as the notion of rights is alien to the Greek mind, so also it is alien to the Christian inspiration whenever it is pure and uncontaminated by the Roman, Hebraic, and Aristotelian heritage. One cannot imagine St. Francis of Assisi talking about rights. (SE 20–21)

The difference between the cry of the violated, "Why am I being hurt?" and the cry for fairness, "Why has someone else got more than I have?" is that the first comes from the *impersonal* human depths of the soul (like the baby's cry for milk or the lover's cry of desertion), while the second expresses the calculated demands of the social self (or personality, as Weil uses the term). Because we confuse the primal individuality with which we are born (but which is easily wounded for life) with the socially developed personal shell (the guise we develop to deal with the world in years four, five, and six), we confuse two different kinds of wrong. The cry "Why am I being hurt?" comes from the same part of us as the baby's cry for food and love. Neither is like the complaint of the older boy that he is being treated unfairly because another gets a bigger piece of cake than he does. (John Rawls restricts his discussion of justice largely to the second realm.)

Obligation arises from primal need, from complete dependence and expectation of good. Here is the bond upon which the concept of justice finally rests. The expectation that good will be done to us by other human beings is the one thing sacred in a human being. In all probability nothing else stands between us and mutual destruction when the forces of hate and bloodthirstiness, combined with modern technology, are let loose.[10]

The universal needs that nations serve (or should serve) in vastly diverse ways are, Simone Weil says, "arranged in antithetical pairs which have to combine together in order to form a balance" (NR 12). She lists fourteen needs in seven pairs, though it is not always clear in what the pairing consists.

We have already mentioned the most sacred and supernatural need for and obligation of *human respect*, based solely on being human without further qualification. The other supreme sacred and supernatural need and obligation is *truth*. Both have to be embodied in nations, or else nations fail in their primary obligations. As it was for St. Augustine, but with a meaning of "among us" more than "within us," truth (along with Plato's Good) is the supreme value for Simone Weil. We will see the many ways in which it intersects with national life.

The balanced needs which a nation exists in order to meet she lists as follows:

1. *Liberty* and *obedience*. Liberty means being able to choose from among possibilities limited by sensible comprehensible rules a sufficient part of our life so that we do not feel constrained in it. Obedience has to be based primarily on consent and not on punishment and reward. When either one of this pair of needs is not met, the other is not met either.

2. *Equality* and *hierarchy*. Equality means identity in respect and consideration; hierarchy "a certain devotion towards superiors, considered not as individuals, nor in relation to the powers they exercise, but as symbols" (NR

19). This emphasis on the purely symbolic nature of rank and status under-lines Simone Weil's belief in the essentially illusory nature of all social power and prestige as such. Although the entire social order is defined by power and prestige, these things in themselves have no religious or spiritual significance and in fact interfere in the most serious ways with the true dimensions of human life. Nevertheless the symbolic significance of hierarchy is a human need.

3. *Honor* and *punishment.* Honor also has a purely social and symbolic meaning, and in Weil's view should be separated also from power and pres-tige. Punishment should be regarded as a need rather than an imposition or correction. "By committing a crime a man places himself of his own accord outside the chain of eternal obligations that bind every human being to every other one" (NR 21). "Men who are so estranged from the Good that they seek to spread evil everywhere can only be reintegrated with the Good by having harm inflicted upon them" (SE 31).

4. *Security* and *risk.* Security means freedom from fear and terror. But we also need "the permanent presence of a certain amount of risk in all aspects of social life" (NR 34). Quite clearly, neither total security nor total risk is a need of the human soul, but only each tempered by the other.

5. *Private property* and *collective property.* "It is desirable that the majority of people should own their house and a little piece of land around it, and, wher-ever not technically impossible, the tools of their trade" (NR 35). With this should go a sense of personal owning of public places, display, and ceremonies. State ownership and giant private corporations have no place in the small-scale communal world which Weil regards as the most natural and normal.

6. *Responsibility* and *freedom of opinion.* The first means that "a man should often have to take [part in] decisions in matters great and small affect-ing interests that are distinct from his own, but in regard to which he feels a personal concern" (NR 15). The subject of freedom of opinion raises so many difficult questions that it calls for special consideration.

7. *Order* and *truth.* Both of these occupy special positions: order because it concerns the harmony of all the other needs and the special obligation to try to work to reduce incompatibilities between them, and truth because this is the ultimate significance of human life. Works of art supply models for order. The mutual infusion of both science and religion with the spirit of truth—lacking, Weil says, in both of them now—would bring truth back into the national life.

∞

By far the most difficult and controversial and easily misunderstood part of Simone Weil's political and social philosophy concerns freedom of thought and the use of the law to prevent totalitarian control of the mind. Perhaps there has been nothing written by a major philosopher since Plato's attempt to censor the poets that will seem more breathtakingly extreme than this. On the other hand, we must see that what motivates these passages in *The Need for Roots* is a passionate attachment to *the freedom of the human mind* and an equally passionate desire to resist all attempts by *mass suggestion* and *indoctrination* to interfere with this. Since we are far from understanding what creates the totalitarian mentality even in Western democracies, we ought not to dismiss what she says too quickly (and especially if it comes from those who themselves have this disposition toward "group-think" against which she is warning).

Two principles appear to underlie her proposals. First,

> complete, unlimited freedom of expression for every sort of opinion, without the least restriction or reserve, is an absolute need on the part of the intelligence. (NR 23)

Second, law must prevent interference with this, for

> the need of freedom itself, so essential to the intellect, calls for a corresponding protection against suggestion, propaganda, influence by means of obsession. These are methods of constraint [that is] not accompanied by fear or physical distress, but which is none the less a form of violence. (NR 26)

Simone Weil believes that all forms of group-think should be forbidden by law. Since groups cannot think, but only individuals can, it is intrinsically dishonest to put forward opinions as the opinions of groups, rather than of individuals.[11]

> Protection of freedom of thought requires that no group should be permitted by law to express an opinion. For when a group starts having opinions, it inevitably tends to impose them on its members. Sooner or later, these individuals find themselves debarred, with a greater or lesser degree of severity, and on a number of problems of greater or lesser importance, from expressing opinions opposed to those of the group, unless they care to leave it. (NR 27)

All orthodoxies, party lines, regimentations of thought, indoctrinations, and sloganizing were, for Weil, crimes against the most precious thing we have—the freedom of the individual human mind—which is the capacity to receive truth. Those who deliberately promulgate lies and deceit should be punished, whether they be politicians, journalists, educators, clergymen, or novelists (often dressing up their tendentious ideas in fiction).

We all know that when journalism becomes indistinguishable from organized lying, it constitutes a crime. But we think it is a crime impossible to punish. What is there to stop the punishment of activities once they are recognized to be criminal ones? Where does this strange notion of nonpunishable crimes come from? (NR 37–38)

In the more sophisticated forms of lying and deceit, such as putting "spins" on stories, managing news by leaks and half-truths and disinformation, it becomes increasingly difficult to identify the crime or the criminal. When almost everything that appears in the mass media is a form of manipulation, it is difficult to see who is responsible for it.

Simone Weil is well aware that nothing can take the place of the spirit of truth itself, which must come in the first instance from those in authority.

> There is no possible chance of satisfying a people's need of truth unless men can be found for this purpose who love truth. (NR 40)

It seems clear that she has no objection to groups or political parties which attempt to promote openly and freely their interests and ideas. What she opposes is ideological thinking and the covert ways it spreads lies and deceptions or mass thoughts promoting secret agendas. This is treason against freedom of thinking itself through forms of mass suggestion and control of public opinion.

One of her most profound observations on this subject is to be found in her *Letter to a Priest*:

> Intellectual adherence is never owed to anything whatever. For it is never to any degree a voluntary thing. Attention alone is voluntary. And it alone forms the subject of an obligation. (LP no. 27)

This amounts to an enlargement of Wittgenstein's statement that the philosopher belongs to no community of ideas.[12] Neither, says Simone Weil, does *any* human being. All beliefs as rigid orthodoxies are imposed from outside; they are never the result of voluntary efforts. We have it in our power only to give attention. And this alone is our obligation. (These are words of such depth and difficulty that we must leave it to the future completely to unravel them.)

There is an inner tension in Simone Weil's thought between the realization that uprootedness (i.e., homelessness) is "by far the most dangerous malady to which human societies are exposed" (NR 47), and her equal realization that for Christians (and for Jews in a very different way) there is "only one country that can be the object of [absolute] patriotism and [that] is situated outside the world" (NR 132). As against any claims linking God to any worldly power, she affirms the words of Christ, "My kingdom is not of this world."[13] And yet there are, tiny as a mustard seed, forms of the implicit love of God in the world, such as science and the order and beauty of nature, love of neighbor, sacraments, friendship in the spirit, and love in and despite and even because of affliction. There are no divine covenants conferring special status on any nation or any collective, but there are individual expressions of divine love in every nation. The sacred condition is not God ruling the world by *command* and law as something imposed, but rather God forming the world as germinal *love* from within.

The idea that Judaism and Christianity must uproot human beings from ancient pagan, natural, and national roots in order that all may submit to a higher divine social law has been expressed by the French Jewish philosopher Emmanuel Levinas in an essay on Simone Weil. He asks:

> Is not Europe's unhappiness due to the fact that Christianity did not sufficiently uproot it?[14]

Such uprooting may conform to the original Hebrew experience in the desert of Sinai, but it seriously violates the experience of other nations.

Forgoing dreams of national glory, divine destiny, or the final settling of accounts, we are left with love of a nation as something fragile and perishable like all other human institutions. Simone Weil says the attitude toward the nation should be one of compassion. It should be a

> poignantly tender feeling for some beautiful, precious, fragile, and perishable object [that] has a warmth about it which the sentiment of natural grandeur altogether lacks. . . . A perfectly pure love for one's country bears a close resemblance to the feelings which his young children, his aged parents, or beloved wife inspire in a man. (NR 171, 172)

Such a compassionate national feeling "gives the poorest part of the population a privileged moral position" (NR 175): this certainly should apply also to strangers in the nation, who present a special moral responsibility.[15]

To bring about this new perception of the nation, Simone Weil says, requires changing the meaning of the term "greatness" especially as this is used in the education of children. No longer should it be applied to military conquerors like Alexander, Caesar, Napoleon, Hitler, and Stalin. Every time we call such men "great" we add to the prestige of force and help to prepare the way for future men of the same stamp. Those who do not wish to give Hitler future victories should take to heart these words:

> The only punishment capable of punishing Hitler, and deterring little boys
> thirsting for greatness in coming centuries from following his example, is such
> a total transformation of the meaning attached to greatness that he should
> thereby be excluded from it.
>
> It is chimerical and due to the blindness induced by national hatred to imag-
> ine that one can exclude Hitler from the title to national greatness without a
> total transformation, among the men of today, of the idea and significance of
> greatness. (NR 227)

In Vaclav Havel's analysis of totalitarianism, *The Power of the Powerless*, Communist ideology is described as a kind of pseudo-religion that provided a substitute home in a world where uprootedness and homelessness have become
overwhelming and intolerable.

> To wandering humankind it offers an immediately available home. . . . Of course
> one pays dearly for this low rent home: the price is abdication of one's own rea-
> son, conscience and responsibility, for an essential aspect of this ideology is the
> consignment of reason and conscience to a higher authority.[16]

A "monstrous alienation" at the heart of the ideology itself turns everything it touches into a vast lie, worse than the disease it sets out to cure.

To avoid ideology and begin growing roots, there are two fundamental
steps to be taken, aimed at what might called the two greatest weaknesses in
our civilization—the split between religion and nationalism, and the split
between religion and science. These have been the wounds producing the
inner conflicts which have all but torn us apart.

The first essential step is the reintroduction of religion into our schools.
Simone Weil says that ours is the first civilization that has deprived its children of their religious heritage. It has helped to make them vulnerable to cults
and drugs, violence, sexual license, and crime. Without the ballast of religious
teaching, education becomes superficial and emptily technical. The public
and the private spheres are torn apart, each lacking what only the other could
provide.

We have the absurdity now of students graduating from college having
learned about and sometimes read Dante and Milton but not the Bible from
which these works stem, and becoming aware of Chinese and Indian civilization in books but not of Buddhism and Hinduism as living faiths. At the
moment when the spiritual teachings of all humankind are available, a nar-
row-minded secularism keeps them out of the schools. A fearful exclusivism,
no longer viable in the economic and technological spheres, eviscerates public education. The greatest wound is done to the souls of children:

An educational course in which no mention is made of religion is an absurdity. ... The soul of a child, as it reaches toward understanding, has need of the treasures accumulated by the human species through the centuries. We do injury to a child if we bring it up in a narrow Christianity, which prevents it from ever becoming capable of perceiving that there are treasures of purest gold to be found in non-Christian civilizations. Laical education does an even greater injury to children. It covers up those treasures, and those of Christianity as well. (NR 92, 91–92)

As we move toward global civilization, it is not just Christian and Jewish religious teachings and traditions that belong in our schools, but all the spiritual treasures of all the religions of the world. The full recognition and appreciation and acceptance of human differences depend on this kind of openness, which in any case proceeds apace in hundreds of institutes, study groups, centers, and magazines, where, in Western countries at least, every kind of religious teaching is now examined.

The second wound to be healed, that caused by a false conflict between science and religion, has been responsible for the "bad conscience" of each. Science has become an idol (justifying the amoral politics of force) while religion has become self-help and ego-promotion. Lacking the great human goals that the religions used to represent, our civilization destroys itself in the pursuit of money, success, and power.

Instead of looking for changes in science to make it more compatible with religion (e.g., speculations in quantum physics) or in religion to do the same (e.g., cosmic evolutionism), Simone Weil points to something missing from both of them, missing indeed, she says, from virtually the whole of thought today. This is the spirit of truth. As Havel struggled in his country to escape from the totalitarian "living in a lie" so as to "live in truth," and Heidegger called attention to how "that which calls us into thinking" more and more withdraws from us, Simone Weil saw in truth and the inner openness to truth something more valuable than any attachment, any past or any future, and more valuable than life itself.

How is this missing from science?

Since the spirit of truth is absent from the motives behind science, it cannot be present in science. . . .

The spirit of truth can dwell in science on condition that the motive prompting the savant is the love of the object that forms the stuff of his investigations. That object is the universe in which we live. What can we find to love about it, if it isn't its beauty? (NR 260, 261)

We know what motivates science—national subsidies, technological results, consumer applications, prestige, and prizes. And we also know the possessive attitude toward particular theories and doctrines that marks the history of science.

In national life the feeling that it is not possible to get the truth any more about matters of public concern, because so many powerful interests conspire to cover it up, produces a poison of distrust that must end in making democratic government impossible. Without an obligation to the truth there will be in the end no freedom or justice either.

To define the central point we have to question the philosophy of pragmatism, which already permits an element of expediency by looking at truth as that which serves life or produces beneficial results. (The notion that truth is "what works" easily slides over into "what pays off.") Simone Weil says this must be reversed: it is not truth that must serve life, but life that must serve truth. The matter is stated with great eloquence in this passage:

> In this world of ours life, the élan vital, so dear to Bergson, is but a lie; only death is true. For life constrains one to believe what one has to believe in order to live; this servitude has been raised to the rank of a doctrine under the name of pragmatism. . . . But those beings who have, in spite of flesh and blood, spiritually crossed a boundary equivalent to death, receive on the farther side another life, which is not primarily life, which is primarily truth; truth which has become living; as true as death and as living as life. (NR 249)

Truth becoming life—we recognize this as the Christian experience, which simply means that there is nothing anywhere that cannot be faced and understood; for everything [else] has already been lost and it is certain that Truth is enough.[17]

CHAPTER 8

Heidegger, Science, and Technology

S IMONE WEIL MAKES CONTACT with Heidegger not only in her attention to truth but also in her criticism of modern science and technology. She died in 1943, two years before the nuclear bombs were dropped
on Hiroshima and Nagasaki. Had she lived to see that, her reaction might have
been similar to that of Ludwig Wittgenstein, who wrote:

> The bomb offers a prospect of the end, the destruction of a dreadful evil (*eines
> gräßlichen Übels*)—our disgusting, dishwatery science.[1]

Martin Heidegger did not comment on the nuclear bomb directly, but he did
say that what was most important about it was that it showed the danger to
the essence of humanity as it falls into the possession of technology.

All three—Simone Weil, Ludwig Wittgenstein, and Martin Heidegger—recognized three truths about this which are still not generally grasped. First,
modern science and technology go together and cannot be separated; for it is
false that science is neutral, while it is only the use of it that does good or
harm. Second, it is the spirit of modern science and technology itself that
threatens the spirit of humanity. And third, science and technology properly
understood by being put in true human context would no longer threaten us.[2]

It is correct to say that all three rejected "the spirit of the modern age," the
spirit of scientism and technologism. Weil pointed out that our science is
entirely without relation to the Good. Wittgenstein said that the spirit of our
age is one of constant movement outward until the human center is entirely
forgotten.[3] And Heidegger spoke of the growing danger of losing the human
essence of openness and free relation to Being as Presence.

In this chapter we concentrate specifically on Weil and Heidegger, both of whom represent a "reversal" or movement out of traditional "humanistic" metaphysics onto an emphasis on what is given us by the revealing of the Good or of Being. Heidegger's complete midlife abandonment of metaphysics parallels Weil's abandonment of humanistic reason and natural theology in favor of the theology of intellectual grace. Heidegger's history of the revealing of Being as Presence parallels, and does not contradict, Weil's mathematics and science as the revealing by analogy of the human relation to the Divine.

In her book *Oppression and Liberty*, Simone Weil gives a remarkable analysis of contemporary life (see pp. 108–122), in places approaching a level of insight that is truly prophetic.

The thread that ties the analysis together is what she calls the human tendency to substitute means for ends, to lose sight of the ends of human life in the proliferation of means and our fascination with them.[4] This produces what she calls the greatest evil of our time, the growth of the power of the social at the expense of the individual.

> Never has the individual been so completely delivered up to a blind collectivity, and never have men been less capable, not only of subordinating their actions to their thoughts, but even of thinking. Such terms as oppressors and oppressed, the idea of classes—all that sort of thing is near to losing all meaning, so obvious are the impotence and distress of all men in face of the social machine, which has become a machine for breaking hearts and crushing spirits, a machine for manufacturing irresponsibility, stupidity, corruption, slackness and, above all, dizziness. The reason for this painful state of affairs is perfectly clear. We are living in a world in which nothing is made to man's measure; there exists a monstrous discrepancy between man's body, man's mind and the things which at the present time constitute the elements of human existence; everything is in disequilibrium. (OL 108)

It is a terrible dialectic that Weil describes. As the social power increases, the individual becomes weaker; as organization, rationalization, and centralization grow, so do disorder, confusion, and violence. Politicians who decentralize the state build up the centralized military. We are crushed by deadly paradoxes: never was our power so great and never were we so powerless; never was there so much control and never were we so vulnerable to accidents; never so much interdependence and so much fragmentation.

Weil points out that the power and force of nature have been replaced by the power and force of the collectivity. The instruments of the social power— arms, gold, machines, magical or technical secrets—oppress the individual as much as the natural forces of cold, number, and disease ever did. Humans are simply the plaything of a different kind of brute force.

> It seems as if man cannot manage to lighten the yoke imposed by natural necessities without an equal increase in the weight of that imposed by social oppression. . . .
>
> The efforts of the modern worker are imposed on him by a constraint as brutal, as pitiless and which holds him in as tight a grip as hunger does the primitive hunter. (OL 78, 79)

War, wealth, production, power—all these are means that finally acquire an autonomy and assert themselves as ends. We become the playthings of our own instruments, the victims of our own creations and doings. The inversion of means and ends invades every sphere of life. Science does not increase clarity of thinking but fragments knowledge; machines do not serve life but dictate conditions to it; money does not facilitate exchange, but goods are exchanged to keep money in circulation; groups do not use organizations but turn into organizations.

We might imagine that at least methodical thinking has increased, but even this is not so.

> In appearance, nearly everything nowadays is carried out methodically; science is king, machinery invades bit by bit the entire field of labor, statistics take on a growing importance, and over one-sixth of the globe the central authority is trying to regulate the whole of social life according to plans. But in reality methodical thought is progressively disappearing, owing to the fact that the mind finds less and less matter on which to bite. . . . Thought has been reduced to such a subordinate role that one may say, by way of simplification, that the function of verification has passed from thought to things. (OL 109, 113)

In the economic and political spheres a kind of unreality creeps in because the connection between human actions and the results of human actions tend to become arbitrary and random. The growth of organizations and bureaucracies, the development of finance capitalism less and less related to actual production, all this increases the dizziness.

> Everywhere, in varying degrees, the impossibility of relating what one gives to what one receives has killed the feeling for sound workmanship, the sense of responsibility, and has developed passivity, neglect, the habit of expecting everything from outside, the belief in miracles. (OL 117)

All this produces the dizziness that is unreality.

Heidegger's conception of science and technology is concerned with the fundamental attitude toward the world that they embody and that they have translated into the actualities of modern life all over the earth. This attitude may be described as that of traditional humanism and metaphysics, which has developed in the Western world from the time of the Greeks and which has now achieved worldwide acceptance. It is the attitude that attempts to know the world, to penetrate it fully and to seize control of it.

Heidegger notes the enormous success of this point of view. Science and technology are the success story of world history, perhaps its only one. They have triumphed beyond anyone's wildest dreams, fathomed the secrets of the natural world, and accomplished what metaphysics envisages and rationalizes. For Heidegger they are not a chapter within the history of metaphysics; they are the essence of metaphysics, its complete fulfillment. They show what the "reality" they represent really is, namely, to be no more than what they can grasp. Science puts an end to metaphysics by fully realizing it in theory and practice. In science metaphysics has achieved its own conception and thereby brings itself to an end. In this it is seen to have been something different all along from what it supposed itself to be, to have been part of a different and much larger story.[5]

The moment of the end of metaphysics is the moment at which it reveals what it always was, in a context that until now was hidden from us. We see simultaneously what the essence of science and technology, and therefore metaphysics, is and how this relates to the still larger history of self-revelation that includes it. This essence of science and technology as representation of the world Heidegger calls *Gestell,* or "enframing." This coined word has both the connotation of a "scaffolding" used in a construction and the slang meaning of a "frame-up" or something "rigged" to produce a predetermined result. Science "rigs" its results by framing only questions that elicit a certain kind of answer. This is not full, open, free thinking, only calculation where the question "forces" the answer.

Being accepts it, up to a point. It is a revealing of Being, its becoming present: not a way in which we manipulate it, for that is impossible, but a way in which Being shows itself. That science and technology are such a revealing emerges at the moment when they seemed entirely our own doing, when we had forgotten Being completely and imagined that we had taken everything into our own hands. At that moment there appeared the great danger which they harbor, that they would be the end of the road, the permanent freezing of human openness in one kind of revealing that would hold us fast forever. This threat to the human essence, which is *to be open to and free for Being as*

Presence, is balanced by the saving grace to be able to see the larger and more original "enabling and favoring" of Being which alone can work the "reversal" by which the human essence will rightly surround and include the essence of technology.

Heidegger is very clear on a point that Simone Weil also recognizes, that not only is the essence of technology not technological, but that to the problems of technology there is no technological answer.[6] The answer is the revealing (and concealing) of Being. That is what includes among its possibilities representationalism and what it produces, namely, metaphysics and humanism, two terms which for Heidegger are indissolubly linked.

Metaphysics exhausts its possibilities when its startling success and its equally startling limitations stand side by side in the starkest contrast. The same paradoxes Simone Weil noted show up there: that just when we seem to have almost complete control of the natural world, we find that that by which this was brought about is completely beyond our control; that just when we appear to have unlimited energy at our disposal, that energy threatens to destroy us; that just when we can know everything, we find that we understand nothing.[7]

This is the situation in which the reversal Heidegger speaks of takes place and Being emerges again in its archaic pristine Presence, ever more significant than anything science and technology might have to offer for deciding even the significance of science and technology.

What is the connection between Simone Weil's perception of science and technology as the growth of collective power, at the cost of the increasing oppression of the individual human being, and Heidegger's awareness of science and technology as the end point of metaphysics, finally revealing itself in its moment of success as a threat to the human essence that is openness and freedom? Each of these two analyses—the one concentrating on the relation between the individual and the group, and the other on the relation between human beings and the world and Being—seems to catch a part but only a part of the problem.

The connection between them can be seen in what Heidegger calls the "subjectivism" of modern philosophy (which cuts people off from each other and from the world and Presence and confines them in a metaphysical privacy) and what Simone Weil calls "personalism" (which reduces the human being entirely to the dimensions of the *I* and *we,* the psychological and the social, not recognizing anything about them that belongs to the superpersonal). The modern oppression of the individual by the social (found in

both Communist and non-Communist states) and the metaphysical humanism of scientism and technocracy, while they may appear to have nothing in
common, actually contain the same element, a false individualism that produces the lonely, locked-away solitary ego, a ready victim for the exploitations
and manipulations of mob consciousness. This is the nationalistic or ideological man whose normal and sane intelligence has been smothered by commercial and political indoctrination. For both Heidegger and Weil, this is the
closed private individualism of modern philosophy, the counterpart of the
world of scientific and technological objects. The absolute privacy of the
Cartesian thinking *I* is the horror of the modern human self.

In answer to this, Heidegger finds the essence of the human being in an
openness to Being as Presence, an openness receptive to all its self-revealings
and self-concealings, while Simone Weil finds a supernatural element in every
human soul, which is the basis for all justice, the universal expectation that
good will be done to us.[8]

To *open* the human being, not privately and inwardly but outwardly, that
is, to what comes from without, this is the one factor that makes possible a
"falling back" out of metaphysics and scientism and technologism. Apart
from this, these threaten the human essence and may cut us off forever from
any further revealing of Being, and from love and a Good beyond all that is
subjective and private.

Weil considers that as long as the relation to the Good and the religious
significance of mathematics found in Plato and the Pythagoreans were main-
tained, science still belonged to a larger world. Heidegger would say that as
long as Being was understood as *physis* and "coming into presence," not
merely as rationally grasped forms, metaphysics was not yet triumphant.
But Heidegger ignores the religious element in Plato, which for Weil is all-
important; Weil ignores the phenomenological element in Aristotle, which
for Heidegger is all-important. For this reason they come to opposite conclusions about Plato and Aristotle (and also about the relation of nature to
religion). This leads to different ways of reading the history of Western philosophy, one favoring Plato and the other Aristotle.

What matters more than this, however, is something Weil and Heidegger
share: the *reversal* of the relation between the human and the divine in the
case of Weil, and between the human and Being in the case of Heidegger. The
metaphysical attitude puts the emphasis on the human, at least in religion
with regard to natural religion. Simone Weil rules out natural religion completely. To her all authentic religion involves revelation and grace, never
unaided human intelligence. And something similar may be said in the end
for science and mathematics. As for Weil, in religion the primary role of the
human is to respond to the divine, so for Heidegger in philosophy the primary
role of the human is to respond to Being.

For Weil the good reveals itself in three main ways: in the beauty of the world in art, in the order of the world in science, and in the divine human capacity for love in the face of affliction. For Heidegger the Divine reveals itself in nature to the poet and artist, while Being reveals itself to (and conceals itself from) the philosopher and thinker. In putting the emphasis on revealing, Weil and Heidegger both reverse the position of traditional humanism.

To forget the Good and to forget Being as Presence reduces mathematics and science to purely human tools, and nature to "the model of work" (Weil) and "a standing reserve of energy" (Heidegger). This reductive picture makes the claim to be *true* in the only still-accepted sense of "true," that is, corresponding to what is called reality. In Heidegger's understanding in terms of *Gestell* ("enframing"), it is indeed true, but this is a very limited truth and revealing. The more primal original meaning of *truth* as "unconcealing" returns again, as the limited metaphysical and scientific meaning exhausts itself.

While Heidegger finds in Greek poetry and the poetry of Hölderlin a response to the divine and the holy in Nature, Weil finds in mathematics and particularly geometry a supreme analogy for the relation between the divine and the human. The exact intellectual formulations of the relations between the infinite and the finite in mathematics (where even self-contradiction is dealt with in a precise and exact way) is for her the best of all models for the paradoxical relation between the human and the divine. (Her view is that intelligence concerned with the divine is more exact and precise than that concerned with merely human things.) If to Heidegger Hölderlin is the forerunner of the return of "holy poetry," for Weil modern mathematical logic—when it realizes how incommensurate with its understanding of itself are the perfection and precision of its techniques—will be the forerunner of "holy mathematics."[9]

For Simone Weil the human intellect has no access to the supernatural except by way of grace, revelation, and analogy. And even our relation to the natural will fall into darkness without the supernatural. Thus she writes in her *New York Notebook*:

> This is the essential and unrecognized truth: Everything that is good is of divine and supernatural origin, and proceeds directly or indirectly from the celestial, transcendental source of all good.
>
> Everything that proceeds from another source, everything whose origin is [merely] natural, is alien to the good. (F 120)[10]

Let us compare this with Heidegger's remarks in his *Letter on Humanism*:

> All working or effecting lies in Being and is directed toward beings. Thinking, in contrast, lets itself be claimed by Being so that it can say the truth of Being. . . . Before he speaks man must first let himself be claimed again by Being.[11]

What lies ahead now? Both Weil and Heidegger warn against deceiving our-selves about what the future holds. They drew the most somber conclusions. Weil says that we must not fall victim to the fanaticisms and delusions that will come. Heidegger makes it clear that he does not believe that there is much that thinking can do. Here is what Weil says:

> The pivot around which revolves social life [now] . . . is none other than prepa-ration for war. . . . This development will only give disorder a bureaucratic form, and still further increase confusion, waste, and misery. Wars will bring in their train a frantic consumption of raw materials and capital equipment, a crazy destruction of wealth of all kinds that previous generations have bequeathed us. When chaos and destruction have reached the limit beyond which the very func-tioning of the economic and social organization becomes materially impossible, our civilization will perish; and humanity, having gone back to a more or less primitive level of existence and to a social life dispersed into much smaller col-lectivities, will set out again along a new road which it is quite impossible for us to predict.
>
> To imagine that we can switch the course of history along a different track by transforming the system through reforms or revolutions, to hope to find salva-tion in a defensive or offensive action against tyranny and militarism—all that is just day-dreaming. There is nothing on which to base even attempts. (OL 116–117)

Weil's remarkable ability to distinguish freely what we really can do from what we only imagine we can is shown in her succinct statement:

> To sum up, it seems reasonable to suppose that the generations which will have to face the difficulties brought about by the collapse of the present system have yet to be born. As for the generations now living, they are perhaps, of all those that have followed each other in the course of human history, the ones which will have had to shoulder the maximum of imaginary responsibilities and the minimum of real ones. Once this situation is fully realized it leaves a marvellous freedom of mind. (OL 121)[12]

Heidegger's last word appears in an interview in the German magazine *Der Spiegel*. The interview took place in the spring of 1966 and was published in the spring of 1976 shortly after his death at the age of eighty-eight. He dis-cusses the circumstances in which he joined the Nazi party for five or six months in 1933. That he could have been misled in this way shows something about the spiritual and philosophical situation in this century, which he later addressed in his writings on the spirit of technology which combined with rampant nationalism and socialism (especially in Germany) to produce so many horrors. Here is what he says:

The task of thought is to help limit the dominance of technology so that man in general has an adequate relation to its essence. Nazism moved in that direction but those persons were far too limited in their thinking to achieve a really explicit relationship to what has been happening now for three hundred years.

To put it briefly, perhaps a bit ponderously, but after long thought: philosophy will not be able to effect any direct transformation of the present state of the world. This is true not only of philosophy but of any simple human contemplation and striving. Only a god can save us now.[13]

Every morning's newspapers confirm that the belief that *technology* will save us is as strong as ever and permeates the thinking of the world's so-called leaders in virtually every field. The economic, political, and cultural momentum of this belief in the last three hundred years and what lies behind that for another two thousand years, is too strong to undergo the necessary changes as Simone Weil and Martin Heidegger understand them.

In a recent symposium on nuclear policy at the Columbia University School of Law, one of the participants, Thomas Powers, summed up the situation in this way:

From the very beginning the (nuclear) weapons have been telling us what to do. First they told us they could be invented; then they told us they could be numerous; now they're telling us they can be accurate and versatile. My hope is that fifty years hence will somehow have reversed this relationship, that we will finally have found a way to tell the weapons what to do. My fear is that we won't have.[14]

CHAPTER 9

Love in Abandonment

H IDDEN IN THE BEGINNINGS of Western civilization, so it has often been said, was a Promethean Will to knowledge and power that was restrained for long centuries but broke free in the modern world and has finally led to disastrous consequences in our times. In the Greek age it was limited by the jealousy of the gods, which forbade human beings to cross the line between human and divine. Even Plato, when he came to talk directly about the soul and especially concerning life after death, had to resort to myths. But a still deeper prohibition restrained the Promethean Will. This was the idea that all true knowledge concerns a realm of perfection and there can be no genuine knowledge of the practical ordinary world. In the ordinary world there are no straight lines or perfect circles. As the heavens were perfect and therefore sacred, knowledge could disdain to concern itself with the mundane. When the Alexandrians found the principle of the steam engine, it never occurred to them to apply it to anything but children's toys. There was a sacred cosmos on which one could not lay profane hands.[1]

With the Romans, who were nothing if not practical, it was intellectual curiosity that was missing. The Will went into war and practical life. The theoretical speculations of the Greeks meant little to the Romans. They organized and built and were like Americans forever busy, entirely taken up with the problems of daily life, the moralistic how-to-do-it and how-to-get-on-with-other-people books, the politics of the everyday. The two great Roman cosmologies, of the Epicureans and the Stoics, were materialistic. The fact that they called Nature *Zeus* has little or no religious meaning.[2]

In the Christian centuries, or at least the early ones, the European world was too concerned with the soul's life, the drama of the soul's salvation, to direct itself toward either knowledge or power.[3] The Inner Turn, which we see so dramatically in St. Augustine, meant that one listened to a subjective teacher and affirmed the second principle of Christian philosophy (after the Greek principle that *form precedes matter*), namely, that *the inner is superior to the outer.*

It is in the twelfth century in the Crusades and the Gothic cathedrals that the Promethean Will begins to stir. What the historian Spengler called the Faustian principle, the upward thrust symbolized in the spires of the Gothic cathedrals, is the first powerful expression of this. Something similar is created in the Scholastic philosophical systems, great intellectual syntheses as they were. Paralleling this is the outburst of magic and occultism that led to alchemy and astrology and various schemes of correspondences, which anticipated the birth of modern science. The impulse of this science from the start was to take control of the natural world, to wrest secrets from nature for the sake of human power.

When the Greek spirit returned in the Renaissance, it entered a world in which curiosity and the desire to explore and control were already in full swing. The Greek idea that the particular is too imperfect to be the object of knowledge remained in place. The really new idea of Galileo and the other founders of modern science was that by *rigging* the natural, that is, by creating a drastically simplified situation (later called an *experiment*), the perfection of mathematics could after all be *made* to apply to everyday reality. The simplicity of this idea is so vast that it still amazes us, involving as it does a new kind of human being and seeing this being mirrored in a new and different world. We *forced* the mind onto phenomena by first creating a mechanical picture out of phenomena.

In less than two hundred years the basic framework of this alliance between ancient knowledge and practical occultism was thoroughly worked out: a mechanistic view of the universe in which the pushes and pulls of material bodies were the basic reality; the distinction between primary and secondary qualities, which Whitehead called *the bifurcation of nature* and which corresponded to the distinction between absolute objects and absolute subjects; the emergence of the physical and the psychological, materialism and idealism—all this defined a world and a knowledge entirely unsacred and unholy.

Thus was born the idea of scientific progress through the ever-growing conquest of nature and the extension of controlling knowledge for the sake of human betterment. This has been the prevailing religion of the modern world, not seriously questioned until this century, when it became self-destructive.

In the writings of Francis Bacon in the seventeenth century we have a full-blown affirmation of the faith in scientific progress to liberate the human race and restore the perfection of the Garden of Eden. As fifteenth-century humanists had spoken of human beings as "like gods" in their enthusiasm for the restoration of classical learning, Bacon spoke of the "dominion of man over the universe"; of "interrogating nature with power"; and in one of the most revealing passages, of "putting nature on the rack thereby uncovering the hidden processes and secrets of excellent use still laid up in her womb." The cat is out of the bag: science *rapes* nature.[4]

The unconcealed anti-feminism of this vision comes through clearly. He is talking about the feminine, the pagan, the energies of life. "Bind her to our service and make her our slave," says Bacon. Four thousand years of patriarchal arrogance finally come to a head. It is not the yoke of the biblical Law that is to be clamped down now, but the experiments of modern science that are to subordinate all to the Promethean Will. It is a hierarchical view in which the human dominates the natural as God dominates the human, as man dominates woman, and as both dominate children and animals. The rational mind aims at taking possession of the secrets of the physical, taking control for the sake of establishing an order and making use of it. Nature exists for the sake of human beings, as woman for the sake of man. This was not new. What is new is seizing hold of things in this way, extracting their resources, unleashing their powers, piling and manipulating them.

Knowledge as an imposition of the will in order to increase human power defines our relation to the world in the technological age. With each new scientific discovery, involving the most profound depths of physics and now extending into molecular biology and genetics, we have the impression that our power is increasing and that the earth is becoming more and more interrelated and the goal of a universal secular order and prosperity is getting closer. Into this happy dream, however, there has intruded in this century a fearful realization, something completely unexpected, an awareness of an opposite result. It is the awareness that the whole process has turned against human beings, that we are going to be the victims of it and not the beneficiaries. It is dawning upon us that science and technology will destroy what is most human and may very well make of the earth a poisoned planet, if not an atomic wasteland. Something is missing from the equation, and it is more and more clear what this is. It is the human being. We ourselves will be the victims of our own will to conquest.

Two names symbolize this century: *Hiroshima*, in which we brought the powers of the sun down to earth for the purposes of war and destruction, turning fifty thousand people into radiation in three seconds; and *Auschwitz*, where whole categories of men, women, and children were treated as utterly worthless, no better than vermin, and fit only to die or be worked to death. These were breaches of the human continuum as barbarous as anything ever done before. The poisoning of the air, water, and rain by toxic waste and chemical pollutants, oil spills and radiation, the threat to the ozone layer, the extinction of animal species—these follow as further examples of the Promethean Will unleashed by modern science.

It is against this background that we must examine the alternative visions of two women, two prophets who are leading voices of a great protest, a change that is now taking place as we enter a new era. The first philosopher of China, Confucius, stated twenty-five centuries ago that when we alter the balance between the masculine and the feminine, everything else changes too. This is one crucial aspect of what is happening. It is no accident that the two figures who take the lead here are both women—Hildegard of Bingen (1098–1179), who belongs to the Christian Renaissance of the twelfth century, and Simone Weil (1909–1943), a French woman of Jewish ancestry. Although these two women represent very different points of view, there are striking similarities between them. If we can see what it is they have in common, we can begin to formulate the parameters of the new world-view.

It was understood in the past, not only by primitive peoples but by all peoples, by the Greeks as well as by the biblical Jews, that as it is said "they alone shall possess the earth who live from the powers of the cosmos." But the powers that we have tapped turn out to be only the powers of death. What other powers are there? Or what other teaching is to be found in the cosmos? This is the question we want to put both to Hildegard of Bingen and to Simone Weil.

There are, to begin with, striking differences between them. They are the differences between the medieval cosmology and the modern one. Hildegard lived in the closed structure with the earth and humankind at the center, surrounded by nine divine circles reaching out to the heavenly spheres. It was essentially the universe of Aristotle in the medieval Neoplatonic Pseudo-Dionysian version. Inwardly these were the nine circles of heavenly choirs revolving around the ultimate mystery at the center; the earth is surrounded by the planetary spheres and that of the fixed stars, and all of this is within the Divine. What distinguishes Hildegard is the way in which she interprets this.

The modern universe of Simone Weil, on the other hand, is an open world: the earth no longer at the center, space opening endlessly it seems with billions of galaxies and systems of galaxies reaching out inconceivably far. Distances of immeasurable vastness separate one from the other. The sun is a quite ordinary star in a quite ordinary galaxy. We are unable so far to enter into communication with any other living or intelligent beings anywhere else in this vastness.

What are the theological meanings of these two pictures? How do they bear on our understanding and religion?

What has made Hildegard so important for us, made her the patron saint of the environmental and ecological movements, is her awareness of the *life* of the earth, the immanent energy that she feels in every thing that exists, above all in the greening of the earth, but also in the sparkle of the water, the burning of the sun, and the growing and dying of the moon. To her all this living energy is divine. Her philosophy has much in common with the ideas of Bergson, Whitehead, and Teilhard de Chardin. It centers on a vital potency which she feels moving the world from within. Motion is not merely mechanical and the result of pushes and pulls from without, but comes from an inner source. It is as if we are to understand the forces of physics by analogy with the energies of life, rather than the other way around.

To Hildegard, God is in these living forces. Her most important idea is *greening power*, or, in the word which she apparently devised, *viriditas*. It has inspired the Green Party in Germany. Living in the Rhineland, where she was founder and head of an abbey at Rupertsberg, she was aware of the bursting into greenness that happens every spring. In some of the visions that began to come to her in middle age and that she had painted and turned into magnificent mandalas, it is the ancient symbol of the Cosmic Tree appearing at the center. In one of them picturing the Cosmic Wheel, we see the head of Christ emerging from the top of the head of the Cosmic Mother. The greening power seems to be female, as if Hildegard were incorporating a fourth and feminine nature into the Christian Trinity, as Carl Jung proposed.

Her intuitive visions, full of female symbols as they are, particularly circles and ovals (at first she conceived of the cosmos in the shape of an egg and then changed this to the Aristotelian circle), sometimes show the soul beset by dangers from dark spirits and winds and humors that threaten the cosmic unity and wholeness, as if to show that the greening power and the energy of life may be overcome by dryness and disease and inner conflict.

In the very first of the *Ten Visions* that make up her *Book of Divine Works*, a voice speaks from within the mystery of God:

> I, the highest and fiery power, have kindled every spark of life, and I emit nothing that is deadly. I decide on all reality, with my lofty wings I fly above the globe, and with wisdom I have rightly put the universe in order.[5] I, the fiery life of divine essence, am aflame in the beauty of the meadows, I gleam in the waters, and I burn in the sun, moon, and stars. With every breeze, as with invisible life that contains everything, I awaken everything to life. The air lives by turning green and being in bloom. The waters flow as if they were alive. The sun lives in its light, and the moon after its disappearance is enkindled once again by it and revived. The stars, too, give a clear light with their beaming. I have set pillars that

bear the entire globe as well as the power of the winds which are moderated by lesser winds that resist them and make them safe. . . .

I am hidden in every kind of reality as a fiery power. Everything burns because of me as breath constantly moves animals, like the wind-tossed flame in a fire. All of this lives in its essence, and there is no death in it. For I am life. I am reason, which bears within itself the breath of the resounding Word, through which the whole of creation is made. I breathe life into everything. . . .

I am life, whole and entire, not struck from stones, not blooming out of twigs, not rooted in a man's power to beget children. All life has its roots in me. Reason is the root, the resounding Word flowers out of it.

To Hildegard, God's perfect power is the "green freshness of life," which he pours into the hearts of women and men so that they may bear good fruit. It is not the dominational power that imposes itself on the world by force and authority. She recognizes God as ruler and in an orthodox way an ultimate judge. But to her this is not primary. There is a different balance. In *Vision Three* she puts it this way:

God, who has created me and who has power over me like a ruler, is also my own power because without God I am unable to do any good deed, and because I have only through God the living spirit through which I live and am moved, through which I learn to know all my ways.

These passages may remind us of D. H. Lawrence. (From *Mornings in Mexico* and the first version of *Studies in Classical American Literature* we can judge that Lawrence in writing of the Hopi Sun Dance may also have been thinking of the Kundalini energy in Hindu philosophy.)

In *Vision Six* in her other book, *Scivias,* Hildegard speaks of the Christian idea of God's renunciation of power even in reference to the serpent, the ancient symbol worldwide of the feminine, always treated with respect by this woman despite its biblical manhandling:

The ancient serpent was conquered by God's humility and justice. God did not wish to overcome the ancient serpent with power and strength, because God is just and does not wish evil.

There are no hells or everlasting punishments in Hildegard's visions. When she speaks of justice, it is a form of love rather than something imposed by force and punishment. Matthew Fox says that he regrets that Hildegard did not speak out against the Crusades or the persecution of the Jews, but we cannot expect of her an ecumenism that belongs to a later time and which a great many Christians have still not attained today. It is sufficient that she recognizes the importance of so many feminine elements and incorporates them into her Christianity. It is these elements that make her so relevant today. In her we are being reminded of symbols going back to pre-Neolithic times.

We want to turn now to the other prophet, Simone Weil, and to a viewpoint far removed from Hildegard. If Hildegard reminds of the ancient *Living Cosmos,* Weil speaks for a very different feeling and vision—what we must call the *Abandoned Cosmos.* In her view the world is still shot through with beauty and order that manifest the love of God. This beauty and order are made known to us by the supernatural gift of mathematics. But the principal fact discerned from the vast reaches of cold cosmic space and cosmic time is *the absence of God,* and it is in this absence or *abandonment* that Weil paradoxically discovers something like the supreme manifestation of his love. We can understand the beauty and order of the world as expressions of this love, but how can the abandonment of the world, which she discerns in the modern astronomical universe, express it too?

Let us look at two apparently unrelated subjects that together may well alter our conception both of creation and of Divine Love. We will be looking at a new myth, a modern myth, which has a close relation both to modern science and to modern feeling in general. The two ancillary matters are the idea of creation in the Jewish Kabbalah of Isaac Luria in the seventeenth century and a recent book by John Boswell, a historian at Yale, entitled *The Kindness of Strangers: The Abandonment of Children in Western Europe from Late Antiquity to the Renaissance* (Yale University Press, 1988).

The idea of conception that we find in Hildegard, like that in most medieval writers and indeed in the *Zohar,* a twelfth-century Jewish Kabbalistic text, is *emanation.* The world streams out of God as a flow of divine power. It is an outgoing action of his, as in the book of Genesis. At his command his Ideas are realized in space and time, an outpouring of love and power. In the century after Hildegard, Thomas Aquinas described God as Pure Act, and creation as a supernatural event that we understand as conferring upon the world a secondary capacity to act. God thus creates space and time as the scene of a semi-autonomous being. This is not a part of God, but it contains knowable aspects that are like him and an affirmation from him. The Kabbalist Isaac Luria thought of creation in a very different way: not as a putting forth of power but as an act of withdrawal, a stepping back to make room for the world. God's power did not stream out from him into an independent or semi-independent realm, but he withheld it as a parent might make room to allow a child more free space. He created by getting out of the way and permitting an open place which is what we call space and time. Luria called this creation by withdrawal a *Zimzum.* There is a profound awareness here of the nature of human creativity, which likewise involves putting aside our own egos in order to let something else, not ourselves, come into being, in the way people open a circle to allow a stranger in. Such making room is a high manifestation of love.[6]

Luria describes *Zimzum* not as abandonment but as withdrawal. For him something else happens that separates the world from God, what he called *the breaking of the vessels*. Even after creation the beauty of God is too overwhelming. The finite vessels cannot contain the divine glory, and they burst. This means that every single object loses its original meaning and assumes a corrupted possessive ego meaning, since the creation tries to be completely independent of God, forgetting its origin in the Divine Love. The whole universe falls into the condition of what Weil calls *gravity*.[7]

Nothing in Weil corresponds to this conception of the breaking of the vessels, but the notion of *abandonment*, being much stronger than that of withdrawal, in a way covers this greater possibility of evil. An abandoned world is farther from God than a *Zimzum* world; it has much greater possibilities of suffering and evil. But we face a much greater dilemma. How can abandonment be an act of love?

This is where John Boswell's extraordinary book comes in: *The Kindness of Strangers*. First, we learn that the abandonment of children was a very common practice throughout the ancient world and during Christian medieval times. There was not enough food, and families were too large; parents had to trust that strangers would feed the children that they could not. Second, children were abandoned out of love and probably more out of love than for any other reason. We must not allow our middle-class American prejudices to mislead us here. Most of us are horrified by the act and can only conceive of it as a callous, selfish behavior. We tend to confuse it with the more ancient one of exposure, with death foreseen and intended. If there are already ten children in a family and not enough for them to eat and no hope of getting more, no Social Security or rich relatives, it is not an act of cruelty to put the child out as a foundling. Third, most abandoned children were found and brought up by strangers. In effect, they were being put for adoption, without the bureaucratic machinery we have today.

A further common practice existed of giving the tenth child to the church, and this is what happened to Hildegard. She was a tenth child, and at the age of eight she was put into an abbey and did not see her natural parents again. We recall that in pre-biblical times the eldest child was sacrificed to God[8] (and even in the sixth century B.C. the priests in Jerusalem appear to have enforced the rabbinical law by a threat that this old ritual might be restored).

We sometimes forget, as Boswell points out, that Moses himself was abandoned, Oedipus was abandoned, Romulus and Remus were abandoned, Ishmael, the father of Islam, was abandoned. Simone Weil sees the ultimate demonstration of the divinity of Jesus in the fact that on the cross even in expressing his abandonment he could not help but call upon the all-loving God.[9]

Being abandoned raises in the most extreme form the tension between our connection to the natural realm and to the supernatural. In the ancient legends of heroes, a child is raised by more or less ordinary folk only to discover later that his real parents are people of high nobility, perhaps a king or queen. This can be taken as a parable about the divine parentage of all human beings.

In his book *Moses and Monotheism*, Sigmund Freud argues that whereas in the biblical version Moses is a Hebrew child brought up by Egyptian royalty, it is more probable that the reverse was true, that he was an Egyptian brought up by Hebrews. The usual myth, he says, is that the real family is the noble one, while the humble family is fictitious. The Jewish myth seeks to transform Moses, probably a high-born Egyptian, into a Jew by making the ordinary family into the original one.

Boswell points out that Christianity itself was a foundling:

> born into Judaism but rejected by it, it was adopted by Rome, it grew up to be much more a part of its foster than of its natal family. Indeed, Roman language and culture achieved their greatest impact on the Western world chiefly through their *alumnus,* Christianity—an abandoned child reared to greatness by a loving foster parent.[10]

Since Christianity is a *Son* religion, as distinguished from Judaism and Islam, which are both *Father* religions, we have to say that this Son is reconciled not to a Jewish Father or Father-God (neither of whom would abandon the world or his people, whom he continues to govern), but to a New Testament God, who alone could abandon the world out of Love.

Such a God surely cannot be the judging, punishing, and rewarding God of the Old Testament, who has ordained the Law and still rules as Lord and Master. That God never abandoned the world. And, on the other side, we have never abandoned him. But, as Weil says, this latter is not the God of the New Testament, all-embracing, all-forgiving, all-encompassing. For her love is a gift, not earned, any more than a child earns the love of the mother. The love of God is bestowed not in a covenant or contract but as a gratuitous unconditional gift.

The abandonment of the world in Weil's thought helps us to understand the role of force, in both the natural and the human spheres. What has the world been abandoned to? In a sense, to the possibility of evil; for the main evil is force. This is symbolized by the opposite of grace: gravity. It is not merely space and time in their vast emptiness and meaninglessness but gravity which plays such a large part within them. And in the human place we must add prestige, egotistical prestige, which makes up the power and glory that are the realm of illusion. New Testament love in Weil's view shares one great thing with mathematics: it is *impersonal*. We are not used to thinking of mother love in these terms, but it is amazingly impersonal as well as personal. The little baby already has a name and is unique, not to be confused with its brother or sister, who are loved no less. At the same time it has no personality, no ego, nothing to like or dislike; not even resemblance matters. The mother does not see the baby as an other. This is something that the male baby will have to struggle for; to have that granted might be the greatest boon to it. Abandonment out of love grants the maximum of otherness, without violation of love.

The miracle of the Gospels is that the transcendent God, whose beyondness made him forever incomprehensible, was revealed as the all-surrounding, loving Mother.[11] This is what the church was not able to do justice to and what Hildegard and Simone Weil were in their different ways trying to express. In Christian theology the ancient Hebraic lawgiving God of authority is incorporated into the Trinity. It is Christ who recovers the original and deeper principle of all-embracing love, but this applies mainly to the individual, and the nations are still under the old God of law and anger. There is a great difference between the jealous wrathful punishing Yahweh and the all-forgiving God of *agapē*.[12] The first sanctions war in the name of power and justice and demands intolerance to pagans, heretics, and idolaters. The second advocates nonviolence and nonresistance. All through Christian history, the followers of the first have dominated the followers of the second, and have succeeded in persecuting other Christians, Jews, Muslims, and pagans.

In the Platonic system the mathematical predominates as in the universe of theoretical physics today, where we see abstract structures: non-Euclidean geometry, differential equations, tensor calculus, non-commutative algebras. Physics finds it impossible to drop the concept of force entirely and speaks of four fundamental forces, even though the term itself has a more and more and more abstract use than it is given in ordinary language. In a philosophy like that of Leibniz, even space and time become illusory ways in which the confused perceptions of monads—something like little souls or little drops of cosmic consciousness—perceive patterns that are wholly abstract.

These are the differing orientations of Hildegard and Weil. What are the theological implications? Hildegard reaches much further back than Aristotle for her feminine imagery, for example, for the World Tree at the center of the cosmos. Nothing might seem more out of date. Aristotle first introduced the word that we translate as "matter": the word *hulē*, which originally meant "wood." For him the world was made out of "wood."[13] The word "matter" is cognate to the Latin word *mater*, "mother." All these *ma* words have a common root in European languages; the word "mathematics" also is related to *mater*.[14] (*Ma*, the sucking sound, should be contrasted with *Da*, the expelling sound.) As long as we think in terms of progress we think there is a decided improvement in introducing the more abstract concepts. But of course we lose a certain concreteness, the relation to our own bodies, and to our feelings.

Which is more true, the World Tree, or Einstein's Relativity? It depends on what we mean by "true." It is interesting that the word "true" is cognate with the word "tree." They have a common root: something that *stands by itself alone*. We now think of what is *true* as the most abstract and most general representation of the world, the pure reduced structure mirrored in equations. But we might also think of what is true as that which corresponds to our most primal bodily feelings and particular responses.[15]

Let us take as an example the moon. In ancient mythology it is a goddess or the appearance of a goddess, dying and being reborn every twenty-eight days, like the rhythm of a woman's menstrual cycle. Today we say that men have landed on the moon, and *our* mythology does not include it as a goddess any more. But have we entirely finished with the original connection between the moon and the month and the menses and measurement?

In order to sharpen the connection, consider that Hildegard of Bingen connects us with the prehistoric *Mother Goddess*, that is, the immanent principle of *life*, while Simone Weil speaks for a transcendent *Mother God*, a principle of unfailing *love* put forward by Jesus Christ and concealed within Christianity. And these are the two poles of our answer to the ecological, environmental, and human crises. The Mother Goddess reminds us that the ultimate source of all our reactions is a supernatural love not based on any natural connection to our own deserts, surviving even abandonment.

In Weil's view the basis of all claims to rights and justice as well as the only transcendent thing in this world is what she calls *the expectation that we carry with us all through our lives that good will be done to us.* This is our incorrigible humanity, our predisposition to trust in the goodness of others. We are born into the world, as it were, expecting to be fed and looked after. We go on expecting that others will not harm us or permit us to be harmed, often in the teeth of all evidence to the contrary. What else can we do? Are we not dependent on the kindness of strangers (the first of whom is our mother)[16] whether we want to be or not? And now in this century perhaps even more than ever?[17]

We come down to these two: the energy of life in the child and the mother, and the implicit trust of the child in her and others' care. These are fundamental *facts*.[18] Even if the baby is abandoned and someone else adopts it, this trust is usually not shattered. Then the love, if it continues in the foster situation, is more gratuitous, more gracious. The father with his fearsome anger and his rewards and punishments does not appear until later, although his shadow may be in the background and certainly is in the practice of circumcision. There is no *quid pro quo* sought in the mother's love, though there is in the father's. The first is pure gift, the second demands a return. Here is the ultimate quarrel between justice and love as to which comes first, and on this point Hildegard and Weil are both clear that love, that is to say a mother's love, comes first.

In Saint Bartholomew's Church in New York over the altar there is an extraordinary mosaic depicting three men, Jesus flanked by Saint Peter and Saint Paul. All three of them stand against the background of the four primary feminine or goddess symbols. Below the Christ figure is *water*, from which all life originally came and in which each individual floats in the womb. On either side are *trees*, representing the greening power and the ancient World Tree. Above all hovers the *dove*, prime symbol of the Mother Goddess, and then of the Holy Spirit, connecting heaven and earth. Finally, Jesus himself stands inside the oval of the *yoni*, or vulva. This is the shape, too, of the *vesica piscis*, or vessel of the fish, the worldwide sign of the feminine creative energy, also taken over by the early Christians. The picture as a whole thus shows that Christianity exists against the background of the primordial Great Mother and far from being hostile to it still depends on it.

Today our civilization does not protect this living matrix. The waters on which we exist are slowly being poisoned, the forests destroyed, the doves replaced by hawk missiles and planes, birds of prey, and the *yoni* by the commercialization and technification of sex and motherhood.

We are becoming the victims of our own assault on nature, and this points to a profound principle emphasized by the philosopher Heidegger: the solution to the problem of technology cannot be *more* technology. The essence of technology is not technological. It lies in metaphysics, the essence of which appears now to be the Promethean Will to *seize* and *control* the world.

CHAPTER 10

Recovering the Sacred
in Humanity

> He who seeks will not find; he who does not seek—will be found.
>
> —Franz Kafka[1]

I T IS TRUE OF SIMONE WEIL, as it is true only of outstanding philosophers at historical turning points—Wittgenstein is another one in our
century—that in order to understand her we have to learn to think in a
new way.[2] We have to learn, for example, not to think that religions are, or
should be, cut off from each other in water-tight compartments, or that there
is no religious significance to the products of culture, or that there is something admirable about force and power.

A good starting point is to think, as Wittgenstein did—and Simone Weil
would have agreed with him—that "all religions are wonderful."[3] Not that
some are right and others are wrong, but that all spiritual traditions are worthy of respect and have something to teach us. We mistakenly compare religions with scientific truths, but they are more like ways of life, which need
not, and should not, exclude each other.

For example, Jews and Christians have found it possible to be Buddhists,
even Buddhist *roshi*s, or masters, without any sense of "betraying" Judaism
or Christianity by this. Or can't one be a Christian and a Muslim, or a Jew
and a Muslim at the same time? More and more have found that they can.
Rosenstock-Huessy, Franz Rosenzweig, Eric Gutkind, and Martin Buber come
to mind as judaized Christians and christianized Jews.

Quite clearly, however, the vast majority of Jews, Christians, and Muslims
are rigidly sectarian in implacably separatist ways. Orthodox Jews, for example, to this day refuse even to mention the name of Jesus (quoting Exodus
23.13, "Make no mention of the name of other gods").[4] Jesus is regarded not
as a treasure of the human race, but as a religious traitor, an apostate. The case

is no different with fundamentalist Christians and Muslims, who have an arrogant sense of superiority to Buddhists, Hindus, and Confucianists.

A sympathetic study of the Qur'an might be required in every American school. But the schools do not even allow reading the Bible. We speak of water-tight compartments. A better analogy might be that the religions are like tigers kept in separate cages for fear they would tear each other to pieces. This is the world in which there are Hiroshimas and Auschwitzes. It is the world in which "no one speaks for humanity." Simone Weil, however, does speak for humanity.

She refused to join the Catholic Church despite her love for Jesus Christ, for the same reason that she rejected traditional Judaism: its lack of respect for other religions and spiritual traditions. The contempt which Muslims, Christians, and Jews have for those whom they have labeled "pagan," "heathen," and "idolaters" has justified a multitude of crimes: slavery, colonialism, exploitation, and genocide, and at the same time has set the pattern for persecution of each other, particularly the persecution of Jews by Christians.

There is one place where Simone Weil did not find the spirit of fanatical separatism, but rather of all-embracing acceptance of all human beings. It was in the teachings of Jesus Christ in the Gospels. Something of the same spirit was in the book of Job and here and there in the Hebrew prophets; and in Hinduism and Buddhism and the ancient religions of Egypt and the Celts; but mainly in the Gospels.

Perhaps the single most important sentence defining her understanding of Jesus is in the *Letter to a Priest*, the document in which she explains, in effect, why she will not join the church. She says in section 9 that the disciples misunderstood Jesus, not realizing that his teaching was to be *added* on to other religions rather than to *take the place* of them. Thus a man or woman could remain within whatever religion he or she was and be in addition a Christian. He meant, Weil says, that a person could be a Hindu and a Christian (like Gandhi), a Jew and a Christian (like Brother Daniel), a Muslim and a Christian (like Titus Burckhardt). Unfortunately, the church, still pervaded by the exclusionist spirit of the Hebrew Bible and the power and forms of Rome, lost this universality.

Robert Coles, a Harvard psychologist, in a recent book about Simone Weil suggests that she had a "deep antagonism to the Jewish tradition."[5] It would be nearer the truth to say that she had a deep antagonism to *antagonism* itself, that is, to the idea that the fundamental human relation is one of fear and hostility, even if it masquerades for a time as love and respect. The notion that God wants any particular group of human beings to have a favored status seemed to her profoundly wrong, even if this is qualified by some such phrase as "until messianic times" or "until the second coming."

There will never be any possibility of understanding Simone Weil from *within* the conflicts of religions, as if she shared in this rather than having been freed from it. Her perspective can only be seen from *outside* it.

The question has been raised whether it was right for her to attack the Wrathful God of the Hebrew Bible at a time when the Jews themselves were being subjected to the utmost intolerance and cruelty of the Holocaust. The answer depends on whether we see it primarily as part of *Jewish history*—in which case it appears religiously as God's punishment or test of the Jews[6] or secularly as one of the crimes of Christian Europe against them—or as belonging to *world history*, where it appears as part of the entire tradition of inhumanity in the name of nation or religion, a tradition in which Judaism itself has played a considerable part.

Was she being fair to the Jewish people, the people of her ancestors though not of her own life and experience, in not adopting the narrower Judaic perspective? Did she represent it fairly in rejecting it? In answer to this question it may be helpful to cite one of the spiritual leaders of modern Judaism, a chief rabbi of Palestine in the 1920s and 1930s and the only Jewish writer of this century to be included thus far in the *Library of the Classics of Western Spirituality* published by Paulist Press: Rabbi Abraham Kook (1865–1935). The following, written in 1910, refers to the people of Amalek, the chief enemy of Israel, whom God ordered Israel to exterminate:

> Prophecy, which looks with the spirit of the living Lord into the soul of nation and man, attested that the opposition of the race of Amalek to the light of Israel is intrinsic, and that it has no remedy but annihilation in order to clear the path of Jewish history of its greatest obstacle. . . . When the day comes that mankind will no longer have need of acts of hatred, then we may be sure that Amalek has finally been obliterated. [For] because of that same remnant which we stupidly spared, we brought upon ourselves physical and spiritual calamities and we learned to perform all their abominations.[7]

It was a stupid mistake to spare any of them—this is what Simone Weil finds so appallingly wrong, said by any people about any other people. No human beings are appointed by God to annihilate other human beings, although many have thought they were. The quotation from Rabbi Kook continues:

> Christianity wished to eliminate the attribute of hate woven into the tapestry of the Divine Light of Israel, but have we not come to realize that it shed blood and magnified malevolence in the name of the elimination of hatred more than any battle of hatred ever did? Moreover in its haste prematurely to bring the eradication of hate and its adherents while the chaff still remained, it separated the light of the divine faith from the entire social order of life.[8]

Rabbi Kook is right in saying that Christians have behaved in a more inhuman way than Jews ever did; but we do not know whether this was because Christians had the power to do so while Jews did not, and in what way the Jews would have behaved if they had had the power. If we think that God has given orders to annihilate enemies, would *any* Christians have been spared at all? Would the Jews have been more thorough in their annihilation? *If God does not protect the enemy, then who will?* And cannot *anyone* find oneself to be the enemy?

Simone Weil has often been compared to the ancient Christian heretic Marcion (85–159), who wished to separate Christianity from Judaism completely and take the Old Testament out of the Christian Bible. He believed that there are two *gods*, the Wrathful Creator God who gave the Law to the Jews, and the Loving Redeemer God of Jesus Christ. This "two-god theology" of Marcion anticipated the teaching of the Persian Mani a century later and was condemned by the church for the same reason that Manicheanism was—that it destroyed the unity of the Christian God. Christianity had its own way of dealing with the problem: these were two *aspects* of the same God in the Christian Trinity.

Simone Weil's rejection of Judaism goes further than Marcion's (without however violating the Trinitarian Unity as Marcion did). She, in effect, christianizes the Creator God by seeing Creation itself as an act of Divine *Love*, rather than as an act of Divine *Power*, as it has always been seen by the church and as it seemed even to Marcion. In Weil's view there is no room at all for the power aspect of God shown in the Old Testament even in the relation of God to the people of Israel. The true God is *beyond power*.[9]

The Old Testament God is, first of all, a ruler, the prototypical ruler, the very principle of masculine power. The New Testament God, on the other hand, is a loving father, as all-embracing and forgiving as a mother. Is it the same God? The oppositions expressed by Paul between law and grace, the first Adam and second Adam, the two covenants, sharpened the contrast. And yet Paul visualized the loving God returning at the end as the ruling and judging and wrathful God that he had been at the beginning. The wrathful God is still there for those who reject the loving salvation offered by Jesus.[10] Paul thinks of the love and grace of God as a way provided by God to avoid his wrath. But the wrath has not disappeared; it has only been circumvented. The fearful punishing God, rejected by Marcion and Weil, is very real to Paul.

Marcion, like Simone Weil, could not reconcile the jealous intolerance of the Old Testament God with the universal love and goodness of the New Testament one. The Greek spirit of cosmopolitanism and free intellectual curiosity was violated by a God who threatened the most terrible punishments even for showing interest in other religions. Unlike the democratic spirit of the

Greeks, the attitude of the Hebrews was like that of a family held together by a single dominating father who, while he looks after them, is merciless in punishing disobedience. Such a father rules by fear, of course for everyone's own good.

Nothing could be more different from the New Testament God. Love and forgiveness replace fear. Like a mother's love or like the sun, this God's love shines freely and indiscriminately on all, playing no favorites between men and women, free men and slaves, Jews and Gentiles, older sons and younger ones. Furthermore, this love works miracles; it gives joy and spontaneity; it brings us into the present. The central human situation is not the child at the age of six about to be submitted to the discipline of the rod (as the Puritans called it, the "breaching"), but rather the infant in the presocial love and joy and freedom of complete dependence upon the mother; and yet still with individuality.

Simone Weil's thought is the more remarkable because it avoids a second heresy of Marcion, *Docetism*, separating the illusory human body of Jesus from the real divine nonbodily spirit of Christ. She understands that without the full humanity and full divinity of Jesus Christ, *both* together, Christ's teaching itself fails. But in her view, this does not require accepting the Old Testament God. (We could begin to see here the beginning of the end of the torments of the hostilities of Judaism and Christianity.)

The tension in Weil's philosophy and in her life between body and spirit, necessity and grace, affliction and joy is everywhere as strong as it could be, but it never turns into cosmic or metaphysical dualism. She never permits these opposites to come apart completely. She is no Manichean and no Docetist (whatever the superficial impression to casual readers).

It is in understanding creation itself as sacrifice that Simone Weil makes her most innovative step. It is her idea of *the creation of the world by the cosmic absence of God as the fullest expression of divine love.* There are affinities to this in ancient Hindu and Buddhist mythology; but the closest thing to it in modern times is in the Jewish Kabbalist Isaac Luria in the seventeenth century. Luria described God's creation as his withdrawal (*Zimzum*) to make room for the world. The human creator too pulls back his ego to allow inspiration to enter. This is an act of sacrifice as well as compassion and mercy, which here for the first time appears as the primary factor, though Luria does not develop this.

Simone Weil sees creation and the world by analogy with the crucifixion. The world is the realm of matter and necessity, which is at the farthest remove from love and grace (even though it also reveals the order and beauty that are implicit forms of Divine Love). The Spirit of God is crucified upon space and time, on and throughout the continuum of the material world, and yet this is the greatest manifestation of love, to be faithful even in and through the far-thest removal and the most total absence.

Since such theological language is more or less impenetrable to the mod-ern mind, we must look at this in a more familiar philosophical way. The absence of God, insofar as it is the absence of not just anything, but specifi-cally of *God*, is the supreme manifestation of the Love of God in somewhat the way that Hegel says that *the negative is the crucial moment of the positive.* What we cannot help calling out to in its absence is what we love most. This is the way Simone Weil thinks about Jesus on the cross when in his darkest moment he calls out, "My God, my God, why have you forsaken me?" This is the moment of supreme truth because there is nothing else to call out to in that moment of desertion. Love calls out and is called out to then, because then there is nothing else, no other last expression. Hence, what some have regarded as Jesus' moment of doubt is for Weil the seal on his divinity. With-out this, something would have been omitted: the utter abyss of human aban-donment and isolation and the cry ringing out from that.

When we consider the short life of Simone Weil (she died in 1943 at the age of thirty-four), it seems nothing short of miraculous that she could have left such a wealth of brilliant writings on so many different subjects: science, his-tory, social and political philosophy, spiritual direction, and comparative reli-gion. These writings display a quality of near clairvoyant insight and originality that continues to amaze us.

If there is anything that she did not reflect on, it may be in the area of the deeper connections between Judaism and Christianity. As a Marcionite and a student of Greek philosophy—her essays on the *Iliad* and on Plato and the Pythagoreans are among the best ever written on these subjects—she saw in a strikingly new way the intellectual nexus between Euclid and Christ, while not exploring the connection between Isaiah and Christ.[11] Her imagination tended toward the geometrical and the spatial, rather than the temporal and the historical.[12] The peculiar character of the Hebrew experience of time with its language lacking present tense and its past and future given together as both always present (as in prophecy)—this she did not investigate.[13]

Similarly, though she recognized the reality of miracles as gifts of grace, she did not consider their role in the histories of Judaism and Christianity and hence also the great importance of the messianic and the eschatological. It was the possibility of the miraculous (what we today call the paranormal) and of sudden individual, historical, and cosmic eruptions and discontinuities that furnished the background for the appearance and significance of Jesus Christ.

While traditional Christian thinkers have regarded prophecy and miracle as among the vindications of the truth of Christianity, they do not have this significance so much today, and Simone Weil in this respect reflects the character of the modern mind. It is Jesus' teaching itself, its universality and sanctification of the individual, the ways in which it ties together the heights and depths of life, the meaning it gives to misery and affliction and its capacity to release the greatest joy out of the greatest sorrow—this was for her the primary evidence.[14]

All of this would, of course, be recognized by traditional Christianity within the context of its combined Jewish and Greek inheritance. What proved to be the uneasy combination of Hebraic and Hellenic (Christianity, as it were, attacking each of these in isolation and insisting on its own version of their combination), we have come to take for granted, even despite its destructive and pathological aspects.

What the world can no longer accept is the element of fanaticism and exclusivism in the three monotheistic religions that makes them enemies of each other and of the Third World, each jealously guarding its dream of ultimate domination. If we return to the church fathers, and particularly to Tertullian's five books attacking Marcion, we can see the fundamental assumptions about human life that these religions share and that only today we are beginning to call into question. These are the assumptions Simone Weil discards on behalf of a humane and fully human world.

One of the most important of these is the belief that *fear* must come before love in human life in order to impose the necessary discipline that makes love possible, both in the upbringing of children, in social and political life, and in our religious understanding. Justice, so it has been believed, must come before love, and justice is not possible except in alliance with fear and punishment. In the Jewish view hate and fear will only become unnecessary in human affairs at the end of time when justice has finally been established worldwide; whereas for Christians love shows itself in the middle of history as available for individuals now, although not for nations until the end of time. For Christians love is still framed by divine wrath and punishment, the principle of life on this earth for families and governments. Tertullian makes this clear in ridiculing Marcion's view that God is only good and never uses evil. Tertullian believes that it is only the fear of punishment that makes people behave morally, and this applies to Christians in general too (although not to the saints).

The church fathers (there were no church mothers)[15] believe that goodness is not strong enough to have created the world or to maintain justice. Tertullian writes:

> Pure dupe of a Marcion, it is not only to the Creator's thunderbolts that you lie
> exposed and to war and pestilences and his other heavier strokes but even to his
> creeping insects. In what respect do you suppose yourself liberated from his
> kingdom when his flies are still creeping upon your face. . . . You display him as
> a merely good God, but you are unable to prove that he is perfectly good because
> you are not by him perfectly delivered.[16]

The possibility of the self-limitation of God out of Love does not exist for
Tertullian; rulers always exert their power to the fullest in order to make
things the way they want them to be; and this applies to fathers, husbands,
kings, magistrates, and all in patriarchal authority.

Simone Weil's view, against both Marcion and Tertullian, is that the vast
distance at which we lie from the God of Love requires neither a separate God
of power and wrath to have made the material world (as Marcion thought) nor
a different aspect of the God of love (as Tertullian did), but rather an awareness of how this vast distance and absence itself expresses love.

Tertullian is frequently sarcastic about Marcion because he cannot imagine God as anything but a ruler, and rulers cannot rule except by combining
love and hate, and love and fear.

> Listen, you sinners. A better god has been discovered, who never takes offense,
> is never angry, never inflicts punishment, who has prepared no fire in hell, no
> gnashing of teeth in the outer darkness, is purely and simply good. He indeed
> forbids all delinquency, but only in word. He is in you if you are willing to pay
> him homage for the sake of appearances that you may seem to honor God, for
> your fear he does not want. And so satisfied are the Marcionites with such pre-
> tences that they have no fear of their god at all. They say it is only a bad man who
> will be feared; a good man will be loved. Foolish man, do you say that he whom
> you call Lord ought not to be feared, whilst the very power that you give him
> indicates a power that must be feared?[17]

These words were written in 207, about fifty years after the death of Marcion. In the year 1988 they elicited the following comment from a feminist
friend, "Of course if you are going to lord it over people, you have to make
them afraid of you; that's the way you do it." She was thinking of the long history of human beings with power suppressing human beings without power,
supported and justified by just such an all-powerful, fearful, punishing God.
Tertullian speaks of the "punitive evils" that those in authority use against
those without authority. How could it come to an end? Only by expunging
the punishing God, or rather by shifting his sacredness to the loving God.

In Simone Weil's philosophy love is not based on justice, but the other
way—*justice is based on love.* (By the same token, peace is not to wait upon justice, since for this we may wait until the end of the world; first there must be
peace and then justice.)

We have to begin all over again, reversing these relations. What *is* justice? Is it revealed law? Is it the requirements of the powerful enshrining the mystique of the masculine will? Is it the conventional customs and mores of a people? Is it the superior rule of the superior race or a superior religion? Is it the recognition of natural individual civil and human rights?

For Simone Weil it is, in the end, none of these. They are all tainted by power. And all attempts to base justice on power (whether the power of God, the state, or nature) inevitably encounter the difficulty that power has no intrinsic worth, however much it frightens or overwhelms us. There is no workable context for justice except each human being, simply because he or she is human, and not because of any status or power. The true locus of justice cannot be anything else than *humanity* individually and universally.

In her remarkable essay "Beyond Personalism," Simone Weil poses the crucial question, What prevents me from gouging your eyes out if I have the power and desire to do it? The answer in the past may have been the fear of God. But what if this does not deter us, as it has not deterred the mass criminals of this century nor indeed of past centuries? Weil's answer is that there is only one thing that could deter us, and if it does not then indeed (as we have seen in this century) there is nothing at all. It is the realization that if I do it, I will be violating your expectation (that expectation which we all share and which alone unites and protects us) that good will be done to you by others. In other words, although we may not know it, we are all defenseless against force and violence in the end and have nothing to save us from it but the innocence of expectation in each human soul.[18] Atrocities follow from the absence of this bond, for there is nothing else to prevent them. The God of power is no longer available.

Where does this expectation that good will be done to us come from? In Weil's view we are born with it, and it is supernatural—indeed, it is the *only* thing that is supernatural about us. How are we to understand this? Let us recall that in our earliest experience is an unconscious or half-conscious reliance upon another human being (usually our mother) upon whom our well-being and our survival depend. However abused, this trust from the moment of birth is not disappointed; others do look after us, and the trust remains at the center of our souls for all of our lives. It is a human dependence lodged in us prior to any question of fear and punishment. Whatever our subsequent suspiciousness and hostility and betrayal, it is secondary to our need for the help of others. The abuse from God, from parents, from rulers, from members of other religions and races and nations cannot drive it out completely.

Why does Simone Weil regard such an apparently natural human dependence as supernatural? Not reason, not free will, nor consciousness, but this *expectation of good*? It is because it is outside the patterns of necessity and causality, ego and pride, force and compulsion. What is given to us is given to us as a gift, for no reason and for no recompense.[19]

It may surprise us that the church fathers, many of whom impress us as deeply human, should nevertheless have believed to a man that the supernatural factor in human life is power making use of fear and punishment and only occasionally making use of love and grace.[20] Inhumanity has not been restricted to the monotheistic religions. The Greeks exposed their unwanted children to die of starvation; Arabs buried them alive (a practice against which Islam protested). The biblical God, however, yielded to none in his inhumanity. It is an inhumanity that we are now compelled to reject.

Many who attempt to read Simone Weil for the first time have the experience of feeling strongly that there is something important there to understand, yet not actually understanding a word of it. They feel themselves to be in a *terra incognita* where they cannot find even a single landmark. It is the total position that is unfamiliar, even though individual words are those from traditional theology and philosophy. (Wittgenstein once observed that if a lion could speak, we wouldn't understand him. The reason is not that we wouldn't know the meanings of the individual words, but that we wouldn't know the *point* of what the lion was saying. Its world and life would be too different from ours.)[21]

Psychology and sociology and even philosophy will not help us with Simone Weil. Her messages are messages of grace, received by those who wait and not by those who grasp. (The very premises of psychology and sociology and philosophy are grasping, willed knowledge.)[22] We are used to people who impose interpretations on the world, not those who wait and let it come to them. It is this that puts the world into a new context, a sacred human one.

"To recover the sacred"—this has been put down as one of the great aims of the coming age. There are two great sacralizing steps in Weil's philosophy: the sacralizing of culture and the sacralizing of humanity. What do we mean by this term, which, after all, indicates something that is not within our own unaided capacity? It is the recognition that everything that matters most to us comes as a gift. After thousands of years what we can do by will and effort has come to an end because it has become self-destructive. A reversal is under way.

Simone Weil is the opposite of a secularist, because for her a true human culture comes from beyond the merely human. Science, art, poetry, music, philosophy, to the extent that they come unannounced to human attention waiting in patience,[23] she calls forms of the implicit love of God; they are sacred deliverances. This is not romanticism or sentiment because it is not egotism. True making, like true doing, is not ours. Indeed *we* cannot do or make, only wait and receive.[24] (Weapons of destruction do not come from beyond, but entirely from individual and collective egos.)[25]

Even more important is the sacredness of *the human bond*. The root human situation is not pride and disobedience and need for discipline but the vulnerability and dependence of each of us on others, which is our initial situation in the world. It is just because we have failed to acknowledge this (standing by only the masculine authority) that we have opened the door to mutual annihilation. We have accepted only a togetherness and universality defined by and limited to our own nation or religion.

The primary human situation is not our coming under the discipline of the powerful God of authority (which happens to us at the age of five or six). Prior to this (though blocked out later by our amnesia of childhood) is the truly sacred experience of trust in other human beings. This is what "socializing" destroys in favor of regard for power. But it does not have to happen. We can learn the transcendent worth of the human as easily as or more easily than we learned the transcendent worth of the God of power and authority and our own group.

It is a striking fact that we have not been able to get from the Old Testament principle of *the holiness of the people* or the New Testament principle of *the divinity of the individual* to *the holiness and divinity of humanity*, the whole of humanity. This step, for which the world is groping, eludes it. Joachim of Fiore at the end of the twelfth century described a coming Age of the Spirit, following the Age of the Father and the Age of the Son, but he did not see the basis on which this Third Age would have to arise. Sacred humanity can only exist if culture too and the human bond become sacred to us.

Simone Weil's God of grace is a God divorced from power and necessity, which are after all nothing to admire and worship. To her, God has an influence in human affairs and in history that is decisive but subtle and that the world can never understand, for it is entirely beyond human control. The human principle, like Plato's Good, has an inexorability about it too, but it is a providential one beyond natural causality. Higher dimensions show themselves only at scarcely recognizable points. This is how love makes itself felt.

The love she speaks of is not emotional or romantic or possessive. She calls it *impersonal*: it is impartial, unconditioned, objective. The closest to this love of Christ may be the love a mother gives her child, asking nothing in return. It is not cold, but it is not passionate. It wants what is best for the child. It seeks out not the personality of the child, which has not yet developed, but the unique human essence, which is individualized from the start. What keeps this love from continuing into our adulthood are collective identifications (e.g, French, Catholic, working-class) and individual egotisms and possessiveness. In the grip of these two kinds of egotism we cannot see things as they are (we always have an ulterior motive of self-interest) and we cannot relate to human beings simply as fellow human beings.

One of the most important lessons we learn from Simone Weil is to distinguish between the *psychological* and the *spiritual*. It has been a delusion of our age (one already beginning to disappear) that it is possible to "explain" the spiritual psychologically (Freud, Jung, Reich, and the rest). We have myths that have the appearance, but not the reality, of science. They have to be taken on faith, "believed in," like pseudo-religions. (The kind of psychology that people accept is already determined by their predispositions, not scientific evidence.)

Simone Weil herself has been the victim of such psychological "explanations," which in effect ignore her philosophy and try instead to fit it into categories of masochism or anorexia or self-hatred, in the way that psychologists have attempted to explain Leonardo da Vinci's art as a mother-fixation or Dostoevsky's as parricide. In the case of Simone Weil, such "theories" may fulfill a useful purpose by forming a protective shell around her that guarantees that only those who are seriously interested will be able to see through it. This will prevent her from being turned into a cult. Those who cannot recognize her genius because of the screen had best stay away. Thus, her intellectual and moral and spiritual integrity will remain protected until such reductive psychology has disappeared and we are able to meet her truly.

CHAPTER 11

The Life and Death
of Simone Weil

Summing Up

O NE OF THE REMARKABLE THINGS about Simone Weil is the degree
of self-understanding that we find in her writings. As everyone
knows, self-understanding is not always associated with great minds.
But it was so with Simone Weil.[1] A consequence is that those who think that
they understand her better than she understood herself—for example, by referring as some critics do to psychoanalysis or ethnic inheritance—are far off the
track. All they have done is to translate her into terms that are not hers, violating the first principle of hermeneutics, that everything can only be understood in its own terms.[2] We learn from these more about the authors of such
attempts to "explain" her, and about the prevailing myths of the day, than we
do about Simone Weil herself.

In a document that she wrote on May 15, 1942, the day before sailing from
Marseilles to Casablanca and on to America, she left a Spiritual Autobiography
in the form of a letter to Father Joseph-Marie Perrin,[3] which for its succinct-
ness and precision in telling her story will never be matched.

The letter falls into three main parts. First is the description of what she
absorbed of Christianity as a child, that is, as a cultural inheritance in a family which, though Jewish by ancestry, retained no Jewish interests or practices.
She begins the Autobiography by describing the Christian attitude with which
she says she was born and grew up and in which she remained. Some specific
notions went back as far as she could remember; she knows when others first
came into her life.

Second is what she calls the "three contacts with Catholicism" that really
counted. These were experiences leading her into the actual company of

116

Christ, quite beyond the sphere of cultural Christianity. They culminated in a daily realization of the presence of Christ through a recital with total attention of the Lord's Prayer in Greek.

Third is a discussion of the incarnation of Christianity in society and culture and how this relates to her "vocation" from God and Christ "to remain outside the church."

I will discuss each one of these three parts in detail and conclude with some words on her death and her life and the prayers in which she gave meaning to these.

Cultural Christianity

Simone Weil tells Father Perrin at the outset that he neither brought her the Christian inspiration nor brought her to Christ, for both of these happened "without the intervention of any human being." The first came from the life that surrounded her as she grew up, and the second from a series of particular religious experiences.

About all of this she says, "Never at any moment in my life have I sought for God. I do not like this expression, and it strikes me as false" (WG 62).[4] She goes on,

> As soon as I reached adolescence I saw the problem of God as a problem the data of which could not be obtained here below, and I decided that the only way of being sure not to reach a wrong solution, which seemed to me the greatest possible evil, was to leave it alone. So I left it alone.

Something protected her from following any path but her own, and this vocational compass was evident in her from the beginning.[5]

She now proceeds to list the notions and attitudes that she absorbed in growing up, concerning:

1. *Death*

> I never allowed myself to think of a future state, but I always believed that the instant of death is the center and object of life. I used to think that, for those who live as they should, it is the instant when, for an infinitesimal fraction of time, pure truth, naked, certain and eternal, enters the soul. (WG 63)

These words, in conjunction with one or two of her last letters, are critical for understanding the riddle of her death in Ashford Kent, August 29, 1943.

2. *Vocation*

> I saw that the carrying out of a vocation differed from the actions dictated by reason or inclination in that it was due to an impulse of an essentially and man-

ifestly different order; and not to follow such an impulse when it made itself felt, even if it demanded impossibilities, seemed to me the greatest of all ills.[6]

3. *Obedience*

The most beautiful life possible has always seemed to me to be one where everything is determined, either by the pressure of circumstances or by impulses such as I have just mentioned and where there is never any room for choice.[7]

4. *Truth.* Here focuses a major crisis of adolescence involving months of bottomless despair arising from the feeling of being shut out from "that transcendent kingdom to which only the truly great have access and wherein truth abides" (WG 64). This occurred in connection with her close relation to her brother, André, who was a child prodigy in mathematics and from whom she first learned what genius is. The crisis led to the first great breakthrough of her life:

> After months of inward darkness, I suddenly had the everlasting conviction that any human being, even though practically devoid of natural faculties, can penetrate to the kingdom of truth reserved for genius, if only he longs for truth and perpetually concentrates all his attention upon its attainment.

5. *Beauty, virtue, and every kind of goodness.* She says she included these "under the name of truth." She was convinced that they too reward one's longing for them with purest and fullest attention.

6. *The spirit of poverty*

> I do not remember any moment when it was not in me . . . I fell in love with Saint Francis of Assisi as soon as I came to know about him. (WG 65)

These words imply a need for *equality* with other human beings almost in direct proportion to her awareness of her uniqueness and difference.[8]

7. *Acceptance of the will of God*

> I found it set down in Marcus Aurelius under the name of the *amor fati* of the Stoics.

This is one of many examples of her capacity to find Christian parallels in non-Christian traditions and to take what she could wherever she found it.[9]

8. *Love of neighbor*

> From my earliest childhood I always had also the Christian idea of love for one's neighbor, to which I gave the name of justice—a name it bears in many passages of the Gospel and which is so beautiful.[10]

9. *Purity.* The idea of purity . . . took possession of me at the age of sixteen," and she adds, "with all that this word can imply for a Christian," which may be to say chastity.[11]

As she observes, these items by themselves constitute a Christian conception of life. But they do not include going to church, which to her was associated with dogma.

> Of course I knew quite well that my conception of life was Christian. That is why it never occurred to me that I could enter the Christian community. I had the idea that I was born inside. But to add dogma to this conception of life, without being forced to do so by indisputable evidence, would have seemed to me like a lack of honesty. I should even have thought I was lacking in honesty had I considered the question of the truth of dogma as a problem for myself or had I simply desired to reach a conclusion on this subject. (WG 65–66)

Here she pinpoints the severity of her own mind in leaving nothing unexamined.

> I have an extremely severe standard for intellectual honesty, so severe that I never met anyone who did not seem to fall short of it in more than one respect; and I am always afraid of failing in it myself.[12]

Both Father Perrin and Thibon learned to respect this intellectual honesty. But how could she possibly convince them that God and Christ wanted her to remain outside the church? How could this be in their eyes a *Christian* vocation, as she asserted it to be?

Entering the Company of Christ

She now rehearses three episodes that, taken together, make up a classic case of conversion, one that could bear comparison with the conversion of Saint Augustine, who also had something of a Christian upbringing—at least to the extent that his mother was a Christian. To understand what happened to Weil, we must, as in all such cases, look at the immediate crisis of her life that set the stage for these experiences.

It was two weeks after she had finished a truly harrowing period of eight months' labor in metal-working factories in Paris, during which she felt for the first time "the affliction of others enter into my flesh and soul" (WG 66). She discounts her own affliction, her incessant violent headaches, because these are only "biological" and do not in themselves involve the social humiliation of factory life, though later her own affliction will play a role. What happened in the factories was that

> There I received forever the mark of a slave, like the branding of the red-hot iron the Romans put on the foreheads of their most despised slaves. Since then I have always regarded myself as a slave. (WG 67)

Two weeks later comes her first powerful Christian experience on a visit to Portugal with her parents. She feels torn to pieces, and

> In this state of mind then, and in a wretched condition physically, I entered the little Portuguese village, which, alas, was very wretched too, on the very day of the festival of its patron saint. I was alone. It was the evening and there was a full moon over the sea. The wives of the fishermen were, in procession, making a tour of all the ships, carrying candles and singing what must certainly be very ancient hymns of a heart-rending sadness. . . . There the conviction was suddenly borne in upon me that Christianity is pre-eminently the religion of slaves, that slaves cannot help belonging to it, and I among others.[13]

At this moment the flaming social revolutionary activist, dedicated to the revolt of the workers against slave conditions, suddenly, in some altogether different context, accepts an ultimate slavery in a religion that she now sees as a religion for slaves and "I among them." What has happened? What brought about this reversal?

Let us look more closely at Weil's situation at the end of the *Factory Journal,* included in the volume *Formative Writings.* It is one of complete humiliation, powerlessness, counting for nothing at all in the world, being wholly at the mercy of others, much of the time too exhausted even to think clearly, the other workers too tired and harried even to be able to speak with each other. When she has a little energy, she is seething with rage underneath.

It is impossible to live this way, and she knows it. The social basis for self-respect is gone. The concluding entries point to the only alternative as a stoic acceptance.

> The feeling of self-respect, such as it has been built up by society, is destroyed. It is necessary to forge another one for oneself (although exhaustion wipes out the consciousness of one's ability to think!) Try to hold on to this other kind. (FW 225)

The final entry reads:

> At Renault, I had arrived at a more stoical attitude. Substitute acceptance for submission. (FW 226)

Note the self-exhortations here. *Forge another. Try to hold on. Accept.* But of course she cannot do it.

In the fishing village the whole stoic framework gives way.[14] The slave condition becomes a world-renouncing sign putting the human situation in a wholly different light. The social order has to be abandoned as a basis for human worth. Henceforth, willy-nilly, Weil is oriented elsewhere. The fishing women, each with her own candle, are demonstrating a supernatural dignity. Weil has gone through both the bottom and the top of the secular natural world.

Her letter now jumps over a year and a half, which includes the ill-fated enrollment in the anarchist militia in Spain, showing that social action is by no means canceled out for her by what happened in Portugal. Now we are in Assisi for two days in the spring of 1937. Here in the twelfth-century Romanesque chapel of Santa Maria degli Angeli, where Saint Francis used to pray—a building that, in keeping with her preference for the Romanesque over the Gothic, she calls "an incomparable marvel of purity"—she says that "something stronger than I was compelled me to go down on my knees." We should not underestimate the concentrated expressiveness of this physical act, as integral to Christianity as prostration to Islam and the lotus position to Buddhism. Religion goes down into the body.

Still another year later at Solesmes during Easter Week begins the third episode.

> I was suffering from splitting headaches; each sound hurt me like a blow; by an extreme effort of concentration I was able to rise above this wretched flesh, to leave it to suffer by itself, heaped up in a corner, and to find a pure and perfect joy in the unimaginable beauty of the chanting and the words. This experience enabled me by analogy to get a better understanding of the possibility of loving divine love in the midst of affliction. (WG 68)

She does not say that the pain ceased. Rather something happened not unfamiliar in the literature on pain: she separated herself from it. She detached her attention from it.

At Solesmes she meets a young English Catholic, John Vernon, who introduces her to George Herbert's poem "Love," which brings about the culminating experience a few weeks after leaving Solesmes.

> I learned the poem by heart. Often at the culminating point of a violent headache I make myself say it over, concentrating all my attention upon it and clinging with all my soul to the tenderness it enshrines. I used to think I was merely reciting it as a beautiful poem, but without my knowing it the recitation had the virtue of a prayer. It was during one of these recitations that Christ himself came down and took possession of me. (WG 68-69)

She says that this presence came as a complete surprise. She had not read any mystical literature or envisaged such a possibility. She did not like paranormal experiences and tried to stay away from them. She describes what happened in a detached way—her intelligence, she says, still half refusing it.

> In this sudden possession of me by Christ, neither my senses nor my imagination had any part; I only felt in the midst of my suffering the presence of a love, like that which one can read in the smile on a beloved face.

But as it turned out this was not an isolated event, a supreme ecstatic experience not to be repeated. On the contrary, it was the beginning of a continuing presence of Christ in which it became "infinitely more real, more moving, more clear than on that first occasion when he took possession of me" (WG 72).

This continuation came about in this way. She had studied the Lord's Prayer in Greek with Gustave Thibon and recited it every morning before going out to work in the vine harvest and even during the day if she felt so moved. If her attention lapsed or she made a mistake, she would start the whole thing over until it had become a single act of pure attention.

> At times the very first words tear my thoughts from my body and transport it to a place outside space where there is neither perspective nor point of view. The infinity of the ordinary expanses of perception is replaced by an infinity to the second or sometimes the third degree. At the same time, filling every part of this infinity of infinity, there is silence, a silence which is not an absence of sound but which is the object of a positive sensation, more positive than that of sound. Noises, if there are any, only reach me after crossing this silence. (WG 72)

There is an echo here of Cantor's notion of the three degrees of infinity, actually experienced. If this is not what Hindus call "continuing seventh-stage *samadhi*," what is it? Can one contemplate a reality beyond the third degree of infinity?

The Incarnation of Christianity

The last part of the letter deals with what Simone Weil calls the incarnation of Christianity, or the conditions that must be met for Christianity to permeate the whole of culture and society, and the relation of this to her vocation as a Christian outside the church.

What is meant by the *incarnation* of Christianity? It means that its spirit has to find itself in places where it has not been found before: in the distant past, in other races and civilizations, in the secular economic world, and among those who have been branded as heretics and idolaters. Weil's universalism is all-embracing:

> Christianity should contain all vocations without exception since it is catholic [from Greek *kath' holou*, as a whole, thus *katholikos*, universal]. In consequence the Church should be also. But in my eyes Christianity is catholic by right but

not in fact. So many things are outside it, so many things I love and do not want to give up, so many things that God loves, otherwise they would not be in existence. All the immense stretches of past centuries, except the last twenty are among them; all the countries inhabited by colored races; all secular life in the white peoples' countries; in the history of these countries, all the traditions banned as heretical, those of the Manicheans and Albigenses for instance; all those things resulting from the Renaissance, too often degraded but not quite without value. (WG 75)

In the Christian religion there are three incarnations: the creation itself, an incarnation of the Divine in the cosmos and nature; Christ, an incarnation of the Divine in the human; and still ahead lies the incarnation of the Christian spirit in human society and culture. In all these cases incarnation is not an imposition by force from without, but an outward manifestation *from within*.

What is needed are not new legal formulas, but a renewed spirit. (D. H. Lawrence once said that unless we learn to act with great generosity as a society, we are doomed.)

One of the obstacles to this is the mistaken attempt of religion to control the thoughts of men and women, especially as expressed in those dreadful words *anathema sit*, "Be accursed!" the expression by which the church damned those who disagreed with it (WG 77). These words, Weil says, epitomize the spirit of totalitarianism, which has come to life again in political and ideological forms in our own century.

After the fall of the Roman Empire, which had been totalitarian, it was the Church that was the first to establish a rough sort of totalitarianism in Europe in the thirteenth century, after the war with the Albigenses. This tree bore much fruit.

And the motive power of this totalitarianism was the use of those two little words: *anathema sit.*

It was moreover by a judicious transposition of this use that all the parties which in our own day have founded totalitarian regimes were shaped. (WG 82)

She says that the church should declare openly and forever that it has changed with regard to interfering with the human mind.

Otherwise who could take her seriously when they remembered the Inquisition?

While the notion of the church as "the collective keeper of dogma" is indispensable, the church

is guilty of an abuse of power when she claims to force love and intelligence to model their language upon her own. This abuse of power is not of God. It comes from the natural tendency of every form of collectivism, without exception, to abuse power. . . .

> The special function of intelligence requires total liberty, implying the right
> to deny everything. (W 80, 78)

Weil now reminds us also that the doctrine of the church as the mystical body of Christ is especially dangerous and seductive because it conjures up a false picture of the same kind that supports the collective delusions of our day. It is another myth confusing the organic with the spiritual.

> Our true dignity is not to be parts of a body, even though it be a mystical one, even though it be that of Christ. It consists in this, that in the state of perfection, which is the vocation of each one of us, we no longer live in ourselves, but Christ lives in us; so that through our perfection Christ in his integrity and in his indivisible unity, becomes in a sense each of us. (WG 80–81)

The distinction between the collective and the individual, that is, between the social order and the individual life, forces us, Weil says, to recognize two different uses of language, ordained as different by nature and God, and recognized as different by Christ and by the Spirit of truth.

> Christ himself who is Truth itself, when he was speaking before an assembly such as a council, did not address it in the same language as he used in an intimate conversation with his well-beloved friend. . . . For by one of those laws of nature, which God himself respects, since he has willed them from all eternity, there are two languages that are quite distinct although made up of the same words; there is the collective language and there is the individual one. The Comforter whom Christ sends us, the Spirit of truth, speaks one or other of these languages, whichever circumstances demand, and by a necessity of their nature there is not much agreement between them. (WG 79)

Weil says that an example of this is the case of Meister Eckhart, fifty of whose propositions were pronounced heretical by the church. He spoke of the Godhead beyond God, and of cutting God to pieces if he got in the way of God, very much as great Buddhist sages spoke of cutting Buddha to pieces if he got in the way of Truth. Weil says that Eckhart was a genuine friend of God who was repeating words that he had heard in the silence of the union of love, and if these words disagree with church teaching the reason is just that "the language of the market place is not that of the nuptial chamber." She goes on:

> Everybody knows that really intimate conversation is only possible between two or three. As soon as there are six or seven, collective language begins to dominate. That is why it is a complete misinterpretation to apply to the Church the words "Wheresoever two or three are gathered together in my name, there am I in the midst of them." Christ did not say two hundred, or fifty, or ten. He said two or three. He said precisely that he always forms the third in the intimacy of the conversation. (WG 80)[15]

The word of God, Weil says, is primarily a *secret* word, which means that it comes to the individual alone, though it may come to every single individual without favor or discrimination.[16] When it is announced to the world or read in the context of the world, it acquires a different meaning even though the words remain the same. This requires of us, of course, to listen in a different way to God's words to the people spoken through the Prophets, and even to Christ's words in the Sermon on the Mount or at the Last Supper, from the way we listen to the words which he addresses to each individual alone, to *us*, to *me*, and to *you*.

The philosophical difficulties involved in this distinction between the language of "I" and the language of "We" are immense, especially when we consider what confessions and creeds, prayers and blessings are, and what happens to them when they are collectivized.[17]

The Death of Simone Weil

Simone Weil in her hospital bed in Ashford was not a woman who wanted to die, willfully and egotistically; she was waiting for the call of God.[18] Since we generally know only egotism, it is hard for us to realize this. In her letters she tells us that she has always regarded the moment of death as the supreme moment of human life since it may reveal the truth about the Divine and more especially about ourselves in relation to it that we could not otherwise know.[19]

We may find ourselves unable to enter into her thinking. For we have lost the power of contemplation and the great metaphors of balance and the Cross, and we may only see her death as a form of suicide.

Simone Weil wished to become one with the created universe. This meant total equality with all living things as well as so-called dead matter. As long as anything is excluded from this universal equality, we cannot fully know the truth. We must unite ourselves with the whole in its obedience to God and the necessity by which he defines it in creating it. And we must coexist with everyone and everything in it, apart from the evil we can prevent, as equally present because he loves it and wills it to exist.

There were two great prayers in Simone Weil's life, which we must imagine her constantly repeating in the hospital. The first is the so-called paralytic prayer, considered by her critics to be particularly horrifying.

Example of prayer.
Say to God:
Father, in the name of Christ grant me this.
That I may be unable to will any bodily movement, or even any attempt at

movement, like a total paralytic. That I may be incapable of receiving any sensation, like someone who is completely blind, deaf and deprived of all the senses.
That I may be unable to make the slightest connection between two thoughts,
even the simplest, like one of those total idiots who not only cannot count or
read but have never even learnt to speak. That I may be insensible to every kind
of grief and joy, and incapable of any love for any being or thing, and not even
for myself, like old people in the last state of decrepitude. . . .

May this body move or be still, with perfect suppleness or rigidity, in continuous conformity to thy will. May my powers of hearing, sight, taste, smell and
touch register the perfectly accurate impress of thy creation. May this mind, in
fullest lucidity, connect all ideas in perfect conformity with thy truth. May this
sensibility experience, in their greatest possible intensity and in all their purity,
all the nuances of grief and joy. May this love be an absolutely devouring flame
of love of God for God. May all this be stripped away from me, devoured by God,
transformed into Christ's substance, and given for food to afflicted men whose
body and soul lack every kind of nourishment. And let me be a paralytic—blind,
deaf, witless and utterly decrepit. . . .

Father, since thou art the Good and I am mediocrity, rend this body and soul
away from me to make them into things for your use, and let nothing remain of
me, for ever, except this rending itself, or else nothingness. (F 243-244)

Probably nothing she ever wrote has caused more consternation than this
prayer. And yet it amounts to a prayer for the liberation of the world,[20]
through union with its obedience, or, more precisely, with the will of God
whom it obeys; in other words, to be stripped of our own will, sensibility, and
thought, in order to have none but God's for the good of the world; to die to
self so that God may live in us. As she puts it elsewhere, this is "to give one's
flesh for the life of the world, and to receive in exchange the soul of the world.
. . . So we have to die in order to liberate the tied up energy in us" for a service of human beings as his instruments (N 179).[21]

The other great prayer in her life was the Lord's Prayer. She tells us that she
recited it in Greek every morning before she went to work in Thibon's vineyard, and every time it brought her into the direct presence of Christ.

Both of these prayers must have been in her mind and her heart during her
final days of growing weakness in her hospital bed.

The two may seem to us be in conflict, since one of them appears to disparage human life and the other to lift it to exalted heights. But Simone Weil
would have said that this appearance arises from a false humanism and an
inadequate idea of the supernatural. In fact the two prayers ask the same
thing, that God's will be done, in us as it is in heaven.[22]

This thought is expressed in her prose poem about meeting Christ in the
attic, where they spent some days together, talking and eating bread and
drinking wine as they looked out over the town at the "scaffoldings" and boats
unloading. They were alone, though now and then others came and joined in

and went away again; he had promised her teachings, but he taught her nothing. They simply talked in a rambling way about various things. One day he told her to go, and she went out into the streets, realizing she did not know where she had been or if she would ever see him again or what his exact words had been.[23]

Simone Weil understood in writing this that she was not to have a purely contemplative life, but must first take part in the life of the world.

CHAPTER 12

Time and Timelessness

O NE OF THE WAYS TO UNDERSTAND the great religions is to consider the different patterns of time and timelessness that they represent. The differences here are much greater than we think, and real effort is involved. Sometimes it takes many years to see what a religion is driving at. But if we have a clue we can begin.

In this chapter I hope to provide some clues. The patterns of time and time-lessness that I want to talk about are those of four great traditions: Judaism, Christianity, Hinduism, and Buddhism.[1] Simone Weil was keenly interested in the last three; and had she lived she would surely have sought a deeper acquaintance with the first.

The Jews have been called the timeless people, or the people who live beyond time.[2] They live in and with a past that as a whole and in detail remains present to them as a living collective memory. For example, each year the exodus from Egypt is celebrated in the Passover. This is not ordinary history, but history given a timeless significance, kept alive in the presentness of memory and passed on to each new generation. In the Seder ceremony it is as if it is still happening. The Jews are still leaving Egypt just as they are still standing at Sinai, or being exiled. Timeless events are endlessly repeated. In this realm nothing changes and nothing is new that does not belong to the pattern.

But they are not a people of the past. They are the people of a past and future that is always present. And this kind of present takes the place of what we ordinarily call the present, what is *not* (already) the past *nor* (still) the future but this now. That kind of present, understood as fleeting and ephemeral, seems unreal to the Jews. Events do not become significant and weighty to them until they enter into the collective memory.

The uncanny aspect of the Jewish pattern of time is the way in which the past mixes in with the present. For example, a friend recently showed me a copy of the *Jerusalem Post* with a picture of a group of men visiting a farm in Israel in connection with procuring a red heifer in order to have a purification ceremony in accordance with ancient Hebraic ritual. The article explained that this was necessary before the Temple could be rebuilt in Jerusalem [to prepare the return of the Messiah], and that it might be necessary to send to Scandinavia for frozen heifer embryos in order to get a red one. It was reported as a news story like any other news story.[3]

We might be inclined to think that this is simply an ancient custom kept alive for sentimental reasons like the Maypole or Mummers' dances. But it is not. It is part of a vast timeless system of law and ritual that was the original Hebraic and Jewish way of life. This was a system of rules that regulated every aspect of life from birth to death, including food, sexual intercourse, marriage, divorce, property, inheritance, education, family relations, Sabbath observance. There are altogether 613 laws, including a vast structure of animal sacrifices, that would have to be reinstated if the Temple were rebuilt. All this hangs together as a single system. We might suppose that it could be reformed or updated. Orthodox rabbis, however, have a story comparing the law to a huge synagogue, where removing a single rusty bolt in the ceiling might bring the whole building down.

The law has a timeless character just because it is laid down once and for all as part of the timeless myth or timeless history of the people. Even when it is practiced by only a handful of people, it remains alive and authoritative. These Orthodox people are the demonstration of the original character of Judaism, which did not distinguish the sacred from the secular and united the cultural, the biological, and the religious in one total timeless system.

I turn to the Christian experience of time and timelessness. This is as much a closed book to Jews as the Jewish point of view is to Christians. But as the Jews have their treasure, which is the Treasure of the Law preserved in the Torah, Christians too have their treasure, which is the spirit of Christ preserved in the Gospels.

If we study the Gospels we will find that it is life in the present—not in the timeless present of past and future, but in the [timeful] present of the *Now*—

that is the essence of Christianity. The secret of the teaching of Christ is that *all true life is life in the present*, as distinct from the past and future. This is where *reality* is. If there is no experience of the present as the *Now*, then there is no real *life* at all.

It is the ascendance of the present over both the past and the future that is the actual experience of Christianity. This is the freedom that liberates the individual from past and future, and that means from the people and the collective memory. The individual is discovered in one's own true life where the Now surges up within spontaneous and new. This life coming to birth within each individual in each present moment is the joy of Christianity.[4]

The time frame here is the *day* rather than the week or the month. Sufficient unto the day is the evil thereof. Let not the sun go down on your wrath. Christianity discovers forgiveness because it is not the collective memory that has the most reality but the fullness of life here and now.[5]

It looks like a psychological license for egotism: people following their own whims and immediate desires, abandoning the discipline of the law and doing what they please. But it has to be an abandonment to the spirit, that is, abandonment of self, or it becomes a new form of slavery. Saint Augustine said, Love God and do as you please. The catch is that you cannot love God without doing what *he* pleases.

The ideal of Christianity is for each moment to be fully real. But this is not possible unless we *let go* of it. The timelessness here is the quality of living by the spontaneous Spirit. The New Testament calls it the well of everlasting life, which individuals experience when they are freed from inner domination (by self, from enslavement to sensuality, fantasy, and pride).

The Christian experience is a rebirth of the spirit of childhood. We are talking about the child before the age of six, before the social self or ego defense is known. When in our lives do we live most in the present, most in each day, with most freedom from cares and most reliance on the love of others? We would have to say it is in early childhood. Children have a great faculty for forgiving and forgetting. The world is fresh and new for them, each day a new adventure. Even a sad childhood may have moments of freshness and novelty.

Essential life is the abandoned life. The ego that we build up to protect ourselves about the age of five or so is a prison that falsifies our existence. True individuality predates the social ego. Even an infant has an individuality, as any mother will tell you, but it is prior to personality and before the ego. The child lives within the gift of the mother's love. We are all born trusting that we will be looked after, and we are, or else we do not survive. It is this attitude of expecting that good will be done to us that Simone Weil called the only thing supernatural about us.[6]

In the Christian view God is not primarily to be feared any more than the infant fears the mother. Fear comes later, when the ancient father imposes his

discipline. But even then the original love remains as the underlying first reality even though forgotten and buried, so that it takes a special experience to
remember that first reality.

Christianity appropriated its past from Judaism, but its past is secondary to
its present and exists only for its present. We have always known that the past
was waiting for the fullness of the present. We needed something to demon-
strate what life in the present could be, and this is what the New Testament
does. Timelessness attaches to that present, which is always a present experienced by *individuals,* and not by the collective memory of a people.

We must remember that the New Testament was written in Greek, not
Hebrew. Two of its writers were Greeks, and Jesus himself had a partly Greek
orientation.[7] The Hebrew prophets always spoke *to* the whole people and *for*
the whole people. Jesus spoke as an individual to individuals.[8] He used the
word *I,* "I say unto you." By this single word he separated himself from the
Jewish tradition.

We turn now to another pattern of time and timelessness, that which we find
in Hinduism, the traditions of ancient India, going back to the oldest religious
writings, the *Upanishads.*

The central theme here is a still earlier and more fundamental level of consciousness, prior to individuation itself, that of the universal Self, or *Atman.*[9]
There is in the Hindu experience only one consciousness, related to the fundamental energy of the universe, and the different phenomena of birth and
death are only the manifestations of this.

There is no *mythos* of history but of recurring cycles of nature, and no ultimate attachment to the individual but to the timeless *Atman,* or universal Self,
of all things. The supreme word of Indian philosophy, that the *Atman* is *Brahman,* means that the one true Self is the supreme reality. The *Katha Upanishad*
says,

> The Universal Self knows all, is not born, does not die, is not the effect of any
> cause, is eternal, self-existent, imperishable. How can the killing of the body kill
> him? (2.18)

> When that person in the heart, no bigger than a thumb, is known as maker of
> past and future, what more is there to fear? That is Self. (4.12)

How are we to think of this in terms of actual experience? What is being
recovered here is not the freedom of childhood but something even more
originary and universal, the prebirth consciousness, the experience of life
before birth.[10] This is the primal cosmic condition, the state of bliss and one-

ness in which there is no separation of subject and object, so that we are part of the one great whole in the original condition of life. It is this state of consciousness that is the primordial one and that stays with us throughout our lives whether we know or not.[11] What is called waking consciousness is a ripple on the surface of this deeper ocean of unconscious consciousness.

When Ramana Maharshi, one of the great teachers of modern India who lived into the middle of the twentieth century, was asked by visitors what their true identity was, he often asked them in return what it was that survived through deep sleep and was there before falling asleep and on waking up. This was the primordial Self, of which we have to become aware in order to see our lives clearly.

It follows from this that we should not identify with any social or national group or any individual savior, but allow ourselves to be what we really are, this original blissful state of undifferentiated flow of feeling and energy. Maharshi put it this way. He compared the true consciousness to the screen in a cinema.

> There are scenes floating on the screen. Fire appears to burn buildings to ashes. Water seems to wreck vessels. But the screen on which the pictures were projected remains unscorched and dry. Why? Because the pictures were unreal and the screen is real.
>
> The world is a phenomenon of the single timeless reality which is not affected in any manner.

Hindus locate the universal consciousness not in the head or mind, but in the heart, where feeling flows forth. We have to abide in a thought-free state. To think[12] is not our real nature. What Krishnamurti called choiceless awareness, pure witnessing, comes closer to it.

When women walk with water pots on their heads and chat with their companions, Maharshi said, they remain very careful, their thoughts concentrate on the loads on their heads. Similarly, when a sage engages in activities, these do not disturb him because his mind abides in *Brahman*.

The goal that we try to reach by the ego is really prior to the ego, just as it is prior to both the body and the soul. It is the reality that we already Are. Again Maharshi:

> Doubts arise in the mind. The mind is born of the ego. The ego arises from the universal Self. Search the source of the ego and the Self is revealed. That alone remains. The universe is my expanded Self. It is not different from the Self.

Nothing can alter the ultimate Self, it is not subject to time or change. In the flow of time and causality are the psychic constellations that make up the selves that reincarnate. Individual selves go in and out of the material[istic] world without ceasing, because they are chained [by egoistic possessive desire] to the wheel of existence. These are the forms of time, the manifestations of the universal Self, the images that keep returning in ever so many different forms on the screen in accordance with their own karmas or accumulated necessities.[13] There is no freedom in the realm of time: everything is subject to reappearing again and again until it dissolves itself, by acknowledging its own illusoriness, into the single unchanging reality.

Finally, Buddhism. It will be helpful to think of Buddhism as standing in the same relation to Hinduism that Christianity does to Judaism. That is to say, it is an individualization and universalization of Hinduism as Christianity is of Judaism. We have the experience of a single man that can be repeated or approximated by any other human being. In this case it is not rebirth into the essential Self as in Christianity but enlightenment or awakening into the no-self. Not a universal Self, but having no self at all. This is the fundamental distinction between Buddhism and Hinduism. In Buddhism the ultimate situation is Nirvana, or no-self, a bliss of pure emptiness that is realizable individually and actually. We want to see what it means in concrete terms.

I will concentrate on Zen Buddhism because I have spent many years studying that. I was a student of Daisetz Suzuki in the 1950s and have followed the development of Zen in the United States. There are three main branches of Buddhism: *Hinayana,* which is the orthodox or Catholic form in Southeast Asia; *Mahayana,* the Protestant or reformed branch in China and Japan; and *Vajrayana,* the occult or Gnostic one in Tibet. Buddhism spread from India throughout the East as Christianity spread from Palestine throughout the West. *Zen* is a Japanese offshoot of a Chinese form of Buddhism. It has great appeal to Americans because it is so down-to-earth and practical. Suzuki used to say that the Indians are the most metaphysical people on earth, while the Chinese and the Americans are the least.

Zen goes immediately to the heart of the matter. Nothing could be more simple than what it is after and yet it may also be very strange.

Zen calls us to a sudden waking up. Waking to what? Waking to an immediacy or directness greater than any [other] we can know or say. It is completely unconditioned, free of any memory or association, an instantaneity of timelessness. We are talking about *perception,* just *looking* at what is in front of us, for the first time really seeing *it,* not our words, or our categories, or as we were conditioned to see it even by the Hindu philosophy. In this looking there is no metaphysics, no ideology, no beliefs, no object, no subject.[14] We see it as we would have if we could have seen in the womb, with a pure flash of instantaneous immediacy. It sounds easy, but it might take a whole lifetime or several lifetimes. How do we know it is possible? Because we have the example of Buddha and of the teachers who have experienced it. How do we know it is worth the trouble? Because we feel that something is missing from our lives: we are not really here. Our life is like a dream, as if we were living in various collective illusions. Those who have reached *satori*, enlightenment, report back: yes, it is marvelous, and so simple, no wonder we could not see it before.

Zen is simple as regards method as well as content.[15] There are two main methods corresponding to the two main branches of Zen—Soto and Rinzai. Soto Zen emphasizes a meditation called *zazen,* or sitting, aiming at emptying the mind because the mind is the one thing that interferes. The greatest teacher of Soto Zen was Dogen, who lived in our thirteenth century (1200–1253). He is the greatest philosopher of Japan, who will some day be studied here the way we now study Thomas Aquinas or Immanuel Kant. Rinzai is the school to which Suzuki belonged, and its main method is the *koan.*

The koan is a riddle with which one must struggle possibly for years in order to attain insight. It sounds impossible and yet there is an answer. There are about seventeen hundred famous koans and a single one may occupy us for twenty years. *What is the sound of one hand clapping?* There is no intellectual answer, but there is something to be understood: *how one may be two.* It is always the same riddle, the riddle of our life. In the koan everything is condensed: that there is no place to go, that we already have the answer even though we don't know it, that enlightenment is not a goal that we can reach by any effort. It is like grace or the gift of faith. We must struggle as hard as we can, but our struggle is going to prevent us.[16] All the paradoxes of religion—and every religion *is* paradoxical—are summed up in the koan.

Let me cite a koan very familiar to me, *how to get the goose out of the bottle.* We have a bottle with a goose in it. Our problem is how to get the goose out without breaking the bottle or hurting the goose. The first point is, it can be done, although quite obviously it cannot be. The teacher will keep you at it. *You fool, keep trying. You are not really trying. Think harder.* Year after year. Then one day suddenly a small event, it could be anything, and all at once you will see. Out, out at last. The goose is out. At the same moment, *you* are out. Your imprisoned self is out. How did it happen? There are things you might say, but they won't help. The goose was never in the bottle. There was no bottle, and no goose, and so on.[17]

We labor under a delusion that there has to be a method for doing everything. But suppose that with the highest things there *is* no method, and this absence of method is exactly what we need, that *that* is the method.[18] Then what looked like a defeat is actually the victory. There is a wholly different dimension there glimpsed for a moment quicker than the wink of an eye.

It is the nature of every problem, that the solution is different from the problem. I am imprisoned and I want to be free. I am unhappy and I want to be happy. I am asleep and I want to be awake. I am here and I want to be there. This is the struggle, years of effort chained to the wheel. Then one day something overwhelmingly simple happens: I see that the struggle, the search, the gap was the mistake. There was never any place to go because I was already where I have to be. I was looking for a light with the only light already in my hand.

There is a letting go here as there is in Christianity too.[19] Just when you give up, aid comes.

Everything we have said about perception also applies to action. In Zen we are after a total spontaneity. If there is a moment's hesitation we fail. It is this way in the Old Testament too. When you see what you have to do, there is no more waiting: here I am.[20]

Suddenness is a supremely important religious and ethical category.[21] Everything important happens suddenly, though it may have taken years to mature. Suddenly the whole situation is different. We should look at the way the word "sudden" is used in the New Testament and in the Buddhist writings.[22] A Buddhist teacher I know put it this way: You have exactly four seconds to reply, and if you reply that quickly then what you say will be phony. He was talking about certain types of questions.[23]

Where is timelessness in Zen? In the instant, the instant of everyday life—in washing the dishes, dressing the children, getting on the bus—when if we live it truly there are no self and no ego games, no defensiveness and no grabbing, no hostility and no anxiety, nothing but being fully. There is an experience of timelessness in this fullest reality. [Simone Weil would say that it comes from and *is* the renunciation of all longings and all resentments and regrets for things received or done in the past and all hopes of success and compensation in the future, but—when we have done the right and best thing and avoided the wrong and evil we can—simple acceptance and love of what must be in the present as the reality we are given. It is the surrender of self and time, and the surrender to a Good beyond, that is to say a dependence on grace.][24]

What should be our attitude toward these four great spiritual traditions? I believe that we should accept them all as our heritage. Humankind makes room for them. We should make room for them too. To learn from all human traditions is true humanism.

Notes

Introduction

1. Some may feel that this phrase says much too little, that she is beyond questions of how we come to know and prove the reality of God; that she is concerned (like Frege and Wittgenstein) primarily with meaning, not justification. But she herself writes that "anything less than certainty is unworthy of God" (WG 209); and she repeats Socrates' remark that the highest truth should be known most precisely (N 239, 336, 441; F 109, 182; NR 188; IC 164; Plato, *Republic* 6.504de, cf. 5.477a). Weil begins to work out a theory of knowledge through faith which is not belief but action that brings transformation into what is known: had she survived her illness and the war (she died at thirty-four) she would have developed this into an account of what might be called a connatural knowledge that is fulfillment, living acquaintance, *gnosis*.

2. This idea of truth as a personal quality realized in existence is the core idea of existentialism, at least in the version of Søren Kierkegaard. But it is much older than that. See John 3.21 and 1 John 1.16; and earlier still Heraclitus B 112: "Wisdom is to speak the truth and *do* it, seeing things as they are"; Plato, *Phaedo* 115a; *Laches* 188cd: a true man proves by his life that he has a right to speak of goodness and wisdom, for his words and deeds are in true harmony.

Simone Weil disliked Aristotle for his disregard of Pythagoras and the mystical element in Plato, as well as for his defense of slavery, but she would have approved his words in *Nicomachean Ethics* 4.7: "The best man is truthful both in *life* and in words . . . a truthful man is true both in word and in life, because his character is such"; and 6.2: "Truth is the function of both intellectual parts of the soul," so his theoretical wisdom has truth about what is, while his practical wisdom has "truth in harmony with right desire." That is, he clearly perceives and wholeheartedly desires what is truly good for human beings in general, and he calculates well how to achieve it in particular cases.

3. "Intellect" is a Latin word translating Greek *nous*, a loving grasp of true, pure unambiguous Good and unity and the other transcendentals. See, e.g., Socrates in Plato, *Republic* 6.506–511 (Sun and Line), 7.533e–534a; Aristotle, *Nicomachean Ethics* 6.1–7ff; Plotinus 1.2.3; 4.3.18; 4.8.1; 5.1.11; Boethius, *Consolation* 4.6; 5.4f (cf. 1.6 end); Dante, *Hell* 3.18; *Purgatory* 16.79–81; 24.51; *Paradise* 1.4–9; 2.43–45; 14.27–51; etc. Intellect, Intellectual Love, Love, Spirit: for Dante it is all one.

4. Plato, *Republic* 2.379bc.

5. WG 211; Plato, *Republic* 7.518c.

6. Need of grace: Psalms 119.36: "Incline my heart to thy testimonies, and not to gain! Turn my eyes from looking at vanities; and give me life in thy ways"; Galatians 4.8: "By grace you have been saved through faith; and this is not your own doing, it is the gift of God." See further Luke 11.13; 1 Corinthians 12.1–11: God gives his spirit to all who ask for it, with its wisdom, *gnosis*, faith, discernment, though he gives it differently to different people. Our obscure confused self-consciousness: see chapter 12, n. 13 below.

7. IC 164–165; NB 292; SN 144.

8. Already in the New Testament religious knowledge is or fulfills faith and is not opposed to it: see John 6.69; 17.8; 1 John 4.16. In Ephesians 3.14–19 Paul prays that his readers will through *faith* and *love* come to *know* "the love of Christ which surpasses all [other] knowledge"; also 4.13. Clement of Alexandria (c. 150–220) writes in the *Miscellanies* 7.16 that "*Gnosis* is the perfection of faith." In the Old Testament, faith and knowledge are one in the concept of knowing God as submitting to and obeying him, sc., acknowledging him and going his way: thus, e.g., 1 Chronicles 28.9; Jeremiah 9.24; 24.7.

9. N 333: When the most wretched creature that can love him does so, sc., lets God love himself through it, "the creative act has been completed"; N 428–429: That the greatest love can cross the greatest distance—"This is exactly the opposite of the conception formulated by Leibniz. It is certainly more compatible with the greatness of God: for if this were God's idea of the very best of all possible worlds, it would mean that he was not capable of producing very much." (Here the two ideas of the best do not combine very well together, for she is saying that the worst *is* the best.) Cf. John 9.3.

10. See N 47, 191; F 146, 213; WG 97–98, 128; SN 197; IC 48–49, 133, 186–187.

11. As the Pythagoreans said, God is pure, unambiguous unity that is a limitless limit to unlimited matter. See N 386, 418, 426; F 126–127, 310, 317; SN 79: "Limitation is the law of the manifested world. Only God is without limits." Pascal, *Pensées* (tr. Krailsheimer; Penguin, 1966), no. 199: the two infinites "touch and join by going in opposite directions, and meet in God and God alone"; cf. no. 308: "The infinite distance between body and mind symbolizes the infinitely more infinite distance between mind and charity, for charity is supernatural"; no. 201: "the eternal silence of these infinite spaces fills me with dread," sc., humanly speaking, because they are full of God: thus nos. 148, 166. Kierkegaard usually

calls infinite our right relationship to God (as in "the movement of infinity") but it is because God himself is: e.g., *Journals and Papers* (7 vols.; ed. and tr. Howard and Edna Hong; Indiana University Press, 1967–1978), nos. 1254, 1312, 1365, 1393, 2089, 4571; *Attack* (tr. Walter Lowrie; Princeton University Press, 1944) 275, on serving "the infinite, the idea, God" versus serving "the finite, low things, profit."

12. Infinites of higher orders appear in lower orders as infinitesimals: N 464, 466, 481, 484: "Limit constitutes the presence in an order of the transcendent order in the form of something infinitely small"; N 500: "All supernatural reality here below is something infinitely small which increases exponentially," e.g., the freedom in grace; OL 166, 175: "The share of the supernatural here on earth is that of secrecy, silence, the infinitely small. But the operation of that something infinitely small is decisive," e.g., Persephone's pomegranate seed, the pearl in the field, the grain of mustard; SE 218: the only way to faith for the afflicted is spiritual poverty, which is almost the same as slavery "except for an infinitely small difference. We are always brought back to something infinitely small, which is infinitely more than everything." See further Plotinus 6.4.2: "It is our way to limit Being to the sense-known . . . but our great is small, and this, small to us, is great."

13. N 221: "God does not change anything. Christ was killed out of rage because he was only God"; F 141: "God is only the good. That is why he is waiting there in silence . . . . Beggars who are modest are images of Him"; WG 33; SJ 3; N 626–627; WG 124, 213; SN 197–198: the cry of Christ and the silence of God, a harmony that is unity. Cf. 1 Kings 19.12, the still small voice of God; Isaiah 30.18, he waits; Matthew 6.1–9, he is in heaven and sees in secret; 25.35; 26.53; John 18.36, he is humanly present in a beggar but he is a king of kings whose kingdom is not of this world.

14. This is another form of freedom. For we can be free not only (a) from doing wrong, and (b) to rule and fulfill ourselves, but also (c) in dealing with one another as full equals. A fourth form that is important to Simone Weil, as it is in Spinoza and in Zen, is to be free (d) in accepting limits.

15. It is an act of *justice*, as on the Socratic model in Plato's *Republic*, book 4: it is doing one's task. Weil will compare it to Hindu *dharma*, as in the teaching of Krishna in the *Bhagavad Gita*: it is sacrifice, united to God's own sacrifice, working for the good of the world.

16. See Mary Midgley, *Can't We Make Moral Judgments?* (St. Martin's, 1991), especially chapters 6 and 7; and see below, chapter 6, n. 1, citing Mary Douglas, *How Institutions Think* (Syracuse, 1986); and see below, chapter 7 nn. 11, 12.

17. SL 144–157. "Blood is Flowing in Tunisia," in *Oeuvres Complètes II: Écrits Historiques et Politiques* (Gallimard, 1989), 131. See also the essay draft of 1938, "Who Is Guilty of Anti-French Schemes?" 137: "Perhaps those oppressed in the colonies can find a bitter consolation in the thought that their victors would some day suffer because of them a misery equal to that inflicted on them. When one studies the history of the period before the war, one feels that it is because of them

that the conflict over Morocco poisoned French–German relations to the point of turning in 1914 the assassination in Sarajevo into a worldwide catastrophe. France won and subjugated the Moroccans, but it is because of these defeated and subjugated Moroccans that so many Frenchmen have wallowed for four years in the trenches. This was their punishment, and it was deserved. Today if a new conflict breaks out, the colonial question will once again be its origin. Once again Frenchmen will suffer and will die, and once again they will have deserved it." Steiner's report is in "Bad Friday," *The New Yorker,* March 2, 1992, pp. 86–91, at p. 90.

18. WG 78: "The special function of the intelligence requires total liberty, implying the right to deny everything, and allowing of no domination"; WG 85: "my thought should be indifferent to all ideas without exception, including for instance materialism and atheism; it must be equally welcoming and equally reserved with regard to every one of them. Water is indifferent in this way to the objects that fall into it. It does not weigh them; they weigh themselves, after a certain time of oscillation." Cf. Plato, *Laws* 9.875cd: "Reason, if it is genuine and really enjoys its natural freedom, should have universal power: it is not right that it should be under the control of anything else, as though it were some sort of slave"; *Phaedrus* 245e: "Precisely that is the essence and definition of soul, self-motion" and "it cannot abandon its nature," any more than fire can its heat or ice its cold, for, as R. H. Blyth says, these are jealous and merciless. Immanuel Kant, *Groundwork* (tr. James Ellington; Hackett, 1993), 2.425: "there is neither in heaven nor on earth anything on which philosophy depends or is based," sc., for its authority to judge what is true or false; *Critique of Pure Reason* (tr. Norman Kemp Smith; Macmillan, 1929), A 739: "Reason depends on this freedom [of criticism and self-criticism] for its very existence . . . its verdict is always simply the agreement of free citizens": A 752: "human reason recognizes no other judge than that universal human reason in which everyone has his say."

Similarly, Marcus Aurelius, *Meditations* 4.3; 5.19; 6.8; 7.16, 54; 8.48: nothing *can* disturb the soul's judgment by its own moral and intellectual criteria, sc., provided it gives clear, steady attention to these; and nothing *should.* (For without this attention, anything *does.* Thus Pascal, *Pensées,* no. 48: "Do not be surprised if his reasoning is not too sound at the moment, there is a fly buzzing round his ears." Weil would say that only loving attention to Good opens us to the grace to overcome gravity.)

19. Cf. Exodus 17.14; 23.13; 34.7, 14; Leviticus 26.14–33; Deuteronomy 19.15; 32.39–43; Isaiah 13.6; and Matthew 5.43–48; 28.19; Luke 15.3–32; John 10.16; 14.2. (We might also compare Franz Kafka and Georges Bernanos. William Blake too contrasts the Loving Father with the hidden Angry God, whom he calls the "Nobodaddy," or Nobody's Daddy, invented by falling Albion, inviting the imposture of Satan: see *Complete Writings* [ed. Geoffrey Keynes; Oxford, 1966], 171, 502, 617, 646, 652, cf. 771, 788.) But the Old Testament God likewise loves those who love him and what he loves, and forgives those who repent, while the New Testament

one too condemns those who do not: thus, e.g., Exodus 34.6-7; Leviticus 19.17-18, 34; Isaiah 55.7-8; 56.8; Matthew 10.14-15; 25.31-46; Luke 15.7; 17.3-4. (Thus Blake, who studied Hebrew, calls the true Jehovah a God of Mercy: *Complete Writings,* 694-695, 745, 779-781.)

20. We could say that this compassionate love that is simple justice proves our own humanity, as Christ said that obedience to his word proved our spiritual kinship with him: see Mark 3.33-35; Matthew 25.37, 46; WG 139-140; IC 175-176.

21. This is the tendency of its spokesmen. It is a star example of the *social* thinking, for it is an *institution* thinking in and through its members, and because its members think; and they follow its traditions more or less faithfully and more or less critically.

22. This is called trusting God, relying on Providence, loving one's destiny. Cf. Marcus Aurelius, *Meditations* 3.16; 5.8; 7.57; 10.21; Epictetus, *Manual* 31: "For piety toward the gods, you must know that the most important thing is this, to have right opinions about them, that they exist and govern the universe well and justly, and to have set yourself to obey them [sc., by acting justly] and to surrender to all that happens, following events with a free will in the belief that they are accomplished by the highest mind. Thus you will never blame the gods, nor accuse them of neglecting you"; *Moral Conversations* 1.12.25.

23. Cf. Silent John's remark, in *Fear and Trembling* (tr. Howard and Edna Hong, Princeton, 1983), 104, about the coward who does not know love or manhood or life: he has not even grasped the little mystery that it is better to give than to receive, much less has he any intimation of "the great mystery that it is far more difficult to *receive* than to give." (Emphasis added.)

Chapter 1
Affliction, Love, Geometry

1. See, however, F 157: "If we put obedience to God above everything else, unreservedly, with the following thought: 'Suppose God is real, then our gain is total—even though we fall into nothingness at the moment of death; suppose the word "God" stands only for illusions, then we have still lost nothing because on this assumption there is absolutely nothing good, and consequently nothing to lose; we have even gained, through being in accord with truth, because we have left aside the illusory goods which exist but are not good for the sake of something which (on this assumption) does not exist but which, if it did exist, would be the only good . . .' If one follows this rule of life, then no revelation at the moment of death can cause any regrets." Similarly F 149. And as for Pascal, his wager is formulated "according to our natural lights" and addressed to a worldly gambling man, perhaps Mitton: see *Pensées* (tr. Krailsheimer; Penguin, 1966), nos. 418, 597, 853.

2. Descartes says in the *First Meditation*, "the end I now seek is not action but knowledge"; and in the *Sixth,* "the necessities of action frequently oblige us to

come to a determination before we have had leisure for so careful an examination." In the *Synopsis* he declares that his treatment of error concerns theory, not practice, so that "I do not refer to matters of faith, or to the conduct of life, but only to what regards speculative truths, and such as are known by means of the natural light alone." He is not doubting everything, but treating morality or religion as certain. "Was it because the ethical is in itself certain? But then there was something which doubt could not reach!" as Kierkegaard notes in *Journals and Papers* (ed. and tr. Howard and Edna Hong; Indiana University Press, 1967–78), no. 774.

3. Actually Weil rarely calls the Good itself supernatural, as opposed to its action in the world. For two exceptions see SE 23 and N 410: even here it is good, not the Good, pure and unconditional.

4. That is, we are related to God only through a perfectly just ("four square") man, as these are related to unity only through a number that is to unity's square as their square is to it. For example, 1 is to $\sqrt{2}$ as $\sqrt{2}$ is to 2, for 1 *squared* is to 2 as 2 is to 2 *squared*. The mediation is found by raising the terms to a higher dimension. As 2 is related to and identified with 1 through its proportional mean, so a man is related to and identified with God through justice.

F 80: "Geometrical equality makes a man equal to God. And that poor Callicles, who only wanted to be always acquiring more [Plato, *Gorgias* 508a]! A bad number, not a square, such as 17 for example, may think it would be greater if it was 18. But it doesn't know that the secret, the creative principle of all greatness is nothing other than 1. By becoming 18 it moves further away. It degrades the 1 by reducing it to the plane of number. Its greatness resides solely in its identification with 1 by its own root, $\sqrt{17}$, which is mediation." Thus also IC 161, and N 456, 602f, 614f.

5. That is, the demand for rigor seems pointless today, like art for art's sake; when mathematicians understand its value they will realize its true meaning. Weil is following Socrates in the *Republic* 6.508d–9a: let us see the truth about anything in the good done by the best case, thus see what a true ruler is by seeing what good the best ruler does. Mathematicians will encounter true rigor and purity when they consider the use of mathematical ideas in formulating and contemplating truths about God. See further *Republic* 10.601ce; *Cratylus* 3906d; *Euthydemus* 290c.

6. Numbers 21.4–9; cf. 2 Kings 8.14f; and John 3.24f; 8.28; 12.32.

7. See, e.g., Plato, *Timaeus* 47ab; *Epinomis* 976e, 988ab, 990d.

*8. Weil says that algebra, in its origin, that is, in the way in which it was first understood "corresponds to a fundamental error concerning the human mind," an error found in Descartes and repeated by philosophers down to the present day. It is the error of trying to "think the singular" (F 39). This means taking the value of a variable as itself an object, as if it were a singular and particular object in the world. (To prevent this error Weil recommends where possible substituting infinite series for such "general objects.") When we try to think the singular as a single instance of a general object, we are not of course thinking the singular at all but substituting an abstraction for a concrete particular. In this way the "content" of the world entirely escapes us without our realizing that it has gone. Hence the misleading slogan that has made its way into modern philosophy, *To be is to be the value of a variable.* Single values of algebraic values do not correspond to concrete particulars at all.

9. That is, it is an abstract representation of *any* particular of a special kind, which is not *a* particular.

Chapter 2
Gnosis

1. A middle, or mediator: a *metaxu*, the term Weil takes from Plato's *Symposium* 202, 204b, but see also *Republic* 2.359a, 4.443d, 5.477ff, 6.511d; *Philebus* 16e; *Timaeus* 36a, 50d.

2. That is, the two hands are One in their cause. It is two in its manifestations.

3. "Don't think, but look!" Wittgenstein, *Philosophical Investigations* (Blackwell, 1953), no. 66.

4. *Republic* 6.509b. Cf. 2.379b: the Good is in no way evil, or the cause of any evil, but good, and the cause of all other good; 6.492: only God makes anyone good; *Euthyphro* 15a.

5. See, however, Isaiah 45.15: "Truly you are a God who hides yourself"; 8.14–17; 29.9–14; 54.8; Matthew 6.1, 4, 6, 9: "Your Father who is in heaven," who is and sees "in secret"; Pascal, *Pensées* (tr. Krailsheimer; Penguin, 1966), nos. 228, 242, 427, 921; Plato, *Republic* 2.365d; *Laws* 10.886d, 899d. For these writers, however, God is *also* present in our justice and compassion, though he is absent for the person who lacks these and faith.

Chapter 3
Intellect as Grace

*1. A fourth, more hidden track of Simone Weil's life was to suffer bodily pain, in fact twelve years of constant headaches day and night. Two other women of genius who underwent lifelong violent headaches were Hildegard of Bingen (1098–1179) and Anne Conway (1631–1679). [Editor: More on these headaches below in chapter 5, n. 7, and on Hildegard in chapter 9.]

2. A translation was prepared by Martin Andic and informally published through the American Weil Society in 1988–1990.

3. If this sounds strange, that is because we usually think of a *shaman* not only as finding truth and freedom through asceticism and silence and solitude, through fasting and chastity, but also as taking visionary flight through and over the world into the other world among the dead and spirits, and thus having mas-

tery of space and time and mortality. What shamans and sages know by experience and keep to themselves, philosophers share with others in discussion and analysis and interpretation for the good of all; their secret practice and forbidden knowledge become an esoteric teaching, and then an exoteric resource for the whole community and for every community. See Jean-Pierre Vernant, *Myth and Thought among the Greeks* (Routledge, 1983), 354–357. In this more precise meaning Simone Weil is much more like a philosopher than a shaman or sage. She criticizes everything she can and believes only what she must, she teaches and writes and publishes and popularizes. As for being a *charismatic*, if that is speaking in tongues as well as with authority, she does not always expect to be understood or believed without question, though sometimes she commands attention, as at SL 139; cf. 96f, 200f; WG 93f, 101.

4. Blake, *Complete Writings* (ed. Geoffrey Keynes; Oxford, 1966), 557: "Since all the riches of this world / May be gifts from the Devil and earthly kings, / I should suspect that I worshipped the Devil / If I thanked my God for worldly things."

5. Cf. Thoreau, *A Week on the Concord and Merrimack Rivers*, "Sunday" paragraph 7, "Over the old wooden bridge[s] no traveler crossed." R. H. Blyth (*Zen and Zen Classics*, vol. 1 [Hokuseido, 1960], 96), quoting this comments, "This no-traveller, like deserted roads, empty chairs, silent organs, has more meaning, more poetry, solidity and permanence than any traveller. 'No traveller' does not mean nobody, nothing at all; it means every man, you and I and God and all things cross this old rickety bridge, and like the bold lover on the Grecian Urn can never reach the goal." If for Weil no single instance as such is a single thing (see chapter 1, nn. 7–8), for Zen no instance (sc. any single thing) is everything in God.

6. WG 85: "My thought should be indifferent to all ideas without exception, including for instance materialism and atheism; it must be equally welcoming and equally reserved with regard to every one of them. Water is indifferent in this way to the objects that fall into it. It does not weigh them; they weigh themselves, after a certain time of oscillation." N 334: "A method is necessary for the understanding of images, symbols, etc. One should not try to interpret them, but contemplate them until their significance flashes upon one. . . . Generally, a method for exercising the intelligence, which consists of looking." N 303: "We should be indifferent [in will] to good and evil but . . . when we bring the light of our attention equally on both, good prevails by an automatic mechanism. There lies the essential grace. It is the definition, the criterion of good." N 262: "Attention is non-active action of the divine part of the soul upon the other part."

7. It was an inability and not a willful act; God brought her to it. She writes that we may not rightly seek affliction and the cross, only that when affliction comes it may be or mean the cross, for that is our vocation: SN 184, 193; N 262, 269, 411, 415, 433.

8. Cf. Pascal, *Pensées* (tr. Krailsheimer; Penguin, 1966), no. 840: "This is not the home of truth; it wanders unrecognized among men."

9. F 92. Cf. Heraclitus B 11: "Every creature is driven to pasture with a blow."

10. F 311: "Reality and existence are two things, not one. That is a central thought of Plato's, little understood." N 480: "Reality is transcendent; this is Plato's fundamental idea"; N 365: "Reality represents for the human mind the same thing as good. That is the mysterious meaning behind the proposition: *God exists*. In Plato, *to on* should be translated by 'reality'"; N 220: "We ought to love [absolutely only] what is absolutely worthy of love (Plato). Nothing which exists [relatively] is absolutely worthy of love. We must therefore love that which does not exist. But this object of love which does not exist is not devoid of reality, is not a fiction. For our fictions cannot be more worthy of love than we are ourselves, who are not."

11. Thus Pascal, *Pensées*, no. 44, cf. 665, 554; Weil, F 305.

12. In the sense not exactly of Wittgenstein in *Philosophical Investigations* (Blackwell, 1953), nos. 89, 94, but of alchemy.

13. Whereas the most that could truly be said is, they saw it as it really *appeared*. The idea of perspective created an informative appearance of reality. See Jean Gebser, *The Ever-Present Origin* (tr. Noel Barstad and Algis Mickunas; Ohio University Press, 1985).

*14. Parallels between Ludwig Wittgenstein and Simone Weil are pointed out by Peter Winch throughout his recent book, *Simone Weil, "The Just Balance"* (Cambridge, 1989).

15. That is, we cannot sensibly deny to be true, or assert to be false, what we claim to be senseless, or neither true nor false.

16. The goal is not full description in total detachment, but description detached from self and will, from all desire to acquire and possess and use for worldly materialistic egoistic purposes.

17. That is, it should not be concerned entirely with knowledge as we usually think of this, acquisitive, instrumental. Cf. Socrates' criticism of the sophists' reduction of the moral wisdom that makes us and our lives good to technical expertise in satisfying desires. A wise person knows goodness.

18. See further "Simone Weil: Harbinger of a New Renaissance?" in *Simone Weil's Philosophy of Culture* (ed. Richard Bell; Cambridge, 1993), 295–309.

Chapter 4
Cantor, Infinity, and the Silence

1. *Laws* 7.819d. Sc., indifference to this is, among other things, a failure of piety. Cf. *Timaeus* 47, and *Epinomis* 978e, 988ab, and especially 990d–991b: geometry is "the assimilation by reference to plane surfaces of numbers that are not by nature similar to one another. That this miracle is of divine, not human origin should be obvious to anyone who can understand it. . . . What people who look into these matters and understand them find divine and miraculous is how nature as a whole molds sorts and kinds according to each proportion with reference to

the power that is always based on the double and the half," sc., the series of geometrical, arithmetical, harmonic means, that is to say, mediation.

2. See Malcolm Brown, "Plato Disapproves of the Slaveboy's Answer," *The Review of Metaphysics* 20 (1967): 57–93, reprinted in his *Plato's MENO, Text and Critical Essays* (Bobbs-Merrill, 1971), 198–242.

3. Thus *Timaeus* 53c–57d; and Karl Popper, "The Nature of Philosophical Problems and Their Roots in Science," sections IV, VII–IX, in *The British Journal for the Philosophy of Science* 3 (1952), reprinted in *Conjectures and Refutations*, 2nd ed. (Basic Books, 1965), chap. 2, and in Brown, 128–179. For another kind of mixture of infinite and finite, see *Timaeus* 35a, 52de, 58a, with *Parmenides* 158c; *Philebus* 16c–17a, 23c–30.

4. That is, what is false for the finite is true for the infinite.

5. Kierkegaard comments tirelessly on the wonderful, infinitely deep arithmetic of love that gives infinitely little and receives infinitely much, that sees love giving infinitely more than the most, giving more the less it has (*Works of Love* [tr. Howard and Edna Hong; Harper, 1962], 1.5; 2.7). In the second passage, he is referring to the story in Luke 21 of the widow's mite, and he exclaims, "Wonderful computation, or rather, what a wonderful mode of calculating—not to be found in any mathematics book!" He repeats (2.3 and 6), "Wherever love is present, there is something infinitely profound!": e.g., that love has what it gives and loses what it keeps back (2.3 and 5) that it always goes on and if it ever ceases then it never was (2.6).

6. Perhaps Plato in the *Symposium* 201c, 210–212a, followed by Plotinus 1.6.6–9 and Pseudo-Dionysius, *Divine Names* 4.5; cf. the *hadith* of Muhammad, "God is beautiful, and He loves Beauty," and the Sufi saying "Here God is outward Beauty and inward Goodness, there he is outward Goodness and inward Beauty." Weil, WG 213: "God is pure Beauty."

7. For instances that probe the rule, see N 279: "the fulness of being [is] the good which exists unconditionally"; N 471: "annihilation in God confers the fulness of being"; F 96: his is "the plenitude of being"; F 102: "God desires to be, not because he is himself but because he is the Good"; F 269: "We have stolen a little of God's being to make it ours. . . . We must return it," sc., to receive it again from him as his; F 316: the Good's "being consists in being the Good. But it possesses in fullness the reality of that being. It makes no sense to say the Good exists or the Good does not exist; one can only say: the Good."

8. That is, in the infinite number of terms between first and last, thus in the infinity of terms.

*9. J. W. Dauben, *Georg Cantor* (Harvard, 1979), 290. [Editor: Bracketed phrase added. The Purest Actuality is *all* that it can be and is fully realized (actual), because it is without accidents and *only* what it must be (pure).]

10. Once we contrast the number of something with our knowledge of that number, and say that it is independent of our knowledge, it is not obvious why we should agree that the sand is certainly finite but the stars may be infinite: for that

stars are continually coming into existence and passing away, or have no definite identity-criteria and arithmetic, can be said of *sand* as well.

11. The passage continues: "The distinction to be made between levels is something of the utmost importance. Mathematics provide an excellent exercise in this respect. The relation between the whole and the part, and between the part and the whole in mathematics. Needs to be contemplated. The different forms of demonstration—a great mystery. . . . Analogical utilization of the notion of trans-finitude. . . . Cubes, cubes of cubes, etc. There is more and more of reality, right up to God. It is by this method of proof alone that we can verify the fact that He is what is most real, otherwise this remains an expression devoid of meaning."

12. Cf. N 341: God is "even beyond the infinite."

13. That is, my misery can exhaust itself, and it must do so for so long as it still exists I am imperfectly obedient to the will of God. But it is not my will but obedience to God's that exhausts it. Cf. N 364f, 531; F 262, 306f, 326.

Grace, for Weil, though its power is infinitely greater than gravity, appears within the world of gravity as something infinitely *small*, infinitesimal: see N 464: what is infinitely above an order and above what is infinitely great in it "is represented in that order by something infinitely small"; N 481: its action is infinitely small, only its presence is "infinitely, transfinitely great"; thus N 622 for Nicolas of Cusa: "The absolute superlative is equally well, and without distinction, an absolute maximum and an absolute minimum. . . . The circle is a visible demonstration of the identity between the maximum and the minimum. Cf. Heraclitus. The same point forms the beginning and end of the circle."

14. Letter IV to Father Perrin, WG 61–83, discussed below in chapter 11.

15. Cf. Shakespeare, *The Merchant of Venice* 5.1.58–65, *Pericles* 5.2.225–236.

16. Thus in mathematics we can add 2 to 2 or divide by 2, as if 2s were *many*, all divisible, or add the units in any 2 to those in another to get 4, as if 2 and 2 and 4 were *sums* of interchangeable units. These numbers are not Forms, but they are not the sensible particulars either that collected one way have (or are of) those numbers but differently collected have different numbers (e.g., four single people, two couples, one quartet). *Republic* 7.525d–526a, cf. 528e–531c; *Philebus* 56de; Aristotle, *Metaphysics* 1.5–8.

17. WG 168–169, 130: works of art only reflect this or open the way to it.

18. See, however, Aristotle's report, in *The Complete Works* (ed. Jonathan Barnes; Bollingen Series 71.2; Princeton University Press, 1984), 2.2391, 2397–2399; discussed by Konrad Gaiser, "Plato's Enigmatic Lecture *On the Good*," *Phronesis* 25 (1980): 5–37.

19. N 514: "Algebra reflects the two properties of the circle (as the locus of proportional means, and that of points equidistant from the center). But this appropriateness translated in this way remains just as mysterious"; IC 191–192: "When one contemplates the property which makes of the circle the locus of the apices of the right-angled triangles having the same hypotenuse, if one pictures at the same time a point describing the circle and the projection of this point upon the diam-

eter, contemplation may extend far toward the depths and toward the heights. The affinity of the movements of the two points, one circular, the other alternating, includes the possibility of all the transformations of circular movements into alternating ones, and conversely, which are the bases of our technology. This is the principle of the operation by which a grinder sharpens knives. On the other hand, the circular movement, if one conceives not a point but a whole circle turning upon itself, is the perfect image of the eternal act that constitutes the life of the Trinity. . . ." Cf. N 493, 505, 512, 515, 528; IC 162.

20. The *ponderous* and the *appropriate* in mathematics are related not exactly as natural to supernatural, but as *brute or opaquely necessary* to *beautiful and good.* Necessity, whether considered as pure mathematics, or in its application to the natural world, becomes appropriate when we see it as a symbol of supernatural truths: N 514, 516: "Genius like grace is the wing by which that which is ponderous is borne aloft," revealing the fullness of its reality.

21. Plato himself seems to follow Pythagoras and Parmenides in associating God and Being and Unity with Limit: see, e.g., *Philebus* 16b–18, cf. *Gorgias* 507c–508a; and so in a way does Simone Weil (see chapter 1 above), who otherwise accentuates the infinity of God. Perhaps like her, Plato would accept the notion of a limitlessness of form in the sense of its exemplary purity and unqualified wholeness, its nonrelativity and nonambiguity; e.g., the Good that is in God, and is God, is nothing but good and in no way evil, it simply and fully *is*—thus it truly, superlatively, actually is—what qualified goods are in some relations only by contrast with others (*Republic* 2.379bc; *Phaedo* 100c). This kind of limitlessness or infinity is not so much quantitative as qualitative (as in Nicolas of Cusa, *The Vision of God* 13–16.) For Weil, God is unlimited, yet he *sets* limits and even *accepts* them, submitting to them in the world that embodies him. His creative act is an abdication, and it is in obedience that we are like him: see, e.g., F 81, 92, 103, 130, 140–142 (cf. Seneca: "The founder and master of the universe himself always obeys and commanded only once"); and chapter 11 below.

When Aristotle rejects the actual infinite in *Physics* 3.6–7, it is for the constructivist reason that there is, for there can meaningfully be said to be, no size greater than the greatest *actual* one, "or there would be something bigger than the heavens" (207b19).

Chapter 5
T. E. Lawrence and the Purification of Evil

˙1. Malraux met Lawrence just once, in a bar in Montparnasse in the early 1930s; Weil never met him. Malraux wrote of Lawrence (in the Preface to the French edition of *The Seven Pillars of Wisdom*) that he was "one of the most religious intelligences of his time, if one means by religious someone who in the very depths of his soul knows the anguish of being a man."

*2. This letter does not appear in *Seventy Letters*, edited by Richard Rees in 1965, but was printed by Louis Allen in "French Intellectuals and T. E. Lawrence," *Durham University Journal* (December 1976): 52–66, at 60–61.

3. IC 116: Force is "an absolutely sovereign thing in all of nature, including the natural part of the human soul, with all the thoughts and all the feelings the soul contains." Cf. her praise of Marx for his "idea of genius" that human society is subjected to laws of force, discussed in the next chapter.

*4. Both died in ways that made it look as if they were "inviting death"—he traveling too fast on his motorcycle; she refusing to eat more than a wartime starvation diet.

5. Weil knew strong will too, despite her longing for purification and freedom from it. See SL 172–174, 178–179; F 262; WG 59. Her biographers report that at five she repeated to herself in her cold bath the words of Turenne: "You shaking carcass, if you only knew where I am taking you"; probably Weil heard them from her brother André who found them in Nietzsche, but Kierkegaard in *Journals and Papers* (7 vols.; ed. and tr. Howard and Edna Hong; Indiana University Press, 1967–1978), no. 6180 indicates that they go back to Plutarch, who says that shaking can have a double cause and meaning, strength or weakness). As a young woman she admired Antigone. Her own later view is that love of true good transforms will into consent and spirit; we should seek release from all (other) will as such.

6. *T. E. Lawrence, The Selected Letters,* ed. Malcolm Brown (Norton, 1987), 237. *Seven Pillars of Wisdom* (Jonathan Cape, 1935), chapter 1, paragraph 4.

*7. "For twelve years I have suffered from continuous pain around the central point of the nervous system, the meeting-place between soul and body; this pain persists during sleep and has never stopped for a second. . . . The result was that the irreducible quantity of hatred and repulsion which goes with suffering and affliction recoiled entirely upon myself. And the quantity is very great because the suffering in question is located at the very root of my every single thought, without exception. . . . Since it is not only my body but my soul that is poisoned all through by suffering, it is impossible for my thought to dwell there and it is obliged to travel elsewhere" (Letter to Joë Bousquet, SL 140, 141).

[Editor: Weil seems to be following Descartes (*The Passions of the Soul,* 1.31–50, and the letters to Mersenne of 1640) in locating the meeting place of soul and body in the pineal gland, which recent studies suggest makes us responsive to periodic changes in *light.* Weil's headaches began to abate in 1938, and treatment for sinusitis in 1939 relieved them further, though they recurred occasionally until her death in 1943. See Jacques Cabaud, *Simone Weil: A Fellowship in Love* (Channel Press, 1964), 187; Simone Pétrement, *Simone Weil: A Life* (tr. Raymond Rosenthal; Pantheon Books, 1976), 365–366; and above chapter 3, n. 1. Considering her struggles to understand and open herself to grace, it is interesting that she compares grace to the *chlorophyll* that enables a plant to feed upon light (N 223, 367–368, 543–544; F 70, 280).]

*Two other women of marked philosophic-religious genius also suffered from lifelong continuous violent headaches, Anne Conway (1631-1679) and Hildegard of Bingen (1098-1179). Anne Conway's husband sent all over Europe for healers, one of whom, the famous Baron von Helmont, came to live with the Conways in England. Hildegard, searching for a medicinal remedy, became an expert botanist.

8. Neal Oxenhandler (*Looking for Heroes in Postwar France* [University of New England Press, 1996], 191-192) follows Juliet Mitchell's diagnosis of hysteric anorexia and writes of her hysteric courage, speculating: "She finally took herself out of the war, by stepping into a basin of boiling oil. . . . She wounded herself in order to stop thinking about the death and destruction all around her." *Is* it hysteria to hunger and thirst after righteousness and to struggle for it? Weil herself calls it supernatural justice, although humanly speaking it is madness (SJ 3-4, 9-10).

9. She remarked to Thibon: "One day I wondered if I had not died and fallen into hell without noticing it and whether hell did not consist of working eternally in a vineyard" (GG xi).

*Thibon at the age of ninety-three still (in 1993) operates the same vineyard.

10. He wrote to Lionel Curtis in 1923: "perhaps in determinism complete there lies the perfect peace I have so longed for. Free-will I've tried, and rejected: authority I've rejected (not obedience, for that is my present effort, to find equality only in subordination. It is dominion whose taste I have been cloyed with): action I've rejected: and the intellectual life: and the receptive senses: and the battle of wits. They were all failures, and my reason tells me therefore that obedience, nescience, will also fail, since the roots of common failure must lie in myself—and yet in spite of reason I am trying it" (*Selected Letters*, 240).

*11. To help other British officers and diplomats posted to the Mideast, Lawrence drew up in August 1917 *Twenty-Seven Articles* advising how to get on with the Arabs. See Jeremy Wilson, *Lawrence of Arabia* (Athenaeum, 1990), Appendix IV.

12. Henry James was born in 1835 and died in 1916. As for D. H. Lawrence (1885- 1930), T. E. Lawrence (1888-1935) read all (and even wrote reviews of some) of his books, admiring them for a darkness and violence showing greatness and genius, but found him astonishingly ungenerous, for the novelist entirely ignored him.

13. *Equal* attention is uniform or steady, held equally on every alternative, "equal as the light of the sun" (N 30, 47, 303). It is like the equal mind with which we should welcome and accept and respond to whatever presents itself, equal to everything.

14. See N 56, where she alludes to *Hamlet* 3.1.85: "And thus the native hue of resolution is sickled o'er with the pale cast of thought." Hamlet is rebuking himself, that his reflection so far only intellectualizes and replaces urgent and timely action.

15. One may not do evil that good may come, but one may often have to do

evil as the necessary cost of avoiding a greater evil. In this way doing *right* may involve doing evil.

16. See further 1 Samuel 15.1–11. Weil does not see how sparing and coexisting with the Amalekites and other peoples in Canaan would have been a greater evil than destroying them to the last man, woman, and child.

*17. The traditional biblical God will surely not give way finally without a furious backlash, and this is the meaning of fundamentalism today in the three biblical religions. But fundamentalism is in a losing struggle with the technological thrust toward multiculturalism. [Editor: William Blake also condemns these atrocities, and calls the true Jehovah "Father of Mercies" (*Complete Writings* [ed. Geoffrey Keynes; Oxford, 1966] 387–388, 780).]

18. Or is it only the human beings committing these crimes for him that we cannot recognize as his servants?

19. That is, a god of returning evil for evil and wrong for wrong is a false god; the true God is a god of suffering evil and wrong rather than doing them even in return or defense.

20. In a letter to Edward Garnett of August 26, 1922, he says he once aspired "to make an English fourth" [to]. . . *The Karamazovs, Zarathustra,* and *Moby Dick,* . . . [these] 'titanic' books distinguished by greatness of spirit." And writing to A. P. Wavell that year, he calls the *Seven Pillars* "a great failure (lacking architecture, the balance of parts, coherence, streamlining): and oddly enough among my favorite books are the other great failures—*Moby Dick, Also sprach Zarathustra, Pantagruel*—books where the authors went up like a shot of rockets, and burst. I don't mean to put mine into that degree of the class: but it is to me as Zarathustra was to Nietzsche, something bigger than I could do."

21. Lawrence means to "understand love."

22. That is, his best chance to know this spirit among the Arabs. He knows the Sufis, for he refers here to "the introspective mysticism of Iranian devotees." For Weil's view that carnal love is a love of the beauty of the world incarnate in a particular human being, and so is an implicit form of the love of God, see WG 133-134, 137-138, 158-181, especially 171-172.

Chapter 6
Marx, Oppression, and Liberty

1. Thus Kierkegaard too: see, e.g., *Journals and Papers* (ed. and tr. Howard and Edna Hong; Indiana University Press, 1967–78), no. 2958: "The numerical does not constitute quality; on the contrary, it is the indifferent quality. . . . But the fact is— the numerical exercises a sensate power over us men. . . . The numerical changes men intoxicates them, obsesses them, as if by being many they were something altogether different from what each single individual is"; no. 2970: "number simply does not exist at all for the eternal. It is related inversely to the eternal—the

greater the number, the easier—if I dare say so—it is to discard it. It is very hard for the eternal to discard a single individual. . . . God is present only for the single individual"; see also nos. 2980–2989, 2999, 3540.

2. Yet we do deliberate and speak differently as individuals and *as* members and *in* the name of and *for* different groups, though it is as individual members of or spokesmen for these. For example, our *moral* judgments are the ones we formulate for *all* of us, as members of a community of equals defined in effect by the golden rule.

The social anthropologist Mary Douglas argues that even if institutions have no minds of their own and do not build themselves and thus even if *they* do not think for themselves, they enable *us* to think for ourselves and for them, so that we more or less self-consciously and critically both rely on them and build them as collective systems of classification and assessment; Douglas gives the example of the varieties of wine (*How Institutions Think* [Syracuse, 1986]). (They shape our thoughts without determining them, unless we allow it by failing to be self-conscious and critical.) If institutions are conventions with legitimacy or authority, encoding information, then Wittgenstein would say that *languages* amount to institutions that we may use to speak for ourselves.

Weil herself complains of the church and the state stifling and punishing the free thought of their members, not tolerating and encouraging it as they should, except where they hold teaching functions and their speculations do harm in practice (WG 78-80). It is the individual officers and spokesmen of the church and the state who have this totalitarian tendency and who need the warning against it. Thus she addressed her criticism of the church to Father Couturier (*Letter to a Priest*) as someone in a position to shape its thinking, and it seems her words had some effect, as Joanna Weber has argued in an unpublished essay. Popes John XXIII and Paul VI were among her enthusiastic readers: see Gabriella Fiori, *Simone Weil: An Intellectual Biography* (tr. Joseph Berrigan; University of Georgia Press, 1989), 309; and David McLellan, *Simone Weil: Utopian Pessimist* (Macmillan, 1989), 268.

3. Except insofar as necessity is itself obedience to the Good that is in God and is God, and the distance is itself the bond between them, between God and us: see N 379: "The beautiful is the necessary which, while remaining in accord with its own law and with it alone, obeys the good. . . . The distance between the necessary and the good is the selfsame distance separating the creature from the creator"; N 424: "This world, insofar as it is completely empty of God, is God himself. Necessity insofar as it is absolutely other than Good, is Good itself"; N 311: "For some people everything that brings God nearer to them is beneficial. In my case it is everything that makes Him more remote"; N 497: "Every separation is a bond," sc., when it purifies and intensifies the real bond which is desire and love.

4. Cf. WG 117: "The men of antiquity used to say: 'A man loses half his soul the day he becomes a slave'": see Homer, *Odyssey* 17.322; Plato, *Laws* 7.776e: half

his *aretē*, worth. Aristotle, *Nicomachean Ethics* 8.11: "A slave is a living tool, and a tool is a lifeless slave."

5. See NR 219–237, also 131–132, 143, 169, 174.

6. Cf. Socrates' view in the *Republic* 4 that justice and doing right are doing your own work, that which you can best do for the good of your community, to make human beings and their lives good, and this is what makes you and your life good. Similarly the *Bhagavad Gita* on your *dharma*, doing what is best for all not for any reward but as a service of God. Thoreau, *Walden* 1.103, 108: work not to do good but to *be* good and let the world take what good it may, true goodness being an unconscious overflow of faith, courage, health, and freedom. A. K. Coomaraswamy, *Why Exhibit Works of Art?* (Luzac, 1943), 24: "The artist is not a special kind of man, but every man who is not an artist in some field, every man without a vocation, is an idler."

7. Thus Coomaraswamy, *Why Exhibit Works of Art?* 14, 33ff, 71f: the best and true artist *freely* conceives the living form of the work to be made and brings it to life in himself and the work, *serving* only the good of the work; he thinks of quality, not quantity and profit.

Chapter 7
Nationalism

1. In March 1939, when the Germans seized Czechoslovakia (SL 158; F 345).

2. More generally she never disavowed her political writing and activism, only raised it to a higher level (N 311).

3. NR 159–160. In a different context Weil writes: "The relation of hunger to food is far less complete, to be sure, but just as real as is that of the act of eating. . . . [For some] the desire for and deprivation of the sacraments might constitute a contract more pure than actual participation" (WG 55). Cf. chapter 6, n. 2, above.

4. They feed what is best in us, the impersonal or selfless love of the good, and building this up consume the rest. See F 284–285, 286; WG 164, 166.

5. Plato would say, when it makes us worse human beings, inciting us to wrong one another and so to harm ourselves: *Laws* 6.770e; *Republic* 1.335bc; *Apology* 29b; *Crito* 47c–48b; *Gorgias* 469bc, 470e, 502d and ff.

6. Which is not to say, no souls can be punished even capitally. See WG 152–157; NR 21–22 (discussed below), 299–300; SE 31, 226. For Haman, see the book of Esther 3–9.

7. Her struggle is not for recognition of her rights, but for the protection that is *due* to her because she is a human being. What has moral weight is her cry for the protection that we *owe* one another from the wrong that harms us by making us and our lives worse, that any human being *deserves* and *ought* to receive from any human being.

8. "It is not true that the freedom of one man is limited by that of other men.

Man is really free to the extent that his freedom fully acknowledged and mirrored by the free consent of his fellow men finds confirmation and expansion of their liberty. Man is free only among equally free men. The slavery of even one human being violates humanity and negates the freedom of all" (Michael Bakunin in 1866, *Revolutionary Catechism*, no. 4). That is, no one is fully free until all are. (Bakunin was a revolutionary comrade of Richard Wagner in Dresden in 1848, and is said to have been the original model for Wagner's Siegfried.)

Cf. the Buddhist story of the vow of Dharmakara Amitabha not to enter Nirvana until he enters that Land of Purity *with* every sentient being, and to save all who call on his name with pure faith: an expression of the idea of *codependent origination*. See WG 182, 188–189, 216f; Frithjof Schuon, *Logic and Transcendence* (tr. Peter Townsend; Harper, 1975), 249–259; cf. Moses in Exodus 32.32; Paul in Romans 9.3; and Simone Weil in WG 48, 75, 77: "I remain beside all those things that cannot enter the Church"; WG 94: "The love of those things that are outside visible Christianity keeps me outside the Church."

9. Leviticus 19.34; Deuteronomy 10.14–19. Women and slaves, however, are not recognized with full equality, as Stephanie Strickland points out.

10. That is, it is our last appeal to the heart. *Human* beings help each other.

11. This is true if the emphasis falls on "rather than" in the sense of *not*.

12. *Zettel* (Blackwell, 1967), no. 455. Cf. Gilbert Ryle, "Taking Sides in Philosophy" (1937), in *Collected Papers* (2 vols.; Barnes & Noble, 1971), 2.153–169. Socrates in *Republic* 9.592 is an exception that proves the rule: for his ideas are not his own thoughts or shared theses so much as divine ideals of which he constantly disavows adequate knowledge, and, while seeking consensus, he also tests and challenges it as well as himself and helps others to test and challenge for themselves. See also *Phaedrus* 247, 250bc: philosophers feast together on the vision of being, but their vision and feast are always incomplete, and they belong to a community of *inquirers*; cf. *Phaedo* 63bc, 67ab. The philosopher is bound for a passion of truth, and this will be isolation before it is communication: see *Phaedo* 64ac; *Gorgias* 521ce; *Republic* 2.360e–362a, 6.496ce, 7.517a.

13. John 18.36; cf. Matthew 8.21. N 298: "One must uproot oneself; cut down the tree and make of it a cross, and then carry it always; uproot oneself from the social and vegetable angles; have no native land on this earth that one may call one's own. . . . But in uprooting oneself one seeks a greater reality. . . . One must acquire the sense of being at home in exile"; see also *Bhagavad Gita* 15.1–14: cut down the tree of life that is the life of ego and materialistic acquisition and comparison.

*14. Emmanuel Levinas, *Difficult Freedom* (Johns Hopkins University Press, 1990), 137.

15. Leviticus 19.34; Deuteronomy 10.14–19.

*16. Vaclav Havel, *The Power of the Powerless* (ed. John Keane; Sharpe, 1985); see also *Living in Truth* (ed. Jan Vladislav; Faber, 1990), 389.

17. John 1.4; 3.21; 1 John 1.6; 5.11. F 47, 342.

Chapter 8
Heidegger, Science, and Technology

1. *Culture and Value* (Blackwell, 1980), 49.

2. The third truth seems to contradict the first one, unless the first is understood as denying the neutrality for good or harm of the spirit of science and technology together when it *is* separated from the spirit of humanity, or understood out of true human context.

3. "Our civilization is characterized by the word 'progress.' Progress is its form rather than one of its features. Typically it constructs. It is occupied with building an ever more complicated structure. And even clarity is sought only as a means to this end, not as an end in itself. For me on the contrary clarity, perspicuity are valuable in themselves. I am not interested in constructing a building, so much as in having a perspicuous view of the foundations of possible buildings" (*Culture and Value*, 7).

4. Given Weil's growing interest in mediation and roots, as central terms of religious morality and politics, it is clear that she is here rejecting more particularly *worldly* means and ends together, those of amoral materialistic egoism. Cf. Wittgenstein in the previous note.

5. Martin Heidegger, *The Question Concerning Technology* (tr. William Lovitt; Harper & Row, 1977); *The End of Philosophy* (tr. Joan Stambaugh; Harper & Row, 1973).

6. Cf. Socrates on *technē*: *Meno* 87e–89a; *Euthydemus* 280b–282a, 288d–289b; *Republic* 6.508d–509b; see further chapter 1, n. 5.

7. That is, we understand nothing rightly and fully, morally and well. Cf. Winston Churchill, speaking at the Massachusetts Institute of Technology, April 1, 1949:

The whole prospect and outlook of mankind grew immeasurably larger, and the multitude of ideas also proceeded at an incredible rate. This vast expansion was unhappily not accompanied by any noticeable advance in the stature of man, either in his mental faculties or his moral character, but it buzzed the more. The scale of events around him assumed gigantic proportions while he remained about the same size.

By comparison therefore he actually became much smaller. We no longer had great men directing manageable affairs. Our need was to discipline an array of gigantic and turbulent facts.

To this task we have so far proved unequal. Science bestowed immense new powers on man and at the same time created conditions which were largely beyond his control. While he nursed the illusion of growing mastery and exulted in his new trappings, he became the sport and presently the victim of tides and currents of whirlpools and tornadoes amid which he was far more helpless than he had been for a long time.

8. See Heidegger, *Nietzsche* (3 vols.; tr. David Krell; Harper & Row, 1979, 1981, 1984); and Weil, "Human Personality" (1943) in SE 9–34, at 10–12; F 73, 124, 284.

9. See IC 154, 160–161, citing Proclus on Euclid: "Plato teaches us many marvellous doctrines concerning the divinity by means of mathematical ideas," explaining that mathematics teaches us to think with exactitude and certainty about things beyond imagination, as are God the Father and the Son and Spirit of God and their relations to one another and to us, the very idea of mediation being the core of mathematics. Cf. NR 292; SN 144.

10. Cf. Socrates in the *Republic* at 2.379bc.

11. In *Basic Writings* (ed. David Krell; Harper & Row, 1977), 193–242, at 193–194, 199.

12. See also OL 87: "A clear view of what is possible and impossible, what is easy and what difficult, of the labors that separate the project from its accomplishment— this alone does away with insatiable desires and vain fears; from this and not from anything else proceed moderation and courage, virtues without which life is nothing but a disgraceful frenzy."

Weil's essay opens with an epigraphic quotation from Spinoza's *Treatise on Political Authority* 1.4: "I have worked carefully, not to laugh or cry or be angry, but to understand."

*13. See *Philosophy Today* 20.4 (Winter 1976): 280 and 277.

*14. *Harper's Magazine*, June 1985, pp. 36–47.

Chapter 9
Love in Abandonment

1. Weil discusses the spirituality of agriculture and metallurgy and all trades and manual labor in ancient times, lost through slavery: NR 295–298; F 173, 268, 337.

2. Simone Weil generally contrasts Roman stoicism with the true stoicism of the Greeks, though she also cites Seneca and Marcus Aurelius with approval. E.g., SN 138–139; NR 288–290; WG 65, 95–96, 160, 175–178, 195; IC 120, 175, 184; N 61, 297, 612, 634; F 20, 142, 155f, 254f, 313f.

3. At least to develop the institutional support for knowlege and technology. The alchemy and astrology of late antiquity are two exceptions that test the rule: they were generally pursued by individuals in isolation and secrecy.

4. Cf. Simone Weil, "Theoretical Picture of a Free Society" (1934), OL 106–107: "For the ancient and heart-breaking curse contained in *Genesis*, which made the world appear as a convict prison and labor as the sign of men's servitude and abasement, [Bacon] substituted in a flash of genius the veritable character expressing the relations between man and the world: 'We cannot command Nature except by obeying her.' This simple pronouncement ought to form by itself the Bible of

our times. It suffices to define true labor, the kind which forms free men, and that to the very extent to which it is an act of conscious submission to necessity." After a year of factory work, she felt very differently: see her thoughts in the Portuguese village (1938), WG 66–67, with OL 144–145; LP 89, 214–216. See chapter 11 below.

5. Cf. Socrates in the *Theaetetus* 173e–174a and *Phaedrus* 246bc.

6. See above, chapter 4, n. 21 end, on God's creative abdication.

7. Cf. Genesis 3.1–7; Plotinus 4.8.5; 5.1.1; Plato, *Phaedo* 81c; *Phaedrus* 246bd, 247b; *Republic* 7.519ab. N 114, 138, 159, 384, 536.

8. See Exodus 13.2, 12–15; 22.29; Numbers 3.13; 8.17; Luke 2.22–24. Sacrificing children to God may be simply giving them to him to be priests or their servants, not killing: Numbers 8.17–19. Ezekiel 20.25f says that he led the faithless Hebrews "to offer by fire all their firstborn, to horrify them"; but this means to offer their firstborn to *idols*, the false gods of their neighbors. See 16.10f; Psalm 106.34–39; Jeremiah 7.31; 19.5; 32.35. He abandoned the faithless to themselves: Psalm 81.12; Romans 1.24.

9. He is quoting David's Psalm 22. But then *David* was made to feel abandoned so that he could find and seek deliverance from his enemies and perhaps more particularly from hatred and revenge (sc., his own, reading it with a Christian accent).

10. Boswell, *Kindness of Strangers* (Yale University Press, 1988), 138.

11. Cf. Job 38.28–29; Isaiah 49.15; 66.13; in Matthew 23.37 it is Christ who expresses a mother's love. See also Deuteronomy 33.27; Psalms 121.3; 139.13.

12. Perhaps more than can be explained by saying God knows and blesses the ways of those who know him and follow his way of justice and mercy, but ignores or punishes those who ignore him and defy that way, so that he is wrathful with the wrathful but forgiving with the forgiving.

13. In this way there is a World Tree in Aristotle's universe too.

14. "Mathematics" comes from Greek *manthanō* (I learn); *mathēsis* (lesson, study, science). Thus a taking in (?).

15. Cf. Socrates' warning in *Phaedo* 83 against taking what most strikes and stings us as most real. (But Plotinus in 6.6.12 says that Unity does this even more than ideal Being.)

16. If *she* is a stranger to us in the sense that we don't know her from the start, who and what she is, *we* are not a stranger to her, who has formed us in her womb and given us life; for we scarcely exist or are anyone with moral standing until she freely recognizes us as her baby whom she wants and will carry and bring forth and nurture and raise. In a way she knows us because she loves us and believes in us, has freely given us her love and her faith in us. Cf. Aristotle, *Nicomachean Ethics* 8.12: she loves her child as (part of) herself, her child is to her "another self, other because it exists separately." Kierkegaard, *Works of Love* (tr. Howard and Edna Hong; Harper, 1962), 1.1: only love recognizes us; 1.2: here knowledge presupposes faith, not the other way. Simone Weil, SE 10–12, 30–31.

17. That is, as our technology makes us more interdependent than ever. It makes us more vulnerable, but also more responsible.

18. They are among what Goethe and Max Picard call *primary phenomena*, e.g., language, silence, beauty, truth, sexuality, color. Goethe says that God shows himself in these to Reason, which grasps active causes, beyond Understanding, which knows only their definite results; God is Reason, he is Understanding. *Conversations with Eckermann*, February 13, 1829, February 23, 1831. Evidently Reason is Understanding turned with loving attention to these elemental phenomena and to God within them.

Chapter 10
Recovering the Sacred in Humanity

1. Franz Kafka, *The Third Octavo Notebook*, December 13, 1917, in *Dearest Father* (tr. Ernest Kaiser and Eithne Wilkins; Schocken, 1954), 80.

2. Cf. the words of Einstein quoted in chapter 3 above, p. 40.

3. Maurice Drury in "Conversations with Wittgenstein," in *Ludwig Wittgenstein, Personal Recollections* (ed. Rush Rhees; Rowman & Littlefield, 1981), 117, from a discussion in 1929. "The symbolisms of Catholicism are wonderful beyond words. But any attempt to make it into a philosophical system is offensive. All religions are wonderful, even those of the most primitive tribes. The ways in which people express their religious feelings differ enormously."

4. Perhaps the sense is, do not swear *by* or speak *for* them, or speak *to* them in submission and prayer, sacrifice and service. Cf. Exodus 22.20: "Whoever sacrifices to any god, save to the LORD only, shall be utterly destroyed"; Deuteronomy 18.20: "The prophet who presumes to speak a word in my name which I have not commanded him to speak, or who speaks in the name of other gods, that same prophet shall die"; Joshua 23.6–8: "Do not mention their gods' names, or swear by them, or serve them, or bow to them"; Psalms 16.4: "Those who choose another god multiply their sorrows; their libations of blood I will not pour out or take their names upon my lips."

*5. Robert Coles, *Simone Weil, A Modern Pilgrimage* (Addison-Wesley, 1987), 48.

6. Deuteronomy 8.2–3, 5, 11–16.

*7. *Selected Letters of Rav A. Y. Kook* (Jerusalem, 1987), 165–166. [Editor: thus Exodus 17.8-15; Deuteronomy 20.17; 1 Samuel 15.]

8. *Selected Letters of Rav A. Y. Kook*, 167.

9. God *looks* powerless (to the powerful) here below, but he *is* power free. Cf. Plato in *Symposium* 196bc.

10. See chapter 9, n. 10.

11. Or not deeply; yet see IC 161: "Christ recognized Himself as Isaiah's man of sorrows"; LP nos. 7, 25; N 501, 506, 538, 583; F 254, 256, 267, 332, 341; cf. N

462f. But she forgets Isaiah's man of sorrows in her list of twenty-eight anticipatory images of Christ at F 321–322.

12. See, however, IC 19, 51, 70–71, 77, 119, 153, 163; WG 192, 208; SN 194; N 564–565; F 91, 178, 302–303; LP nos. 23 end, 35 near end. She certainly read history and literature with her imagination, though some exasperated critics (including some who are otherwise sympathetic) would say with too much, or the wrong kind. For example, J.-M. Perrin, in *Simone Weil As We Knew Her* (tr. Emma Craufurd; Routledge, 1953), 54–70, 75, 93–94, 99, 101; similarly Gustave Thibon, ibid., 140–141, 148–149. Whether she was as arbitrary and subjective and narrow as they say is a question that we must consider still open, until we have examined it fully for ourselves.

13. See chapter 12.

14. And yet she finds "intoxicating" the anticipations of Christianity among the ancient Greeks and others and regards them as proofs. See n. 12 above, and F 80: "It is not that anything that isn't Christian is false, but everything that is true is Christian."

15. Women were active in the early church (see Romans 16.3–16; Acts 18; cf. Galatians 3.28 vs. 1 Timothy 2.12), and scholars have ascribed to women some of the Pauline letters, e.g., Hebrews; but if women wrote theological treatises, these have not survived.

*16. Tertullian, *Against Marcion* 1.24, in *The Ante-Nicene Fathers* (Hendrickson, 1994), 3.290.

17. Tertullian, *Against Marcion*, in *Ante-Nicene Fathers*, 3.292.

18. That is, the humanity, the protection from wrong, that any man owes to and deserves and expects from any man. This is the whole and only foundation of our justice and compassion toward one another, family relative or not, acquaintance or stranger, friend or enemy, saint or sinner. In other words, human kindness is founded on human kinship.

19. That is, no reason but humanity, and no recompense but to have shown our own. Like is known only by like.

As for any sociobiological pattern of necessity and causality—amounting to an evolutionary advantage to our *species*—we respond to one another's expectation of good, and feel and know we "humanly" owe protection and rescue, even when we reflect that there *is* no advantage to ourselves individually or even as a species, beyond the advantage to our species to *acknowledge* our mutual kinship.

20. See p. 58 and chapter 5, n. 21, Finch's criticism of T. E. Lawrence.

21. Ludwig Wittgenstein, *Philosophical Investigations* (Blackwell, 1953), II.xi.223. The territory Weil describes is not foreign so much as it is seen from a viewpoint foreign to our usual materialistic egoistic one. It is beyond our usual thought and language, beyond imagination, beyond and beyond, and yet it is this human world seen as it really is. F 144–148: "Earthly things are a criterion of spiritual things." (It is not just new *as a whole* or in some part, but *wholly* new or in every part; for every part *is* new in its meaning, as in Revelation 21.5: "I make all things new.")

22. We can say that we *apprehend* things, *lay hold* of them, *tackle* and *grapple* and *wrestle* with them (cf. Weil WG 69); we *take* them to mean something, *put* constructions on them, *fit* them together to *make* something of them: "*facts.*"

23. *En hupomenē*, "in patience": a favorite expression of Weil's, taken from Luke 8.15; cf. 21.19; Romans 8.25; Isaiah 30.18; 40.31; 64.4; thus WG 76, 86, 196; cf. F 99, 141.

24. That is, *we* as we are in ourselves, apart from heaven, cannot make or do anything that is truly good, purely and unambiguously: we have no grace of our own to do or make anything truly well. Thus Weil, N 434: for *us* "Good is impossible."

25. Yet consider the swords in Genesis 3.24; Numbers 22.23, 31; Leviticus 26.25; Deuteronomy 32.41f; 33.29; Psalm 17.3; Matthew 10.34; Ephesians 6.17; Romans 13.4. As for biological weapons, there are plagues from God: see Exodus 7.14ff; Leviticus 26.4ff; Numbers 14.12; Deuteronomy 28.15ff; 59ff; 32.39; Revelation 18.4-8, 22, 18.

Chapter 11
The Life and Death of Simone Weil

1. She writes in her *Cahiers* that it is wrong to want to be understood before having explained oneself to oneself.

2. We must understand what an author *means* before we can know whether it is coherent and reasonable and *true*. Otherwise we risk merely condemning a lampoon, like the Athenians who condemned Socrates as they saw him in *The Clouds* of Aristophanes; or like savages "who hear the expressions of civilized men, put a false interpretation on them, and then draw the queerest conclusions from it" (in Wittgenstein's *Philosophical Investigations,* no. 194); or, as Peter Winch has said, like the anthropologists who in their turn misconstrue the beliefs of these same savages and find them illogical. See Peter Winch, *Ethics and Action* (Routledge, 1972), 8–49.

3. This is the fourth of six letters to Father Perrin included in *Waiting for God* (pp. 61–83) (actually the fifth is addressed to Father Perrin's secretary, though the contents and enclosures are meant for him). Perrin has written about Weil in turn in part 1 of *Simone Weil As We Knew Her* (tr. Emma Craufurd; Routledge, 1953; part 2 is by Gustave Thibon), and in *Mon Dialogue avec Simone Weil* (Nouvelle Cité, 1984). See also his preface to *Réponses aux questions de Simone Weil* (Aubier, 1964), and Appendix I, "Concerning Simone Weil," in his *The Church in My Life* (Aquin Press, 1959).

4. "The idea of God going in quest of man is something unfathomably beautiful and profound. Decadence is shown as soon as it is replaced by the idea of man going in quest of God" (*Letter to a Priest* no. 34). She is commenting on the words of the *Days of Wrath* (*Dies Irae*) in the Requiem Mass, *Quaerens me sedisti lassus,*

"seeking me you sat down weary." See further SN 158–159; WG 195–196, 133–134, 210–212, 216; IC 1–6. She means to correct Pascal in *Pensées* (tr. Krailsheimer; Penguin, 1966), nos. 149 end, 472, 919, 929; but he anticipates her at 7, 214, 380–381, 930. See further 631 and WG 69; and the excellent discussion by André Devaux, "Simone Weil et Blaise Pascal," in *Simone Weil, La Soif De L'Absolu* (*SUD, Revue Litteraire*, 1990), 75–97.

5. It was her intimation that the problem of God could not be solved nonreligiously ("here below") and without God's initiative and cooperation. See n. 11 in what follows.

6. Cf. WG 43–45, 50, 67–68, 129 on the the irresistible pressure of God's grace, a *force* beyond any of those operative in the mechanism of nature. Contrast IC 24–55 on *The Iliad* as "a poem of force"; and NR 288–291 on the providential domination of necessity by divine reason's wise persuasion in Plato, *Timaeus* 47e and *Phaedo* 99c.

7. Cf. WG 128–129: "Man can never escape from obedience to God. A creature cannot but obey. The only choice given to men, as intelligent and free creatures, is to desire obedience or not to desire it"; IC 186: "to be free, for us, is to desire to obey God. All other liberty is false"; SJ 6: "Where obedience is consented to there is freedom: there, and nowhere else."

8. Cf. WG 48–49: "I have the essential need, and I think I can say the vocation, to move among men of every class and complexion, mixing with them and sharing their life and outlook, so far that is to say as conscience allows, merging into the crowd and disappearing among them, so that they show themselves as they are, putting off all disguises with me. It is because I long to know them so as to love them just as they are"; see also WG 80–81. Her words also imply a wish to stand beside everyone and everything that cannot enter the church, to remain with everything that one can love, and that God loves or it would not exist, even if it is and because it is excluded by the church that professes to be catholic or universal (WG 75–76, 95).

9. Cf. WG 95–96, 160, 175–178; NR 289; SL 140–141; F 142. This is accepting and cooperating with and willing freely and loving all that must be, as the right thing to be or happen, once we have done right by our own best lights. IC 120: "This is *amor fati*, it is the virtue of obedience, the Christian virtue excellent above all others" (WG 175, 184).

Actually the phrase *amor fati*, as opposed to the thought, is not used by any ancient Stoic nor even by any ancient Latin author; it seems to come from Nietzsche, e.g., *Ecce Homo*, "Why I am so Intelligent," 10; *Nietzsche Contra Wagner*, "Epilogue," 1; *The Will to Power* (tr. Walter Kaufmann; Vintage, 1968), no. 1032. See Pierre Hadot, *The Inner Citadel, The Meditations of Marcus Aurelius* (tr. Michael Chase; Harvard, 1998), 143–147; Marcus comes closest to this in 7.57; see also 3.16; 5.8; 10.21; and 4.23, 29; and 2.16, cited in LP 178; SL 129; N 612, cf. 61, 297. For Epictetus, see Introduction, n. 22; cf. Seneca, *Consolation for Marcia* 16–18.

10. Cf. WG 139, referring to *Matthew* 25.37, 45; cf. 7.23.

11. Purity as freedom from self is, or implies, *humility*, Meister Eckhart's "self-naughting." See WG 46: "humility, the most beautiful of all the virtues perhaps"; WG 109: a fruit of attention in school studies that is "a far more precious treasure than all academic progress"; WG 225: it "crowns all virtues"; F 97, 101, 297.

12. To believe without evidence seemed to her to lack honesty; but since non-religious evidence would be inconclusive and even irrelevant, and religious evidence she mostly ignored by her refusal to attend services in church or to pray, one could say that her decision to leave the problem of God alone and to affirm or deny nothing (WG 62) fulfilled the demands of honesty only in part. Now, however, she would say that acting on faith, without belief, alone gives us the experience that can lead—if God gives light—to certainty and knowledge, the only evidence possible or necessary (WG 107, 209). She has come to see that religious knowledge and certainty are "experimental," empirical.

13. Cf. OL 106: on "the ancient and heart-breaking curse contained in *Genesis* (3.17–19), which made the world appear as a convict prison and labor as the sign of men's servitude and abasement"; OL 144–145: "The man who obeys, whose movements, pains, pleasures are determined by the word of another, feels himself to be inferior, not by accident, but by nature. . . . It is impossible for the most heroically staunch mind to preserve the consciousness of an inward value when there is no external fact on which this consciousness can be based. . . . It seems to those who obey that some mysterious inferiority has predestined them to obey from all eternity, and every mark of scorn—even the tiniest—which they suffer at the hands of their superiors or their equals, every order they receive, and especially every act of submission they themselves perform confirms them in this feeling."

Cf. Kierkegaard, *Journals and Papers* (7 vols.; ed. and tr. Howard and Edna Hong; Indiana University Press, 1967–1978), nos. 386, 991, 4685, citing Matthew 11.5: "The good news is preached to the poor": it is *for* those who suffer and are unlucky, wretched, wronged, crippled, lame, leprous, demonic, who *know* they are (what all men really are) insufficient dependent nobodies (and would suffer *by* proclaiming the Gospel truly); thus 3062: "The more wretched and abandoned, insignificant and unhappy you are, the more God is interested in you."

See also Romans 8.18: "having been set free from sin, you have become slaves of righteousness," with Galatians 4.7: "So through God you are no longer a slave but a son, and if a son then an heir," and see n. 6 above.

14. Cf. Diogenes Allen and Eric Springsted, *Spirit, Nature, and Community* (SUNY, 1994), 6, "The Enigma of Affliction," 97–110, referring to Epictetus's *Moral Conversations* 1.6, "Providence."

15. F 205: "But suppose there are four. Would it be the devil who was among them?" N 290: "Two or three only . . . . This is to eliminate the social element."

16. Cf. Søren Kierkegaard, *The Point of View* (tr. Walter Lowrie [1939], reprinted, Harper, 1962), 128: "The 'individual' is the category through which, in a religious respect, this age, all history, the human race as a whole, must pass. And

he who stood at Thermopylae was not so secure in his position as I who have stood in defence of this narrow defile, 'the individual,' with the intent of at least making people take notice of it."

17. That is, in ceasing to be words spoken by an *individual* to God even in the presence of another—or in the case of blessings, to another in the presence of God with a request to God for confirmation, for we say "[May] God bless you"—they undergo a loss of *meaning* and *truth*. When we repeat them together, a worldly regard for one another's good opinion inevitably intrudes, and purity of heart is compromised. This is one of Kierkegaard's central concerns: see, e.g., *Journals and Papers* (7 vols.; ed. and tr. Howard and Edna Hong; Indiana University Press, 1967–1978), 3.3667; *Purity of Heart* (tr. Douglas Steete; Harper, 1965), 12 par. 5–6, *Works of Love* (tr. Howard and Edna Hong; Harper, 1962), Conclusion end; *Practice in Christianity* (tr. Howard and Edna Hong; Princeton University Press, 1991), 3.6 par. 2–3.

18. As she says in another connection, "It is not my business to think about myself. My business is to think about God. It is for God to think about me" (WG 50–51). In other words, not my will but his will be done.

19. WG 63; SL 178; cf. N 88, 467–468; F 177.

20. See chapter 7 n. 8 above: Dharmakara's vow.

21. It amounts to a prayer for total *humility* and full *obedience*, in imitation of Christ (Luke 22.19–20; John 6.51; 12.24). Let us note that she formulates it as an example of prayer, and that she says that its meaning and truth are beyond her, evidently identifying herself here with her lower, human, all too human, carnal part, from which the prayer asks deliverance. *I* cannot ask this, unless the Spirit move me to it. We can think of it as a prayer that our manual labor may be a work of the spirit: let us labor so that our flesh and blood become wheat and grapes that, made into bread and wine to feed one another's bodies, can be the flesh and blood of Christ to feed them in truth (F 96, 265).

22. See "Concerning The *Our Father*" in WG 216–227.

23. N 638–639; F 65–66. She is entirely on her own now; and yet somehow she cannot help thinking that she *has* his love, that his love is *with* her who desires to be nothing but a way for *it* to flow through the world.

Chapter 12
Time and Timelessness

1. For Islam, see A. K. Coomaraswamy, *Time and Eternity* (Artibus Asiae, Supplement 8, 1957), 86–104; see also pp. 81–85 on the Platonic tradition.

*2. Thus Franz Rosenzweig, for example, in a famous book, *The Star of Redemption* (tr. William Hallo; Holt, Rinehart & Winston, 1971).

3. See Lawrence Wright, "Forcing the End," *The New Yorker*, July 20, 1998, pp. 42–53, citing Numbers 19, and Rabbi Chaim Richman, *The Mystery of the Red*

Heifer: Divine Promise of Purity (The Temple Institute, 1998). See further Hebrews 9.13-14.

4. William Law, *The Spirit of Christianity and the Spirit of Love* (1749-1754) (ed. Sidney Spencer; James Clarke, 1969), 49: "as soon as thou art ready to hear, this eternal speaking Word of God will speak wisdom and love in thy inward parts, and bring forth the birth of Christ, with all his holy nature, spirit, and tempers, within thee"; p. 114: "The spirit of the soul is in itself nothing else but a spirit breathed forth from the life of God, and for this only end, that the life of God, the nature of God, the working of God, the tempers of God, might be manifested in it. . . . God can only delight in his own life. . . . Like can only unite with like"; p. 132: "your power of having the spirit of God and your measure of receiving it are just according to that faith and earnestness with which you desire to be led by it"; p. 214: "The oracle is at home, that always and only speaks the truth to you, because nothing is your truth but that good and that evil which is yours within you. . . . What you are in yourself, what is doing in yourself, is all that can be either your salvation or damnation." (Law generally follows Jacob Boehme, but this is certainly near what Kierkegaard writes at the close of *Works of Love*.) See further Jean-Pierre Caussade, *Abandonment to Divine Providence* (ed. and tr. John Beevers; Image Books, 1975), especially chapter 2.8-10; idem, *The Sacrament of the Present Moment* (ed. Kitty Muggeridge; Harper & Row, 1982). Cf. Weil N 212-213, 282, 618, quoted in n. 24 below.

5. Matthew 25.13, 21, 34, 46; 26.29; John 8.56; 9.4; 14.20. Cf. Isaiah 13.6: "the Day of the Lord is at hand"; Amos 5.17: "Woe to you who desire the Day of the Lord"; sc., for your enemies; cf. Matthew 7.1; Revelation 6.15-17.

6. SE 10, 13: "It is this (expectation) . . . above all that is sacred in every human being"; "so far from its being his person, what is sacred in a human being is the impersonal in him. Everything which is impersonal in man is sacred, and nothing else."

7. Cf. above, chapter 6, p. 58, the thesis of T. E. Lawrence.

8. Thus we can speak both with the impersonal that is sacred in us to the impersonal that is sacred in others, *freely* and with all the attention we owe to *any* and every human being as such; and with *all* our integrity to each as the *very* person that he or she is. Perhaps our most impersonal words are our most personal ones; and the other way. Simone Weil would say that we are then earnestly speaking out of our aspiration for the good to the aspiration for the good in the other, desire speaking to desire: see further F 124, 284. Such communication is a central topic in the writings of Kierkegaard.

9. *Atman* is the presence in us of *Brahman*, the supreme God beyond all. See, e.g., *Brhad-Aranyaka Upanishad* 1.4.8-10; 4.4; *Chandogya Up.* 3.14.4; 8.74; *Mandukya Up.* 6-8; *Bhagavad Gita* 8.3; 15.7.

10. It is not an experience so much as an ideal to be realized in experience. Cf. *Chuang Tzu* (sixth-fourth century B.C.) chapter 2: "The men of old got somewhere. How far? To the point where some of them thought there were no things, that's

the limit. After them there were some who thought there were things but no borders. The next thought there were borders but no yes and no. When yes and no appear, the Way is harmed, and love is complete. But is anything really complete or harmed?" This is a monistic rejection of taking *relative* distinctions *absolutely*, between (a) the One and its many appearances, (b) one appearance and another, (c) appearances as great and small, beneficial and harmful (thus lovable and hateful), and the like.

11. Cf. Plotinus 4.8.8: "our soul does not entirely descend [into body], but there is always something of it in the intellectual world . . . for we do not know everything that happens in any part of the soul before it reaches the whole soul." See further 1.1.11; 6.8.18.

12. That is, to have *thoughts*, to talk to ourselves; not, to *attend*, to be mindful, which is our real nature.

13. Cf. Krishna in *Bhagavad Gita* 7.14–15, 25; 3.38–39; 18.60: "My mysterious cloud of appearance is hard to pass beyond; but those who in truth come to me go beyond the world of shadows. But men who do evil seek not me: their soul is darkened by delusion. Their vision is veiled by the cloud of appearance . . . I am hidden by my veil of mystery; and in its delusion the world knows me not. . . . All is clouded by desire; as fire is by smoke, as a mirror by dust, as an unborn babe by the womb. . . . Because you are in the bondage of Karma, the forces of your own past life, that which you are unwilling to do you will have to do even so." The words adapted from Maharshi have not been traced; but see similar words in *The Spiritual Teaching of Ramana Maharshi* (Shambala, 1972), especially 3–14 (Self and ego), and 27–28, 51–52, and 98 (cinema screen).

14. None as an explicit thought *about* what we see: cf. Weil, N 110–111, 134; cf. N 406: "The idea behind Zen Buddhism: to perceive *purely*, without any admixture of day dreaming"; N 273: We have "to try to love without imagining. To love appearance in its nakedness, devoid of interpretation. What we then love is truly God"; N 283: "To love God through and beyond a certain thing is to love that thing in purity"; N 533: "God is really present [to us] in everything that is unshrouded by imagination."

15. Perhaps it is the *experience* that is simple—it is an experience of simplicity (cf. Plotinus 5.7.35 on being "simplified into happiness," *haplotheis eis eupatheian*)—while the *explanation* of its presuppositions and implications and the method of achieving it are not. The experience is positive; the explanation is negative, a stripping away of every qualification and all relativity. Cf. Weil, F 317: "It is because everything in our world is the wrong way round that the attributes of God appear to us as negations (he is without limits, etc.) and that possession appears to us disguised as desire."

16. Yet it is the struggle that reveals this. The riddle of our life is not solved by thinking but by *life*, yet it is thinking that proves this to us. Not by materialistic egoistic thinking, but the thinking that *is* life; not by the mind, but the mind's living knowledge.

17. That is, *all is out*. Cf. the words of Goethe quoted by Wittgenstein: "Do not look for anything behind the phenomena; they are themselves the lesson" (*Remarks on the Philosophy of Psychology* [University of Chicago Press, 1980], 1.889).

18. Thus the words ascribed to the poet T. S. Eliot: "The only method is to be very intelligent," as a comment on *The Later Analytics* of Aristotle.

19. That is, the aid is *in* giving up after doing our best, as if we had to learn that grace alone fulfills the freedom it nevertheless presupposes. Cf. Matthew 7.7: "Ask, and it will be given you, knock and it will be opened to you," and Revelation 3.20: "Look, *I* stand at the door and knock." Pascal, *Pensées,* no. 631: "It is good to be tired and weary from fruitlessly seeking the true good, so that one can stretch out one's arms to the Redeemer"; no. 793: "It is right that so pure a God should disclose himself only to those whose hearts are purified." Weil, F 262: "The good begins at a point beyond the reach of will"; F 306–307: "A strong will can obtain many things . . . but not the Good"; F 326: we must exercise the will and the discursive intelligence so as to "use them up," destroy them as unaided powers by impossible tasks and contradictions (koans) respectively, in humility "passing beyond" them into obedience that completes them; F 346: we must see our incapacity for perfection and "beseech silently with our whole soul to obtain it, . . . until God's patience is exhausted and he grants it"; F 142: "The good is something which you can never get by your own effort, but neither can you desire it without getting it." Thus the struggle is the mistake, when it is seen as *sufficient* for success, or even as *necessary*, without acknowledgment in humility of the transcendence of the Good and Truth.

Cf. Franz Kafka, *Reflections,* in *Dearest Father* (see chapter 10, n. 1 above), 26: "There is a goal, but no way; what we call the way is wavering"; and 109: "There is no need for you to leave the house. Stay at your table and listen. Don't even listen, just wait. Don't even wait, be completely quiet and alone. The world will offer itself to you to be unmasked; it can't do otherwise; in raptures it will writhe before you."

20. Thus, e.g., Genesis 22.1, 11; 31.11; 37.11; 36.2; Exodus 3.4; 1 Samuel 3; Isaiah 6.8. "Here I am," that is to say, "Ready!" sc., I am ready to hear and to fulfill your word. Cf. Isaiah 58.9 and 30.18.

21. It is the perceived *discontinuity* of the religious and ethical with what precedes. There is a leap—a transition to a higher category or conceptual level or dimension—that has meaning and justification only in retrospect, that is to say, in its own terms. For a transition *from* the higher, whether by its descent or by the lower's intrusion upon it, is fully intelligible only in terms of the higher.

22. See, e.g., Mark 13.36; Acts 2.2; 9.3; also Matthew 24.42–44; Luke 4.5; John 3.8; 1 Corinthians 15.51–52. Cf. Plato, *Symposium* 210e, 212c; *Republic* 7.515c, 516e; *Letters* 7.341d, 344b; and Plotinus, 5.3.17; 5.5.3, 7f; 6.7.34, 36.

23. They are questions not of *words* but of *life*; not what to say but how to live.

24. Words in brackets added by editor. See Weil, N 212–213: "To remit debts is

to remain halted in the present . . . to strip oneself of the imaginary sovereignty of the world, in order to reduce oneself to the point one [actually] occupies in space and time. . . . to acquire the feeling of eternity. Then, indeed, sins are remitted"; N 282: "by contemplating this perpetuity [of pain and exhaustion] with acceptance and love we are caught up to eternity"; N 303: "Obedience—sole means of passing from time to eternity"; N 616: The desire for pure total good applied to the present "pierces right through to the eternal." See also chapter 11 n. 8, on Weil's Stoic *amor fati*.

Bibliography

Allen, Diogenes. *Three Outsiders*. Cowley Publications, 1983.

Allen, Diogenes, and Eric Springsted. *Spirit, Nature, and Community: Issues in the Thought of Simone Weil*. State University of New York Press, 1994.

Allen, Louis. "French Intellectuals and T. E. Lawrence." *Durham University Journal* 29 (1976): 52–66.

Andic, Martin. "Discernment and the Imagination." In Richard Bell, *Simone Weil's Philosophy of Culture*, 116–149. Cambridge University Press, 1993.

———. "Fairy Tales." *Cahiers Simone Weil* 15 (1992): 61–91.

———. "The Love of Truth." *Cahiers Simone Weil* 28 (1995): 389–417.

———. "One Moment of Pure Attention is Worth All the Good Works in the World." *Cahiers Simone Weil* 21 (1998): 347–368.

———. "Simone Weil and Shakespeare's Fools." In *The Beauty That Saves: Essays on Aesthetics and Language in Simone Weil*, ed. John Dunaway and Eric Springsted, 197–215. Mercer University Press, 1996.

———. "Supernatural Justice and the Madness of Love." *Cahiers Simone Weil* 17 (1994): 373–405.

Bell, Richard. *Simone Weil's Philosophy of Culture*. Cambridge University Press 1993.

Cabaud, Jacques. *Simone Weil: A Fellowship in Love*. Channel Press, 1964.

Dunaway, John, and Eric Springsted, eds. *The Beauty That Saves: Essays on Aesthetics and Language in Simone Weil*. Mercer University Press, 1996.

Finch, Henry LeRoy, Letter to the Editor, *The Times Literary Supplement*, July 23 1993, p. 15.

———. "L'universalisme de Simone Weil." Tr. Judith Gordon. *Cahiers Simone Weil* 6 (1983): 275–283.

————. "Simone Weil: Harbinger of a New Renaissance?" In Richard Bell, *Simone Weil's Philosophy of Culture*, 295–309. Cambridge University Press, 1993.

————. *Wittgenstein*. Element Books, 1995.

————. *Wittgenstein—The Early Philosophy: An Exposition of the Tractatus*. Humanities Press, 1971.

————. *Wittgenstein—The Later Philosophy: An Exposition of the Philosophical Investigations*. Humanities Press, 1977.

Finch, Henry LeRoy, and Lucie Gutkind, eds. *The Body of God, by Eric Gutkind*. Horizon Press, 1969.

Fiori, Gabriella. *Simone Weil: An Intellectual Biography*. Tr. Joseph Berrigan. University of Georgia Press, 1989.

————. *Simone Weil: Une femme absolue*. Félin, 1982, 1987.

Goicoechea, David, ed. *The Question of Humanism*. Prometheus Books, 1991.

Kahn, Gilbert, ed. *Simone Weil, philosophe, historienne, mystique*. Aubier Montaigne, 1978.

Little, J. P. *Simone Weil: Waiting on Truth*. Berg, 1988.

Little, J. P., and André Ughetto. *Simone Weil, La Soif de L'Absolu, SUD Revue Litteraire* (1990): 87-88.

McLellan, David. *Simone Weil: Utopian Pessimist*. MacMillan, 1989.

Pascal, Blaise, *Pensées*. Tr. A. J. Krailsheimer. Penguin Books, 1966.

Perrin, Joseph-Marie, Jr. *Mon Dialogue avec Simone Weil*. Nouvelle Cité, 1984.

Perrin, Joseph-Marie, Jr., and Gustave Thibon. *Simone Weil As We Knew Her*. Tr. Emma Craufurd. Routledge, 1953.

Pétrement, Simone. *A Separate God: The Christian Origins of Gnosticism*. Tr. Carol Harrison. Harper Collins, 1990.

————. *Simone Weil: A Life*. Tr. Raymond Rosenthal. Pantheon Books, 1976.

Rees, Richard. *Simone Weil: A Sketch for a Portrait*. Oxford University Press, 1966.

Rhees, Rush. *On Religion and Philosophy*. Ed. D. Z. Phillips. Cambridge University Press, 1997.

Rhees, Rush, ed. *Ludwig Wittgenstein, Personal Recollections*. Rowman & Littlefield, 1981.

Scholem, Gershom. *Origins of the Kabbalah*. Ed. R. J. Zwi Werblowsky and Allan Arkush. Princeton University Press. 1997.

Springsted, Eric. *Christus Mediator: Platonic Mediation in the Thought of Simone Weil*. Scholars Press, 1983.

————. *Simone Weil and the Suffering of Love*. Cowley Publications, 1986.

Strickland, Stephanie. *The Red Virgin, A Poem of Simone Weil*. University of Wisconsin Press, 1993.

Tomlin, E. W. F. *Simone Weil*. Yale University Press, 1954.

Vetö, Miklos. *The Religious Metaphysics of Simone Weil*. Tr. Joan Dargan. State
    University of New York Press, 1994.
Weil, André. *The Apprenticeship of a Mathematician*. Tr. Jennifer Gage.
    Birkhauser Verlag, 1992.
Winch, Peter. *Simone Weil: The Just Balance*. Cambridge University Press, 1989.

Index